AF718554

Industrial Development and Reforms in Myanmar

ASEAN and Japanese Perspectives

Industrial Development and Reforms in Myanmar

ASEAN and Japanese Perspectives

Edited by

Minoru Kiryu

White Lotus Press

© 1999 by The Sasakawa Peace Foundation. All rights reserved.

This book may not be reproduced, in whole, in part, or in any form without written permission from The Sasakawa Peace Foundation. For information, write to: The Saskawa Peace Foundation, Sasakawa Hall, 3-12-12 Mita, Tokyo (Minato-ku), Japan.

White Lotus Co., Ltd.
G.P.O. Box 1141
Bangkok 10501
Thailand

Telephone: (662) 332-4915 and (662) 741-6288-9
Fax: (662) 741-6607 and (662) 741-6287

E-mail: ande@loxinfo.co.th

Website: http://thailine.com/lotus

Printed in Thailand

ISBN 974-7534-06-1 pbk White Lotus Co., Ltd., Bangkok

Contents

Foreword

Unlike some transitional economies where governments retain the main body of their enterprises under state ownership, the Union of Myanmar has been privatizing its state-owned enterprises since 1988 when it announced its economic reform policy. According to government statistics, the percentage of private enterprises vis-à-vis all enterprises (excluding cooperatives) reached 75.9% in 1995, a very high ratio for a transitional economy.

Despite the fact that the country needs to attract more foreign investment and to increase its volume of trade, no study has been conducted to obtain detailed statistics on the privatization of enterprises in Myanmar. Moreover, since it became a member of ASEAN in July 1997, Myanmar has faced even more rigorous international competition. This has compelled it to retool and upgrade its industries.

Since its establishment in 1992, The Sasakawa Southeast Asia Cooperation Fund has been carrying out a diversified program of projects in its targeted countries of Cambodia, Laos, Myanmar, and Vietnam. Among these programs is "Research with Tangible Applications" (to economic reform policies). Given the circumstances touched upon above, in 1997 the Fund initiated a two-year project entitled "Symposium on Industrial Reform in Myanmar." Based on the country's need to enhance its industrial policy and for the government first to obtain an accurate grasp of the overall conditions and trends surrounding the country's enterprises to do so, this project has had three primary objectives:

- To make a comprehensive examination of the problems that Myanmar's enterprises face as the country makes its transition to a market-oriented economy.

- To obtain knowledge of current problems relative to Myanmar's enterprises through conducting research and holding symposia for researchers and policymakers both in and outside Myanmar.

- To prepare a policy recommendation for submission to the government of Myanmar based on the results of these processes, in an effort to aid it in its task of reforming the nation's industrial policies.

This volume of collected papers reflects the fruits of the efforts exerted by professors and researchers from Japan, Myanmar, and Thailand, who participated in this project through the joint implementation of study meetings and research activities in Bangkok, Mandalay, Osaka, Tokyo, and Yangon during this two-year initiative.

We at The Sasakawa Peace Foundation would be delighted if this volume would help people in other countries to enhance their understanding of the circumstances and issues associated with industrial reform in Myanmar.

Akira Iriyama, President
The Sasakawa Peace Foundation
Tokyo

Introduction

Minoru Kiryu
Osaka University of Industry

Since the Government of the Union of Myanmar announced an open economic policy in 1989, many enterprises have emerged in the country. However, as Mr Akira Iriyama, President of The Sasakawa Peace Foundation, notes in his Foreword to this volume, "no study has been conducted to obtain detailed statistics on enterprises in Myanmar." This book provides such data based on research directed at 132 selected enterprises in the country. The results of this research are highlighted in the individual essays. To understand these results fully, a grasp must first be obtained of both the current status and historical background of Myanmar's industrial situation. For this purpose, the volume provides reports compiled by Japanese, Myanmarese, and Thai researchers, who also present various policy recommendations.

Overview

My own paper describes the current situation of Myanmar's industrial sector, giving both historical background and fundamental data. I argue that to advance its industrialization, Myanmar will need to promote the development of small and medium-sized enterprises (SMEs). To do so, I recommend three traditional steps for economic development. First, the development strategy of the government to promote industries that can effectively utilize the nation's advantages, namely its agriculture and agro-industry. Developing these areas will give the country's rural populations increased income, more employment opportunities, and greater purchasing power. The second step is to promote import-substituting industries, such as a parts industry. Reducing imports through increased domestic production will save foreign currency and in turn stabilize the nation's macroeconomy. Lastly, export-oriented industries, such as a software industry, need to be developed. Through technological improvement and the modernization of facilities, even traditional products should contribute to the promotion of Myanmar's export business. In each of these three development stages, small and medium-sized enterprises should play a major role. Finally, I propose that Myanmar actively promote systems of subcontracting with ASEAN companies, particularly by developing SMEs in diverse sectors of various manufacturing industries.

Myanmar's Industrialization: Current Issues and Historical Overview

In the second section, researchers from Myanmar provide four papers. First, Dr Nu Nu Yin introduces the results of her survey, providing a wide range of data. She argues that the 132 surveyed manufacturing firms, which included various types of ownership systems (state-owned enterprises, joint ventures, cooperatives, and private enterprises) have operations aimed mostly at import substitution. She explains that among fifteen industries, only those in the areas of wood-based products, gems, fishery, and garments engage in export promotion. Since domestic demand for these products is sufficiently large, most manufacturing firms do not, according to Dr Yin, look beyond the domestic market. In terms of their product quality, however, there is a crucial need for improvement if these firms plan to enter the export market.

The survey results show the major obstacles to SME business operations to be: shortages of electricity, raw materials, and machine spare parts; a lack of high technology; and the difficulty of hiring skilled labor. To guarantee the survival of these enterprises, she recommends that they develop links, through a framework of subcontracting, with industries in other ASEAN countries as well as with domestic firms.

Next, U Aung Myint argues that because manufacturing industries are a driving force of economic development and social progress Myanmar should pursue a resource-based industrialization strategy. Such a strategy, he contends, is important in a country possessing abundant and varied natural resources. He points out that to enhance the development of the processing and manufacturing sectors the government has set four economic objectives. One is "the development of the economy inviting domestic and foreign investment that will transfer technology and know-how." This has resulted in receiving foreign investment and technical co-operation and in the emergence of joint ventures with firms from various countries including Japan, Singapore, and Thailand. Lastly, he points to the necessity of efficient production, particularly by creating small-scale and supporting industries and integrating them into medium- and large-scale enterprises.

The next essay in this section, by Mr Chit So, explains the historical background of Myanmar's industrial development and presents a perspective on the current situation. He points out the government's stance that a development program cannot afford to emphasize industrialization at the expense of agricultural development but should rather emphasize mutually supportive interaction between agriculture and industry. The government's objective, he states, is to use agricultural development as a base for developing the industrial sector. After the implementation of industrial reforms to form a market economy, the share of industry in Myanmar's GDP remained static. He observes that a heavy reliance on primary commodity exports contributed to the country's limited success in producing non-traditional and manufactured exports. He suggests that Myanmar learn from Japan's economic development example that a nation's most valuable resource is not its cultivable land but its people. To achieve sustainable growth Myanmar will also need to advance its industrialization through technology infusions. Moreover, by improving export performance, the composition of exports can be shifted from primary commodities toward manufactured goods. He concludes that the quickest way to achieve industrialization will be to create a favorable environment for attracting foreign direct investment (FDI). He recommends that the government encourage the private sector to take the leading role while the state plays a facilitating and supporting role.

U Tun Aye then introduces the historical development of industries in Yangon making use of tables. He suggests that Yangon, as the national capital, currently receives preference in industrial investment, despite the fact that the largest number of industries is located in Mandalay. In an effort to upgrade the country's infrastructure and accommodate investment, the government has initiated various programs, including the creation of industrial zones in and near Yangon. He sees the Myanmar Industrial Development Committee and the Myanmar Industrial Development Bank as crucial bodies working to promote the development of private industry.

The ASEAN Experience

The third section elaborates some potentially emulateable development experiences in Vietnam and Thailand. First, Mr Yoshiaki Ueda introduces some Vietnamese examples of potential reference to Myanmar. He points to the very important role of government in fostering a healthy, competitive business environment. For example, he argues that the automobile and tourism industries of Vietnam are facing excessive competition due to the government's failure to provide adequate guidance. For such industries, he recommends orderly investment through a system of government approval. Taking the case of Sony as an example, he proposes that the government nurture successful companies that can serve as development models while promoting investment and economic growth.

He sees government as an "intermediary" in the establishment of an "investment and trade promotion center." For government to be able to respond quickly to the demands and problems of foreign companies, he argues that a permanent official institution be set up to act as an "intermediary." Lastly, he suggests that one lesson to be learned from the Asian financial crisis is a need to alleviate international financial risks by actively fostering export industries instead of import-substitute industries.

Using numerous examples, Dr Kitti Limskul next offers advice to Myanmar's food industry based on Thailand's experience. He says that no strategies for industrial development have thus far been formulated in Myanmar. He suggests that the country look to Thailand's industrial development, which shows the importance of developing a food processing industry both for earning foreign currency and financing economic development. In developing Myanmar's agro-industry, canned pineapple and canned tuna, along with other fruit and seafood products, can be important sources of foreign currency. This is because the country's soil is suitable to growing pineapple, while its labor-intensive plantations provide a cheap wage base.

He further points out that canned products, with the exception of tuna, require few material inputs, which reduces imports and saves foreign currency. He advises Myanmar not to develop a tuna industry for the time being because of the high capital and technical inputs required. He argues that it should seek technical production assistance and international distribution support from its ASEAN neighbors, which can complement its lack of such technical expertise and marketing networks. He suggests that Myanmar first try to develop intermediate products, such as soybean cake and soybean oil for its own as well as Thai markets, and he anticipates that such products can be developed at a level that meets international standards.

The View from Japan

In this section, four Japanese researchers present papers from their respective perspectives as regional experts, financial experts, and economists. First, Mr. Toshihiro Kudo provides a historical viewpoint. He interprets Myanmar's post-independence economic history as being a series of conflicts between nationalist-cum-socialist doctrines and the basic reality that private initiative drives economic development. Whenever each of the governments since independence wanted to accommodate and integrate the energy of private enterprises into the national economy, socialist ideology, anti-capitalist attitudes, and xenophobia stood in the way. He argues that this is why past reform efforts toward economic liberalization have yielded at best lukewarm results.

Although the present government's initiatives are much more committed than in the past to market economy principles that enhance the role of the private sector, there is, to be sure, considerable room for improvement. For example, state-owned enterprises are still more favorably treated than most private enterprises in terms of access to such inputs as raw materials, electricity and petroleum, finance, and foreign exchange. Large-scale privatization programs have long been planned but have yet to materialize. Moreover, the government still tends to resort to administrative and sometimes coercive measures to deal with perceived unstable economic situations. Such an attitude may raise suspicion in the minds of entrepreneurs, evoking the bitter experiences of the socialist period. The only way, he concludes, to instill private sector confidence in its policies is for the government to steadily promote concrete economic reforms toward a free and fair market economy.

Next, Mr Takanori Wajima addresses the financial aspects of industrial development in Myanmar. He points out that after the promulgation of the Financial Institutions of Myanmar Law in 1990, which was crafted in line with the new government's private sector orientation, private foreign banks were allowed to operate in Myanmar. He points out that the Central Bank of Myanmar Law was designed to strengthen monetary control over the financial market while allowing relative independence in the government budget's decision-making process. Along with new financial reform laws, this law is meant to preserve the internal and external value of Myanmar's currency. He adds that the Myanmar Agriculture and Development Bank was created to support the development of rural enterprises through banking services. Since Myanmar's economy is currently sustained by SMEs, in order to guarantee their development, financial mediation will be essential. This means, he asserts, that interest rates must be adjusted so as to avoid inflation and promote savings. Furthermore, money lending by entrepreneurs must be facilitated in order to increase investment.

Professor Tetsuo Minato next explains, based on his field research, how Myanmar might develop its enterprises. He points out that the source of technological progress in developing economies is not product innovation but process innovation. To achieve efficient process innovation, he asserts that it is necessary to make a division between specific and specialized production processes. This is because it is difficult for a single company to handle an entire operation effectively as production processes become more complex and specialized lines become longer. There are two types of corporate sectors, one comprising large companies and the other small and medium-sized companies, each having unique management characteristics. Both are important within an industrial structure. By integrating large and medium-sized companies and separating their production processes so as to maximize the advantages of each, the potential for technological progress driven by process innovation increases. In this way, a substantial rate of technological progress can be maintained and economic growth guaranteed. Developing such a system of the inter-firm division of processes and labor is considered to have strategic importance in Myanmar's economic development. The subcontracting system used successfully by Japan can provide an example for Myanmar, where a model project for production subcontracting is slowly taking shape. He concludes that if technology transfers to SMEs can continue to be implemented and good cooperation maintained between contracting firms, it will be possible for the country to produce internationally competitive products within several years.

Finally, Professor Johzen Takeuchi discusses the formation and features of entrepreneurship in Myanmar and Japan. He explains that Myanmar is still a traditional country, whose economy relies on the primary sector, and whose basic industrial structure, for example, its manufacturing sector, has virtually stagnated. Despite the potential of Myanmar's primary sector and its possible utilization in the country's development, agricultural production has shown a statistical decline over recent years. The bulk of the country's manufacturing sector consists of small workshops. There are within the sector, however, state enterprises that are modernized but relying heavily on the importation of basic products used in production. Development strategies are urgently needed to lighten the dependence of Myanmar's economy. Professor Takeuchi suggests that Myanmar might derive some helpful ideas from Japan's example of SME development, especially in building its manufacturing and labor-intensive sectors. The public sector should, he suggests, take responsibility both for providing new technology for state enterprises and for creating matrixes for fostering SME development. He points out Myanmar's need for skilled human resources as it attempts to introduce new industries and to improve basic infrastructure, and he concludes that in order to promote industrialization in Myanmar the training of government officials should focus on regional development and its impact on local populations.

1

The Role of Small and Medium-Sized Enterprises in the Industrial Development of Myanmar

Minoru Kiryu
Osaka University of Industry

Introduction

Since 1992, Myanmar has developed a market economy and opened its markets to other countries. The results have begun to show. The average annual GDP growth achieved 7.5% from fiscal year 1992 to fiscal year 1995, with a slightly lower rate of 6% for fiscal year 1996-97. Economic growth was made possible by active private investment including foreign investment, extended trade (mostly border trade), and expanded private businesses in various sectors due to the development of a market economy. Myanmar's economic structure has been changing slowly but steadily. There are a number of hurdles to overcome in order to secure the right track for sustainable future economic development. To solve the various problems emerging from the serious lack of foreign currency confronting the country, especially since the Asian financial crisis, it is essential to implement and promote the stabilization of politics and society, to eliminate dual currency exchanges, increase exports, diversify the export structure, and improve the industrial structure. Settling on programs to stabilize macroeconomics should be the strategy whereby these problems are addressed. One improvement strategy for accelerating Myanmar's industrialization is to promote small and medium-sized enterprises (SMEs), and this is the topic of the present essay.

History of Industrial Development after 1962

After 1962 when the former regime inaugurated "The Burmese Way to Socialism," Myanmar's economy fell into a prolonged period of stagnation, especially with respect to industrial development. The average annual growth rate of the industrial sector was only 1.1% from 1962 to 1987. This figure contrasts markedly with industrial development in Thailand during the same period. In 1962, the share of industrial production of Myanmar's GDP was 10%, almost the same level of Thailand's industrial development at the beginning of the 1960s. In the case of Thailand, industrial production developed rapidly after 1960, with the share of industrial production in GDP attaining 31% in fiscal year 1997. But in Myanmar, the share of industrial production decreased gradually and was still only 9% in 1997. Under "The Burmese Way to Socialism," the state's fundamental strategy and industrial policy was to protect and expand State Economic Enterprises (SEEs). This policy severely limited investment in private industry and discouraged industrial development. Most manufacturing industries were nationalized establishments owned by non-Myanmar nationals (British, Chinese, and Indians) previous to being taken over by the government. Many of these non-citizens left Myanmar after nationalization, and only a few entrepreneurs and private enterprises remained in the country.

The production share of SEEs industry was 41.3% out of total production in the manufacturing sector in 1970, and the production share of the SEEs did not increase until 1988. The reasons for industrial stagnation were: (1) confusion due to a radical nationalization policy; (2) a lack of entrepreneurship and human resources for management; (3) lack of a commercial culture and management experience; and (4) unsuitable economic and industrial policies. Each topic will be discussed in turn.

Confusion Due to a Radical Nationalization Policy

The nationalization policy adopted in 1963 was rapidly and radically implemented. The target of nationalization focused on enterprises owned by non-citizens. Until 1965, almost 90% the enterprises owned by non-citizens were nationalized with the exception of small businesses in the service industry. Under this policy, some enterprises owned by Myanmar nationals were also nationalized including rice mills, edible oil mills, cigar factories, sawmills, and cinemas. As the result of this policy, the production share of state-owned enterprises in the industrial sector expanded to approximately 65% for fiscal year 1995. These nationalized enterprises were reorganized as state-owned enterprises at least until the dawn of the 1970s.

Lack of Entrepreneurship and Human Resources for Management

Many non-nationals, especially entrepreneurs of Chinese and Indian origin, who owned or managed various private companies, left Myanmar for other countries as their firms were nationalized in line with the government's nationalization policy. Entrepreneurship in Myanmar decreased at a single stroke, and the country lost well-trained and highly experienced individuals with management skills for developing human resources.

Lack of a Commercial Culture and Management Experience

From 1962 to 1974, under the military government, military officials with no training or background in economics or commercial management managed most state enterprises as the government took over managing the state-owned enterprises it had nationalized. There was a lack of management technology, and the individuals in authority over enterprises lacked commercial instincts, with most management officials simply waiting for orders from a higher authority and making efforts only to pursue set targets.

Unsuitable Economic and Industrial Policies

During the period of "The Burmese Way to Socialism" the basic economic and industrial policy was to protect state-owned enterprises. This tended to discourage private investment, and privately owned enterprises not only lacked government subsidies or support during this period but also were faced with limits on raw material procurement, a lack of finance, and a lack of power supply. There were no linkages between SEEs and private enterprises. Most private enterprises depended on the black market and smuggling to procure raw materials or spare parts. For financing and operations, they also had to rely on informal (private) financial institutions.

Current Situation of Small-Scale Enterprises

Most manufacturers in Myanmar are small companies with fewer than ten employees. When classified by the management body, 80% of large-scale enterprises with more than 100 employees are state-owned or state-affiliated enterprises, while private enterprises comprise only 18.38%. Small- and medium-scale enterprises with fewer than 100 employees comprise 98.9% of all of enterprises, both state- and privately-owned. An obvious structure thus exists in the manufacturing industry: there are a few large-scale, state-owned enterprises and many small-scale, private ones.

1 Inter-Firm Relationships

A characteristic problem of Myanmar's manufacturing industry is that few relationships have been established among enterprises. There is an extremely weak linkage between state-owned and private enterprises. The promotion and protection of state-owned enterprises under "The Burmese Way to Socialism" led to the strict regulation of all private enterprises and prevented their development. Most state-owned enterprises had no relationships with private enterprises in terms of supply or ordering subcontracts, except for certain raw materials.

Relations among private enterprises were also extremely poor. Since most private companies in Myanmar are engaged in rice milling, edible oil extraction, or the processing of other agricultural products, they produce and process final products locally. The same is true of traditional local industries (e.g., textiles, tobacco, timber processing, lacquerware, metalwork, and jewelry polishing) making mono-cultural enterprises and factories the norm. Therefore, relationships among private companies or linkages among different industries have scarcely developed in terms of supply or taking orders. This situation has been changing, though slowly, with the inflow of private investment since the economic reforms of 1988. As the market economy develops, principles of competition work on prices, quality, delivery dates, and so forth, and various relationships have gradually been created with a focus on relationships among enterprises as well as different industries.

2 Ownership and Characteristics

The characteristics affecting manufacturing companies that have been established since 1988 can be categorized as follows: (1) revival of investment by overseas Chinese; (2) transfer from commercial funds; (3) investment by nationals working abroad and returnee workers; (4) enterprises managed by former bureaucrats; and (5) armed forces investment in the economy. Each topic will be discussed in turn.

Revival of Investment by Overseas Chinese

Overseas Chinese funds, which were deprived of their real economic power under "The Burmese Way to Socialism," accumulated in the underground economies such as the black market and smuggling. Since 1988, however, these funds have again emerged in the front-line of the private sector as deregulation has advanced. Although many overseas Chinese were first involved in the commercial and service industries, they are gradually investing in small-scale manufacturing and in construction companies as trade in agricultural products and border trade liberalizes. They are also promoting business with other overseas Chinese formerly resident in Myanmar and now playing active roles in other Asian economies after leaving Myanmar in the post-1962 period. Some of these individuals have established joint ventures in Myanmar with overseas Chinese or others.

Transfer from Commercial Funds
With the opening of trade in agricultural products, the real estate business, and border trade, Myanmar nationals other than those of overseas Chinese origin have increasingly invested in manufacturing industries, such as construction materials, woodworking, and food processing. This is occurring not only in major cities but also in the form of transfers from local commercial funds.

Investment by Nationals Working Abroad and Returnee Workers
Since travel abroad was deregulated for Myanmar nationals in 1988, the number of persons working overseas has annually increased. Deregulation of money remittances from abroad is another factor in sharply rising revenues transferred from overseas. The amount of revenue transferred in the balance of international payments increased from 520 million kyat in 1991 to 2,470 million kyat in 1996. Most transferred revenues were in the form of remittance money from private Myanmar nationals working overseas. For example, about 20,000 Myanmar nationals are working in Japan, approximately 60% of who are illegal workers. These individuals sent an estimated 8 billion yen to Myanmar from Japan in 1996. Although the scale of such money invested in industry is small, it is expected that investment will gradually shift from the service industries such as retailing and restaurants to small-scale manufacturing and construction.

Enterprises Managed by Former Bureaucrats
While the deregulation of private investments has encouraged the establishment and registration of many private enterprises and import-export enterprises, many of the entrepreneurs involved are retired government officials and servicemen. With the position and experience they possessed, they have advantages in approaching related authorities

and customers as well as in credibility. Although many have become agents or dealers for foreign companies instead of starting up their own businesses, they are promising entrepreneurs for the future.

Armed Forces Investment in the Economy

Since military administration was established, the armed forces have been actively involved in the country's economic activities, with the armed forces and the Ministry of Defense establishing enterprises or taking part in management. One such case is the Myanmar Economic Holding Company, Ltd, a private enterprise in which the armed forces invested 50% of the capital. As a single company, the Myanmar Economic Holding Company, Ltd has the most affiliated joint ventures with private foreign investments. The Myanmar Economic Corporation Company is another firm established with 100% of the capital provided by the armed forces after absorbing part of a state-owned enterprise. The company is expanding its business through mergers with private domestic enterprises and planning joint ventures with private foreign enterprises. In manufacturing industries in Myanmar, there is no doubt that these companies, established with public funds, will be among the leading ones in this sector.

3 Types of Industry

Most manufacturing industries in Myanmar are light industries such as food and beverage concerns (58.3%), clothing and apparel (8.7%), construction materials (7.1%). In the food and beverage industry, 80% of factories are rice or oil extraction mills, and various food processing firms. Most are small-scale and traditional private factories with fewer than 100 employees.

Modern industry including firms involved in the manufacture of machinery, equipment, and transport vehicles are mostly monopolized by SEEs. Since the open door policy of 1988, modern and large-scale private factories such as those for making electrical appliances and galvanized iron sheeting have been newly established based on joint ventures with foreign companies.

4 Situation of Private Manufacturing Enterprises

Since 1988, the number of private enterprises in the manufacturing sector has risen sharply. In 1990, there were 35,729 private manufacturing factories. By 1996, the number had increased to 47,592. This represents a 32.9% increase, contrasting with a decline in the number of state-owned enterprises by 9.2% during the same period. During this period, private enterprises showed an average annual growth rate of 6.3% a year, while state-owned enterprises had an annual rate of 5.8%. There is no doubt that this was a result of the effects of the series of investment deregulations, the introduction of a market economy, and the opening of the market to other countries. Under the previous system, state-owned manufacturing enterprises were protected by the government for raw material supplies, foreign currency allocations, bank loans, and so forth, but they have gradually accepted market principles and are now being exposed to competition from private enterprise. State-owned enterprises continue to improve their management through streamlining, such as merging with private foreign investors and selling off unprofitable factories. Another notable aspect is that the number of domestic small and medium-sized enterprises is gradually on the rise and is creating tough competition for state-owned enterprises.

5 Types of Small- and Medium-Scale Enterprises

The types of small- and medium-scale enterprises in current manufacturing industries in Myanmar may be categorized as follows: (1) analog enterprises in rural areas; (2) traditional local enterprises; (3) local urban enterprises; (4) export-oriented small and medium-sized enterprises; and (5) subcontractors for parts manufacturing small and medium-sized enterprises. Each topic will be discussed in turn.

Analog Enterprises in Rural Areas

Most SMEs fall into this category, which includes small cottage industries. Typical enterprises are rice milling, edible oil extraction, tobacco manufacturing (including cheroot), and other industries that target local markets, such as various food processing, drinks, and tea processing firms.

Traditional Local Enterprises

This category includes local homegrown enterprises that process materials other than agricultural products. Included are various food processing, furniture making, metal working (farming tools and mule-cart parts), textile, sewing, jewel polishing and processing, and lacquerware firms, and so forth. These are mostly cottage enterprises.

Local Urban Enterprises

These enterprises operate in Yangon, Mandalay, and other cities and suburbs. Some are manufacturing enterprises dependent upon imported raw material. This group has seen new entrepreneurs as well as investments in plants and equipment since deregulation in 1988. Major enterprises include various food processing (especially snacks, drinks, and instant foods); household-item manufacturing such as kitchen utensils; construction material manufacturing; bricks and stone processing; various printing works; wrapping material manufacturing. These small- and medium-scale enterprises are beginning to receive orders from private foreign companies, such as hotels, indicating the possibility of further development.

Export-Oriented Small and Medium-Sized Enterprises

Until at least 1988, private manufacturing enterprises produced hardly any export products. There were no export-oriented manufacturing firms, except for the rare cases of lacquerware, silk textiles, and handicrafts. Nowadays, firms with private foreign investments are taking the lead in increasing the export of garments, frozen shrimp, and woodwork such as furniture.

Subcontractors for Parts Manufacturing Small and Medium-Sized Enterprises

In the past hardly any business relationships existed for subcontracting or for orders between private and state-owned enterprises. Such relationships were rare among private enterprises as well, and it can be said that there were no subcontracting SMEs. Since 1988, with the progress of deregulation and the development of market principles, subcontractors are slowly being established. However, there are very few subcontracting relationships in parts manufacturing. Subcontracting businesses are seen as receiving orders and deliveries of wrapping materials and other related products. In order to promote SMEs in manufacturing industries, it is essential to reform state-owned enterprises and increase private foreign investment.

Basic Concepts of Industrialization in Myanmar

As the military administration has made clear, the basic strategy for Myanmar's economic development is to develop industries that use the nation's comparative advantages effectively, as well as to push forward a series of economic reforms. The Five-Year Economic Development Program lists the following development priorities: (1) agriculture, livestock, and fisheries; (2) oil, natural gas and various mining activities; (3) processing and manufacturing based on agriculture; and (4) exports. The program targets the economic development of agriculture and the agro-industry as the major focus of state policy. Given the nation's relative advantages, its industrial infrastructure, dependence upon natural resources, and competitive as well as supplementary relations with neighboring countries, the strategy is extremely appropriate. A number of ideas can be developed with respect to Myanmar's industrialization strategies.

First, the fact that agricultural development is the most important factor in Myanmar's economic development will not change drastically for some time to come. Agricultural development helps to increase income, employment, and exports, all of which enable industrial development. To improve agriculture, it is necessary to develop both the supply and demand sectors. From the viewpoint of the supply sector, it is important to develop industries that support agriculture. Among agricultural machinery and chemicals, domestic chemical fertilizer production should urgently be increased. At present it is too import-dependent (51.2% in 1997) although the country possesses the required raw materials. From the viewpoint of the demand sector, it is important to open agricultural processing factories so that drink and food processing industries can develop. These would include sugar manufacturing and edible oil refining, which can substitute for imports effectively, and fruit and vegetable processing industries, which are promising export industries.

The promotion of import-substituting industries is essential, but Myanmar would do well not to follow the ASEAN example and rush to develop modern industries, such as automobiles and electric appliances that require capital equipment and high technologies. Rather, Myanmar should remain dependent for a while on those nations for such high value-added products. It would benefit by concentrating instead on manufacturing parts necessary for modern industries in ASEAN countries, especially Malaysia, Singapore, and Thailand, and promote subcontracting industries for them. However, Myanmar should hasten to manufacture relatively low value-added domestic products that are labor-intensive, require no large-scale capital equipment, and the raw materials of which are easily supplied domestically. Products that are highly effective in substituting for imports include daily necessities such as toilet paper and other paper products, ceramic ware, kitchen utensils, and stationery, metalwork products such as bottle caps, textiles such as towels and fabrics, galvanized iron sheeting, cement, glassware, and plastics.

The development of export-oriented industries is crucial to Myanmar's future economic growth. Ninety percent of the country's exports depend on primary products. Since 1988, the export of garments, processed marine products such as frozen shrimp, processed jewelry, furniture and other manufactured products has slowly increased. An increase in major export products, such as rice and beans, should be aimed for by improving productivity and quality. Timber exports, however, cannot be expected to increase because of deforestation and in the absence of more planned logging. Wood-based products can, however, be a good export, and woodwork is one of the country's promising industries. For an effective exported-oriented policy, it is important to promote such industries as agricultural processing, marine processing, and woodwork, industries that use domestic raw materials, as well as such labor-intensive industries as sewing and manufacturing decorations.

Strategy for Developing Small and Medium-Sized Enterprises

There are a number of issues of concern about implementing industrialization strategies in Myanmar. For instance, an important issue is to organize, streamline, and privatize state-owned enterprises. It is also important to promote linkages among enterprises and to introduce and transfer technologies. The role of small- and medium-scale enterprises in industrialization may be considered from a number of viewpoints.

1 Import-Substituting Small-Scale Enterprises

As stated above, Myanmar is currently heavily dependent on products that can be manufactured with small-scale investments, such as daily necessities, general merchandise, processed foods and drinks, and simple electric and machinery components. When manufactured domestically, these light-industry products can be easily competitive with imports, and small and medium-sized enterprises enjoy numerous advantages. Promoting import-substituting light business is very effective in reducing imports and should be encouraged.

2 Export-Oriented Small and Medium-Sized Enterprises

In order to improve the export structure, which is dependent on primary industry products, Myanmar should actively encourage the diversification of export products. To do so, it is necessary to promote processed export-product industries that use domestic raw materials. Promising industries in this sector include various agricultural processing, food processing, woodwork, metalwork, and marine product processing concerns. Since this type of industry requires cultivating overseas market and a certain standard of quality, it is advantageous to merge with overseas private enterprises to enter overseas markets. It is necessary to encourage bonded processed products, such as sewn products, from the viewpoint of increasing employment and export revenues. Such bonded processed products, which import raw materials and produce revenues of processing charges only, should play a certain role in promoting industrialization and create ripple effects if they gradually increase domestic raw material supplies. Related industries are thereby encouraged. Most export-oriented industries can also be advantageously encouraged by small and medium-sized enterprises.

3 Rural Small and Medium-Sized Enterprises

Since farmers comprise 60% of all workers and the farming population accounts for 70% of the population, the key to Myanmar's economic development undoubtedly lies in developing agriculture and farming villages. In order to expand the country's market, an important goal is to increase incomes and employment opportunities and to raise the purchasing power of farming villages through developing agriculture. It is thus necessary not only to expand agricultural production but also to promote various industries in farming villages. In addition to agricultural processing, it is effective to promote agriculture-supporting industries, such as agricultural machinery manufacturing and agriculture-related equipment manufacturing. It is widely believed that most farmers are landed farmers in Myanmar, but, in fact, there are many landless farmers in farming villages. It is possible to prevent an income imbalance between urban and rural areas and prevent farmers from concentrating in urban areas by establishing industries in farming villages to absorb these only partially employed people. It is necessary to reorganize the establishment of rural small- and medium-scale enterprises as an important development measure.

4 Local and Traditional Small and Medium-Sized Enterprises

Traditional industries in Myanmar have created characteristic products in each region. Typical traditional industries include lacquerware in Bagan, silk in Mandalay and the Inle Lake region, cotton in the Rakhine and Gangaw regions, pottery in Twante and other areas, Buddhist altar fittings and furniture in the suburbs of Yangon, Myanmar cigarettes, silverwork, and jewelry processing in central Myanmar. Among these traditional handicrafts, a number of products can compete internationally through technological improvement and facility modernization. Although most products have thus far been limited to local markets, quality, design, and other aspects need to improve in order to target large markets, like the domestic and overseas markets, in the future. Some local industries will, of course, lose their competitiveness when modern factories and foreign products flow in. However, lacquerware, silk textiles, and the like are promising industries with the possibility of becoming international products through the improvement of technology, design, and materials.

Although some local industries, such as rice milling, oil extraction, and lumbering, are competitive among state-owned and large-scale enterprises as well as import products, small and medium-sized enterprises can have a competitive edge if they cultivate markets advantageous to them and meet extensive market demand.

5 International Subcontracting Small and Medium-Sized Businesses

Myanmar's membership in ASEAN and the ASEAN Free Trade Area (AFTA) will have an impact on it future growth, and AFTA's plans to abolish tariffs in 2008 will impact on the country and region. When planning its future economic development, Myanmar must consider the economic dependence, particularly on ASEAN, that will further develop in coming years. In other words, industry sharing within ASEAN will undoubtedly progress, and Myanmar's economy must be considered an integral part of the ASEAN economic region. Given this aspect of industrialization, Myanmar does not need to promote industries or manufacturers in every field in the country. Rather, it should aim for industrialization and for developing industries in which it enjoys comparative advantages over other ASEAN nations.

Comparative advantages are immovable advantages, such as the diversity of the land, resources, and location, and other advantages such as workforce, price level, technology, and infrastructure that may change depending on the stage of economic development. However, in addition to the immovable advantages, Myanmar currently has advantages over at least Cambodia and Laos, latecomers to ASEAN, in areas such as workforce, price levels, social conditions, legal system, English-speaking ability, industrial expansion, and market size. Myanmar should use these advantages and consider specializing in supporting industries for the more advanced ASEAN members.

Myanmar currently has only a few industries in the manufacturing sector capable of competing with ASEAN's more advanced members. Myanmar is gradually losing its advantages to latecomers to ASEAN in such processing industries as sewing, decoration, jewelry, food, drinks, and timber. Instead of focusing only on these industries, Myanmar should consider actively promoting subcontracting industries related to ASEAN companies. Myanmar would do well to establish a manufacturing system to subcontract for Malaysia, Singapore, and Thailand in manufacturing spare parts for automobiles, electric household appliances, electronic devices, construction machinery, and various other equipment and machinery. In order to achieve this, it is important to develop small and medium-sized enterprises in diverse manufacturing industries. Myanmar can play a bottom structure role in vertical industry sharing within the ASEAN economic region. Subcontracting industries for ASEAN are not limited to manufacturing spare products but, of course, are also related to finished and partly finished products.

Appendix

Table 1.1 Change of Factory Size by Ownership, 1990-98

Number of employees	*1990-91*		*1993-94*		*1994-95*		*1995-96*		*1996-97*		*1997-98*	
	a	b	a	b	a	b	a	b	a	b	a	b
Below 10	909	31324	909	38551	815	43239	808	44683	811	45169	811	49222
10-50	289	1795	292	2089	287	2076	254	2075	251	2142	247	2209
50-100	140	820	142	152	146	417	146	161	148	183	144	199
Over 100	427	25	429	43	427	47	399	5	399	98	398	108
Total	**1765**	**33964**	**1772**	**40835**	**1675**	**45779**	**1607**	**46994**	**1609**	**47592**	**1600**	**51738**

Source: *Review of Financial, Economic, and Social Conditions*. 1990-91, 1993-94, 1994-95, 1996-97

[a] State-owned enterprises

[b] Private and cooperative enterprises

Table 1.2 Change of Factory Ownership by Type of Industry, 1992-98

	1990-91		*1993-94*		*1994-95*		*1995-96*		*1996-97*		*1997-98*	
	a	*b*	*a*	*b*	*a*	*b*	*a*	*b*	*a*	*b*	*a*	*b*
Food and beverages	208	20993	209	23249	210	26842	210	28559	209	28485	209	29036
Clothing and apparel	63	2404	63	2747	63	2974	33	3705	33	4265	33	3916
Construction materials	128	3417	128	3937	127	3899	127	3401	127	3369	126	3614
Personal goods	14	1241	14	1313	14	1402	14	1663	14	1811	14	1381
Household goods	15	168	15	205	15	243	15	457	15	448	15	227
Printing and publishing	28	334	28	348	28	368	28	367	28	364	28	367
Industrial raw materials	928	1870	835	1879	821	1957	826	1312	829	1371	821	1810
Minerals and petro products	23	1925	23	1939	22	2065	22	2691	22	2490	22	2720
Agricultural equipment	3	35	3	6	3	70	3	241	3	330	3	83
Machinery & equipment	7	105	7	111	7	138	7	580	7	539	7	331
Transport vehicles	5	110	5	111	5	123	5	172	5	177	5	201
Workshop & dockyards	305	-	305	-	305	-	305	-	305	-	305	-
Miscellaneous	10	4683	10	5277	12	5453	12	4107	12	3943	12	8052
Total	**1737**	**37225**	**1645**	**41172**	**1632**	**45552**	**1607**	**47255**	**1609**	**47592**	**1600**	**51738**

Source: *Review of Financial, Economic, and Social Conditions*.1993-94, 1996-97.

[a] State-owned enterprises

[b] Private and cooperative enterprises

Table 1.3 Change in Number of Enterprises Registered with the Directorate of Investment and Company Administration, 1988-98

Years	*Myanmar Co. Ltd.*	*Foreign Co. & Branches*	*Partner-ships*	*Chamber of Commerce & Industry*	*Joint Ventures*	*Total*
1988-89	21	2	31	-	-	54
1989-90	154	37	345	-	14	550
1990-91	640	43	189	6	18	896
1991-92	494	51	162	12	9	728
1992-93	961	51	123	11	8	1153
1993-94	1133	113	99	2	13	1360
1994-95	1383	146	106	-	9	1644
1995-96	1888	216	53	1	16	2174
1996-97	2140	336	58	1	20	2555
1997-98	2029	201	48	2	17	2297
1998-99 1-4 to 30.9.98	739	55	9	1	8	812
Total	**11582**	**1250**	**1223**	**36**	**132**	**14223**

Source: Ministry of National Planning and Economic Development, DICA

Table 1.4 Change in Number of Private Business Enterprises and Entrepreneurs, 1989-98

Enterprises	*1989-90*	*1992-93*	*1997-98*
Exporters & Importers	986	4813	8510
Business Representatives	183	947	2075
Myanmar Companies Limited	174	2269	10369
Partnership Firms	376	850	1201
Foreign Companies and Branches	39	183	1152
Joint Venture Companies Limited	15	49	122
Chamber of Commerce and Industry	3	29	35
Tourist Enterprises	-	69	622
Tourist Transport Business	-	71	1620
Hotel and Lodging-House Business	-	46	548
Tour Guide Business	-	87	2763
Total	**1776**	**9413**	**29017**

Sources: Ministry of National Planning and Economic Development, Central Statistical Organization, Statistical Yearbook, 1995 and 1997, Yangon, Myanmar

Table 1.5 Change in Private Production Sector and Growth Rate, 1986-98

Year	*Goods*		*Services*		*Trade*		*Total Production*	
	Volume	*Growth Rate (%)*	*Volume*	*Growth Rate (%)*	*Volume*	*Growth Rate (%)*	*Volume*	*Growth Rate (%)*
1986-87	28107.9	-	3169.9	-	6745.8	-	38023.6	-
1987-88	26752.0	-4.8	3266.6	3.1	7025.2	4.1	37043.8	-2.6
1988-89	23670.0	-11.5	3182.0	-2.6	7142.4	1.7	33994.4	-8.2
1989-90	25318.5	6.9	3255.2	2.3	7615.7	6.6	36189.4	6.5
1990-91	26199.6	3.5	3288.7	1.0	7787.1	2.3	37275.4	3.0
1991-92	25834.1	-1.4	3385.6	2.9	7701.3	-1.1	36921.0	-0.9
1992-93	28834.7	11.6	3785.0	11.8	8557.8	11.1	41177.5	11.5
1993-94	30639.7	6.3	4058.2	7.2	9227.4	7.8	43925.3	6.7
1994-95	32624.7	6.5	4552.2	12.2	10071.6	9.2	47248.8	7.6
1995-96	34644.4	6.2	4931.7	8.3	10717.2	6.4	50293.8	6.5
1996-97 (p.a.)	36858.5	6.4	5409.6	9.7	11330.8	5.7	53598.9	6.6
1997-98 (p)	38322.7	4.0	5924.0	9.5	11784.1	4.0	56030.8	4.5

Source: *Review of Financial, Economic, and Social Conditions*, Various issues

Table 1.6 Foreign Direct Investment by Industry, 1990-97 (US$ million)

	1990-91		*1991-92*		*1992-93*		*1993-94*		*1994-95*		*1995-96*		*1996-97*	
	1	*2*	*1*	*2*	*1*	*2*	*1*	*2*	*1*	*2*	*1*	*2*	*1*	*2*
Agriculture	0	0	0	0	2.7	0	0	0.1	0	0	0	0	6	0
Manufacturing	42.7	18	5.9	0.8	13.3	9.5	18.2	4.3	76.3	13.8	21.3	30.6	923.6	19
Oil & Gas	19.1	178.1	0	228.4	44.5	128.7	19.5	66.5	1039.5	47.4	14.8	189.2	695.6	494.3
Mining	55.1	18.3	0	3.2	33.4	0.4	20.9	0.2	0.5	9.5	155.8	10.9	178.3	41.9
Fishery	77.3	3	0	0	5.9	0	7.6	0.5	148.2	6.7	13.1	2.7	17.5	2.3
Hotel & Tourism	86.4	7.7	0	2.7	3.0	9.4	311.4	18.4	86.1	56.6	79.2	70.5	114.9	129.7
Transport	0	0	0	0	1.0	1.0	0	0	1.3	1.0	118.9	6.3	47.9	26.3
Real Estate	0	0	0	0	0	0	0	0	0	0	251.5	7.3	623.5	38.1
Industrial Estate	0	0	0	0	0	0	0	0	0	0	12.0	0	181.1	20.6
Others	0	0	0	0	0	0	0	0	0	0	1.7	0	8.6	1.1
Total	**280.6**	**225.1**	**5.9**	**235.1**	**103.8**	**149**	**377.6**	**90**	**1351.9**	**135.9**	**668.2**	**317.6**	**2814.3**	**773**

Source: International Monetary Fund Report, May 1998

Table 1.7 Macroeconomic Situation, 1990-97

	1990-91	*1991-92*	*1992-93*	*1993-94*	*1994-95*	*1995-96*	*1996-97*	
Real GDP Growth	2.8	-0.6	9.3	6.0	7.5	6.9	6.4	annual % rate
Consumer prices	21.9	29.1	22.3	33.5	22.4	21.8	20.0	
Total revenue	9.2	9.6	8.1	7.8	7.1	6.7	6.8	% of GDP
Total expenditure	15.4	16.8	13.5	11.9	13.0	12.9	13.3	
Overall balance	-6.1	-7.0	-5.2	-4.4	-6.1	-6.3	-6.5	
Trade balance	-492	-412	-420	-606.6	-560.7	-940.5	-943.6	Million US$
Export	477	431	591	695.4	927.1	890.3	885.6	
Import	-970	-842	-1,010	-1,302.0	-1,487.8	-1,830.8	-1,829.2	
Current account balance	-527	-344	-275	-292.0	-185.8	-420.1	-476.4	
Overall balance	-372	-233	-278	-245.9	-44.4	-18.4	-315.2	
Gross official reserves	311	297	286	338.9	425.9	381.1	287.8	
Official rate (kyat per US$)	6.2	6.2	6.2	6.1	5.8	5.8	6.1	
Parallel rate (kyat per US$)	100.00	120.6	112.0	105.0	109.0	120.0	170.0	
Total debt	4,704	4,873	5,327	5,481	5,511.7	5,479.1	5,388	
Debt-service obligation	286	306	351	321.8	326.2	300.0	339.9	
External debt arrears	587	809	1,103	1,343.9	1,599.5	1,479.6	1,454.7	

Source: International Monetary Fund Report, May 1998

2

A Survey of Selected Manufacturing Firms in Myanmar

Nu Nu Yin

Department of Management Studies
The Institute of Economics, Yangon

Introduction

Industrialization is an indispensable element of a country's general socio-economic growth and development. A country may be classified as a "developed country" or "developing country," depending on the extent of its respective industrial development. Usually, this development follows certain recognizable phases, from a primitive agricultural subsistence economy to a sophisticated one producing manufactured goods for export.[1] Economic activity in the first phase consists mainly of the production of subsistence goods for local consumption, for example, agriculture and fishery products, and so on. In the second phase, the economy undertakes the export of natural materials, such as agriculture, fishery, forestry, and mining products. The local processing of materials begins in the third phase, and the economy shifts to exporting processed, that is, value-added products, rather than raw materials. The economy must now include the acquisition, operation, and maintenance of technology and processes. In the fourth phase, the economy undertakes the integrated manufacturing of modern industrial and consumer products for domestic use. Its industries now have to control all stages of industrial production by determining market needs through product development, design, manufacture, and marketing. In the final phase, the economy has the capability to manufacture products that can compete with those of fully developed industrial economies in the global market. Developing countries have a relative specialization in the earlier phases, and Myanmar is no exception. Accordingly, it is necessary to shift resources from the low-productivity primary center to a high-productivity manufacturing sector for the purpose of development.

Myanmar has been trying intensively to launch the industrial development process. The government has taken steps to improve state-owned enterprises and especially to encourage the development of private enterprises since a market economy was adopted in 1988. The State Law and Order Restoration Council (SLORC), now the State Peace and Development Council, promulgated the Union of Myanmar Foreign Investment Law of 1988, the State Enterprises Law of 1989, the Private Industrial Enterprise Law of 1990, the Promotion of Cottage Industries Law of 1991, and the Myanmar Citizens Investment Law of 1994, and prescribed related rules and regulations. Moreover, the Myanmar Industrial Development Committee (MIDC) was formed in July 1995 by Notification No. 37/95 in order to give greater impetus to the industrialization process. Almost all the activities of MIDC are intended to promote private industries, such as holding industrial exhibitions, conducting seminars and conferences on industrial promotion and technology matters, and assisting smooth operations and advancement. The MIDC has initiated a Five-Year Industrial Plan (1996-97 to 2000-01) concerned with implementing suitable industrial projects in conformity with its policies. Additionally, the Myanmar Industrial Development Bank (MIDB) was established in February 1996 and is now functioning to assist in providing loans to private businesses.

Non-profit organizations such as the Union of Myanmar Chamber of Commerce and Industry (UMCCI) and the Myanmar Industries Association (MIA) are also dedicated to promoting private enterprises. Although the UMCCI was founded in 1919, the MIA was founded only in 1993 with the main objective of achieving growth and development of enterprises in the private sector. The MIA provides a variety of services, such as consultant services, training courses, seminars, workshops, and study tours.

Present Status of Manufacturing Firms

Manufacturing firms in Myanmar can be categorized under three types of ownership: (1) state-owned enterprises, (2) cooperatives, and (3) private enterprises. Control over and management of state-owned enterprises is placed under different ministries, depending on which is most appropriate to their operation. Together with Ministry of Industry No.1 and Ministry of Industry No. 2, other ministries concerned in manufacturing and processing are the Ministries of Agriculture and Irrigation, Commerce, Livestock, Fisheries, Forestry, Railways, Mines, Energy, and Information. In 1997-98, the number of state-owned enterprises under these ministries amounted to 1,600.

The Ministry of Cooperatives is responsible for the affairs of all enterprises run by cooperatives. These include milk factories, rice mills, edible oil mills, mechanical and engineering workshops, textile industries, the plastics and chemical industries, the foundry and metallurgy industries, and enamelware factories. In 1997-98, the number of cooperatives totaled 637. The Cottage Industries Department under the Ministry of Cooperatives gives assistance to handicraft production and cottage industries.

Private enterprises are scattered all over the country. By region, Mandalay Division has the largest number, followed by Yangon and Bago Divisions, respectively. In 1997-98, the number of private enterprises totaled 51,101. The contribution of the three industrial sectors to GDP shows that private enterprises play a major role in the national industrial production (Table 2.1). In recent years private enterprises contributed nearly 72% of GDP in the manufacturing sector.

Table 2.1 Structural Change of GDP by Ownership, Processing and Manufacturing Sector (at 1985-86 constant producers' prices) (million kyat)

Sector	*1992-93*	*%*	*1994-95*	*%*	*1995-96*	*%*	*1996-97*	*%*	*1997-98 (Provisional)*	*%*
State-owned	1,379.6	28.4	1,595.3	27.7	1,672.6	27.01	1,770.5	27.1	1,848.2	26.87
Cooperatives	114.0	2.4	52.7	0.9	61.3	0.99	66.5	1.02	62.2	0.9
Private	3,356.4	69.2	4,108.9	71.4	4,457.7	72.9	4,694.8	71.88	4,967.6	72.23
Total	**4,850**	**100**	**5,756.9**	**100**	**6,191.6**	**100**	**6,531.8**	**100**	**6,878**	**100**

However, the share of manufacturing and processing industries in total GDP was only 9.25% in 1997-98 and remained more or less at the same level during the 1990s. Moreover, the growth rate of this manufacturing sector has gradually been declining from 10.8% in 1992-93 to 5.3% in 1997-98. Despite the endeavors made in the industrialization process mentioned above, such an unsatisfying situation indicates the need to conduct a survey of manufacturing firms to discern the current situation and to seek ways and means for its betterment.

Design and Scope of the Survey

A survey on 132 manufacturing firms was conducted in Yangon and Mandalay during October and November of 1997 and 1998. On this occasion, six purely state-owned enterprises, seventeen foreign joint ventures, two local joint ventures, one cooperative, and 106 private firms were surveyed using a prescribed questionnaire, followed by extensive interviews with industrialists (Table 2.2). Eighty-four firms are located in the industrial zone, and 48 are in non-industrial areas. Purposive and convenience sampling methods were applied to a selection of firms. The selected firms, under three types of ownership, are engaged in fifteen types of industry, located both in the industrial zones and non-industrial areas of Yangon and Mandalay. The profile of each firm, with a focus on production, marketing, personnel, and finance, was identified (see Appendix).

State-Owned Enterprises

Three wood-based firms under the Ministry of Forestry, one pharmaceuticals firm under the Ministry of Industry No.1, one machine shop under the Ministry of Industry No.2, and one textile firm under the Ministry of Defense were chosen for the survey. Among them were five factories situated in Yangon Division and one factory of the Ministry of Industry No.2 in Bago Division (Table 2.3).

Table 2.2 Selected Firms

Type of Industry	*Type of Ownership*					*Location*		*Number of Firms*
	State-owned	*Joint Venture*		*Private*	*Cooperative*	*Industrial Zone*	*Non Industrial Zone*	
		Local	*Foreign*					
Food and beverage		2	3	23		20	8	28
Plastics			1	19		16	4	20
Wood-based products	3		2	8		7	6	13
Machine shop	1			11		9	3	12
Textile and garment	1		6	5		8	4	12
Electrical products				7		5	2	7
Pharmaceuticals	1			2	1	2	2	4
Paper				4		4		4
Metal				4		3	1	4
Construction materials			1	2		2	1	3
Fisheries			2			1	1	2
Gems			2				2	2
Printing				2		2		2
Computer software				12			12	12
Others				7		5	2	7
Total	**6**	**2**	**17**	**106**	**1**	**84**	**48**	**132**

Nearly half the firms were established prior to the installation of military rule in 1962. The others were set up during the period of socialist economy from 1962 to 1988. The Tatmadaw Textile Industry is an exception. Although its year of establishment was stated to be 1989, the firm was originally owned by the Ministry of Industry No.1 and handed over to the Ministry of Defense in that year.

The estimated capital of the state-owned firms ranged from 3.2 million to 577 million kyat, depending on the type of products produced and the size of the firm. As to the number of people employed, the smallest firm had 334 employees and the largest had 2,300. Based on the above factors, it can be generalized that state-owned firms are either medium-sized or large and have been in operation for three or more decades.

All selected firms apply intermediate technology. The firms have installed mostly imported machines, but some have a mixture of imported and domestic machines. In the case of raw materials, almost all firms depend on both imported and domestic materials. Only the wood-based firms of the state-owned enterprises deal with both the domestic and foreign market. Others are entirely devoted to production for domestic use.

Joint Ventures

Nineteen joint ventures (JVs), both local and foreign, were chosen for the survey. All the JVs' foreign partners were found to be Asian: eight companies were from Singapore, three from South Korea, two each from Thailand and Malaysia, and one each from the Philippines and Hong Kong. ASEAN involvement predominates. Only two local joint ventures in the food and beverage industry were included in the survey. The selected magnitude of JVs consist of six garment enterprises, five food and beverage enterprises, two wood-based enterprises, two gem enterprises, two fishery enterprises, one plastics enterprise, and one construction material enterprise (Table 2.4). Among the foreign JVs, foreign partners have a greater share of profits in ten firms, whereas Myanmarese partners have a greater share

Table 2.3 State-Owned Enterprises

Company Name	*Location (Division)*	*Year Established*	*First year of Operation*	*Type of Industry*	*Main Product*	*Production Volume (annual)*	*Estimated Capital (million kyat)*	*Total Number of Employees*
No (1) Plywood Factory, Myanmar Timber Enterprise	Yangon	1959	1962	Wood-based	Timber plywood, veneer	200,000 panels	3.209	334
No (2) Plywood Factory, Myanmar Timber Enterprise	Yangon	1968	1968	Wood-based	Plywood, veneer	400,000 panels	26.6	443
No (4) Saw Mill, Myanmar Timber Enterprise	Yangon	1952	1955	Wood-based	Teak converted timber	4,500 tons	500	780
Myanmar Pharmaceutical Factory	Yangon	1954	1957	Pharmaceutical	Tablets and capsules, powders and liquids, ointment, sterile products, alcohol and allied products, biological products	840 million (tablets), 70,000 liters (liquid), 24 million bottles (injection)	420	2,362
No (3) Factory, Myanmar Heavy Industry	Bago	1965	1969	Machine Shop	Pumps and diesel engines, power tillers, generators, fan motors, hand tools, welding electrodes	Pumps 4,600 units, hand tools 200,000 units, motors 2,000 units, welding electrodes 1,000 tons	577	2,283
Tatmadaw Canvas Weaving and Waterproofing Factory	Yangon	1989	1989	Textiles	Cotton gray canvas, waterproofing canvas, tarpaulin sheets, drills, cellular, web equipment, ribbon	Web equipment 2 million units, cotton canvas 2 million yards	342	1,092

in the other four. The remaining firms are operating with an equal share of profits.

Concerning the contract periods of JVs, eight firms have contracted for five to ten years, two for eleven to twenty years, and five for twenty to thirty years. The estimated capital is normally stated in kyat, but some firms offered figures in US dollars. The majority of firms' estimated capital is found to be in the range of 10-50 million kyat.

More than half of the selected JVs employ labor within the range of 100-500 in the production of wood-based products, foodstuffs and beverages, gems, construction materials, and plastic products. However, the garment industries employed more labor than the others, employing about 2,000 workers. It can be said that these firms create more jobs for the labor force. This element can also be interpreted that foreign partners are enjoying the country's cheap labor costs.

Firms that are producing wood-based products, garments, gems, and fishery products export their products, some totally and others partially. The rest deal solely with the local market. The main reason why these firms do not export their products is that they have huge domestic demand that is as yet more than they are able to fill. The other reason is because of the low quality of their products. However, they have plans to begin exporting in the near future. Such industries include producers of cigarettes, beer, dairy products, and construction materials.

Thirteen firms aimed at export promotion, and five firms aimed at import substitution. One firm producing packing materials represents both aims. Apart from the two gem enterprises that apply labor-intensive technology, all firms apply intermediate technology. Most of the firms are engaged in a processing type of operation, but a few are producing feedstock materials. Basically, forming the joint venture has advantages in acquiring capital, technology transfer, and achievement of greater market potential.

Table 2.4 Surveyed Firms: Joint Ventures

Company Name	Location (Division)	Partner				Year Established	First year of Operation	Type of Industry	Main Product	Estimated Capital	Total No. of Employees	Production Volume (annual)
		Local	Foreign	Profit ratio	Contract Years							
Myanmar Segye International, Ltd.	Yangon	UMEHL*	Segye Corp. (Korea)	60(F) 40(M)	30	1990	1990	Garment	Pants and skirts, jackets, coats, jogging suits	US$ 1.25 million	1,873	1.5 million units
Myanmar Ace Metal Industries Co., Ltd.	Yangon	Myanmar Metal Industries (Ministry of Industry No.1)	Pressure-weld International Pte.,Ltd. (Singapore)	45(F) 55(M)	10	1990	1990	House-hold appliances construction materials	Aluzinc roofing sheets, enamel ware, aluminum ware	1.6 million kyat	173	3,504.23 metric tons
Myanmar VES Joint Ventures Co., Ltd.	Yangon	Myanmar Gems Enterprise (Ministry of Mines)	VES Group Co. (Thailand)	40(F) 60(M)	10	1992	1993	Gems	Jewelry, gem stones	US$2.6 million	375	5,334 pieces
Myanmar Yaung Chi Oo Co., Ltd.	Mandalay	Myanmar Food-stuff industries (Ministry of Industry No. 1)	Yaung Chi OoTrading Pte., Ltd. (Sinapore)	45(F) 55(M)	5	1994	1994	Beverages and soft drinks	Mandalay Beer	106.26 million kyat	95	1.87 million dozens
Myanmar NC Woodwork Co., Ltd.	Yangon	Myanmar General and Maintenance Industry (Ministry of Industry No. 1)	NC Woodwork and Construction Pte., Ltd.(Singapore)	45(F) 55(M)	10	1989	1990	Wood-based	Doors, door frames, architraves, parquet, tongue & groove wall, ceiling paneling, molding, skirting	10 million kyat	178	53.89 million kyat

* UMEHL Union of Myanmar Economic Holding Limited

Myanmar Nouveau Co., Ltd.	Yangon	UMEHL*	Nouveau Marketing Co., Ltd. (Thailand)	49(F) 51(M)	15	1995	1996	Gem	Rubies, sapphires	22.8 million kyat	406	30,049.6 Carats
Rothmans of Pall Mall Myanmar Pte., Ltd.	Yangon	UMEHL*	Rothmans Myanmar Holding, Ltd. (Singapore)	60(F) 40(M)	30	1994	1995	Food & beverage	Cigarettes	38.745 million kyat	217	187,200 cases
Myanmar Daewoo International, Ltd. (Factory I)	Yangon	UMEHL*	Daewoo Corp. (Korea)	55(F) 45(M)	30	1991	1991	Garment	Men's shirts, women's blouses, pajamas, jackets	US$ 1.25 million	2,072	240,000 dozens
Chin Su Myanmar Co., Ltd.	Bago	Myanmar Mayflower Trading Co., Ltd	Chin Su Co., Ltd. (Philippines)	80(F) 20(M)	20	1993	1995	Wood-based	Plywood (3-ply, 5-ply), formica sheets, veneer	50 million kyat	577	251,000 pieces
Myanmar Seafoods, Ltd.	Yangon	Ministry of Livestock Breeding &Fisheries	PL International Pte., Ltd. (Singapore)	65(F) 35(M)	30	1994	1996	Fisheries	Deep frozen prawns	27.5 million kyat	563	US$ 1.6 million
Myanmar Euroworld International, Ltd.	Yangon	Myanmar Textile Industry (Ministry of Industry No.1)	British Virgin Islands (Hong Kong)	50(F) 50(M)	5	1994	1994	Garment	Knit shirts, jackets, hosiery	15.86 million kyat	1,837	72,000 pieces
Myanmar Knitwear Manufacturing Co., Ltd.	Yangon	Myanmar Textile Industry (Ministry of Industry No.1)	Value Knitwear Pte., Ltd. (Singapore)	50(F) 50(M)	5	1995	1995	Garment	Men's wear, women's wear, children's wear	12 million kyat	816	2 million pieces

Table 2.4 (continued)

Dagon Dairy Products Co., Ltd.	Yangon	Myanmar Golden Star Co., Ltd	Myanmar Defence Services**	49 (**) 51 (M)	30	1996	1997	Food & Beverage	Condensed milk	253 million kyat	150	1.2 million cartons
Zabu Poly Pack Factory (Asia World Co., Ltd.)	Yangon	Asia World Co., Ltd	Tego Sdn. Bhd. (Malaysia)	60(F) 40(M)	10	1996	1996	Packing Materials	Jumbo bags, PP woven bags	26.4 million kyat + US$0.3 million	260	12.12 million bags
Myanmar Brewery, Ltd.	Yangon	UMEHL*	Fraser & Neave (Singapore)	55(F) 45(M)	NA	1995	1997	Food & Beverage	Tiger Beer, ABC Stout, Anchor, Myanmar Beer	US$40 million	233	124.8 million cans, 53.04 million bottles,187,200 kegs
Myanmar Daewoo International, Ltd. (Factory No II)	Yangon	UMEHL*	Daewoo Corp. (Korea)	55(F) 45(M)	30	197	1997	Garment	Soft drinks, sparkling, Fruito, Fantasy (orange, Cola)	9 million kyat	526	360,000 dozens
Htoo Htet Co., Ltd.	Yangon	Htoo Htet Co., Ltd.	Malaysia Company		5	1998	1998	Garment	Garment, knitting & woven sweaters, sportswear	NA	300	48,000 dozens
T & T International, Ltd.	Yangon	T&T International Co., Ltd.	Singapore Company	50(F) 50(M)	NA	1996	1996	Fisheries	Deep frozen prawns	US$2 million	234	1050 tons
Diamond Soft Drinks and Ice Factory	Yangon	Loi Hein, Co.	Myanmar Foodstuff Industries Ministry of Industry No.1	NA	5	1926		Food & Beverage	Soft drinks, Sparkling, Fruito, Fantasy (orange, Cola)	118 million kyat	248	9.6 million dozen

** Local partner

Private Firms

Private sector development has been recognized as an important partner in striving for economic growth since the market economic system was adopted. Moreover, the government endorsed five objectives for Myanmar's industrial development, namely: (1) the development of agro-based industries; (2) qualitative and quantitative improvement of industrial products; (3) the production of new industrial items; (4) the manufacture of industrial equipment; and (5) the acquisition of good opportunities required for the industrialization of the nation. For these reasons enterprises in the private sector should be encouraged. The Myanmar Industrial Development Committee (MIDC) reinforces the promotion of these private enterprises through various measures. In this respect, seventeen industrial zones have been established, and private enterprises are gradually establishing their businesses in a variety of sizes.

In order to cope with the present situation, a survey was conducted of 106 private firms, 84 in the Mandalay and Yangon industrial zones and 48 in the non-industrial zone of Yangon. The profiles of the firms are presented in the Appendix. Although the firms differ in size, they are rather small and medium-sized firms. Most private firms produce consumer products, and target the domestic market. These firms are in the early stage of the industrial development process, that is, processing for domestic use. Most apply labor-intensive technology with some exceptional cases applying intermediate technology.

Analysis and Findings

Based on their nature of their product, the surveyed firms are categorized under fifteen types of industry such as food and beverage, plastics, wood-based products, machine shops, textiles and garments, electrical products, pharmaceuticals, paper, metal, construction materials, fishery products, gems, printing, computer software, and others (see Table 2.2).

Main Products

Twenty-eight firms in the food and beverage industry were chosen for the survey. The main products for food include, among others, bread, biscuits, cakes, ice cream, sugar, coconut oil, and rice noodles. The firms produce various types of beverages including soft drinks, beer, and liquor. All products are meant as import substitutes.

In the case of the plastics industry, twenty firms were chosen. Most produce plastic bags; other products consist of plastic sheets, pipes, dishes, baskets, chairs, and so on. These are destined for the local market only.

Thirteen firms were surveyed in the wood-based industry. Their main products are plywood, furniture, parquet, tongue and groove, doors, and doorframes. These products are mainly meant for export, but a few are produced for the local market.

Twelve selected firms in the machine shop industry are producing various products, depending on the firm's size. The largest state-owned enterprise produces pumps and diesel engines, agricultural machines, cutting machines, centrifuging machines among others. But the small machine shops produce only parts and components of machines and render repair service.

Thirteen firms were selected from the textile industry, and most make men's wear, women's wear, hats and caps, and so forth. The garment factories are foreign joint ventures and operate on a CMP basis for foreign markets.

Seven selected firms in the electrical products industry produce transformers, dynamos, generators, spare parts for dynamos, battery boxes, batteries, and battery plates for the local market.

Four firms in the pharmaceuticals industry produce tablets and capsules, and powders, liquids, and ointments for various medical uses. These include ointments for skin diseases, herbal tonics, germitol, methylated spirits, and the like.

Three firms in the paper industry produce voucher paper, harder cards, waterproof harder cards, newspaper-offset paper, exercise book paper, and cards for local use. Only two firms were selected from the printing industry. These print magazines and invitation cards.

Four sample firms in the metal industry produce Chinese shutter frames, regulator parts, antennae, nails, barbed wire, and nuts and bolts for local use only.

Three firms in the construction material industry produce Aluzinc roofing sheets, enamelware, aluminum wares, concrete poles, concrete pipes, and ceiling board. These products are import substitutes.

Two firms in the fishery industry are entirely engaged in exporting deep frozen prawns.

Two firms in the gems industry produce jewelry, gem stones, rubies, and sapphires destined for the export market only.

The computer software development industry was chosen especially for this survey because of its currently expanding market. In total twelve firms are involved in this industry. These provide software for accounting, banking, hotels, integrated systems, manufacturing, staff and payroll, supermarkets, and government organizations, and they produce other customized software products for use in civil engineering, point of sales, travels and tours, HR (Executive Job), and hospitals.

Seven other firms producing cosmetics, toiletries, candles, incense sticks, slippers and rubber soles are grouped under miscellaneous (other industries).

Year of Operation

The first year of operation for selected firms is summarized in Table 2.5. They are found to be in five groups: firms beginning operations before 1960, and those beginning in the 1960s, 1970s, 1980s, and 1990s. Seventy-seven out of 132 firms began operations in the 1990s. This group contains all types of industry, except metal, and they are either joint ventures or private firms. We can, from this situation, infer that due to the introduction of a market-oriented economy, the private sector has been encouraged and flourished, engaging in all types of industry.

Only three firms began operations prior to 1960s. These are state-owned enterprises producing soft drinks, pharmaceuticals, and wood-based products. These firms were established three decades earlier than the others in the survey. Twenty-nine firms were established during the 1960s and 1970s, that is, during the period of The Burmese Way to Socialism. The remaining twenty-three firms began operations in 1980s, and the majority was established near the end of that decade when the market-oriented economy was introduced.

Number of Employees

Since the workforce of selected firms ranges from fewer than five employees to more than 2,000 employees, seven classifications were made, as shown in Table 2.6. It can be seen that 53.79% of the sample size, that is, 71 firms, are operating with five to fifty employees. These can be classified as small firms. Nearly all types of industry are found in this small-sized group, except firms in electrical, fishery, and gems industries. The majority is concerned with food and beverages, plastic products, and machine shops. The second largest group is in the range of 101 to 500 employees and comprises 18.18% of the firms, i.e., twenty-four firms. The types of industry in this group mostly produce wood-based products and food and beverages. The third largest group, 14.39% of the whole, is found to be in the range of 51 to 100 employees producing electrical products, plastic products, and food and beverages, etc. These two groups can be classified as medium-sized enterprises. Among the sample firms, we can find firms operating with fewer than five employees. These can be classified as extremely small. Large firms are those with more than 1,000 employees (Fig. 2.1). These firms are mostly in the garment industry and are foreign joint ventures. The other two are concerned with a private

Table 2.5 Surveyed Firms: First Year of Operation

Type of Industry	*Total Firms*	*Before 1960*	*1960s*	*1970s*	*1980s*	*1990s*
Food and beverage	28	1	1	5	4	17
Plastics	20		1	2	3	14
Wood-based products	13	1	2		3	7
Machine shop	12		4	3	2	3
Textile and garment	12				1	11
Electrical products	7		2	1	2	2
Pharmaceuticals	4	1		1	1	1
Paper	4				1	3
Metal	4		1	3		
Construction materials	3					3
Fisheries	2					2
Gems	2					2
Printing	2				1	1
Computer software	12				3	
Others	7		2	1	2	2
Total	**132**	**3**	**13**	**16**	**23**	**77**

Table 2.6 Surveyed Firms: Number of Employees by Type of Industry

Number of Employees *Type of Industry*	*<5*	*5-50*	*51-100*	*101-500*	*501-1000*	*1001-2000*	*above 2000*	*Total firms*
Food and beverage	1	17	2	7		1		28
Plastics	1	15	3	1				20
Wood-based		1	2	8	2			13
Machine shop		11					1	12
Textile and garment	1	1	1	3	2	4	1	12
Electrical products	1		6					7
Pharmaceuticals	1	3						4
Paper		2	1					4
Metal		4						4
Construction materials		1	1	1				3
Fisheries				1	1			2
Gems				2				2
Printing		2						2
Computer software		9	2	1				12
Others	1	5	1					7
Total Firms	**6**	**71**	**19**	**24**	**5**	**5**	**2**	**132**
(%)	**4.54**	**53.79**	**14.39**	**18.18**	**3.79**	**3.79**	**1.52**	

food and beverage industry and a state-owned machine shop. Based on the size of workforce in these firms, it can be generalized that the manufacturing firms in the private sector are of the small and medium-sized enterprise (SME) type.

Figure 2.1 Number of Firms based on Number of Employees

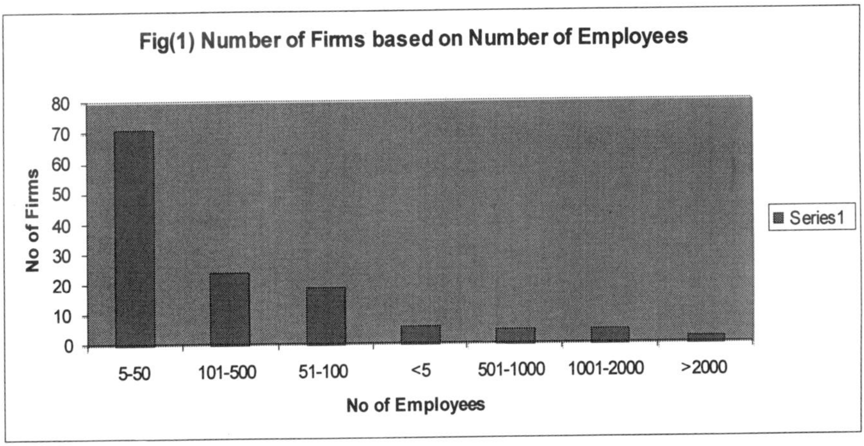

Production Aspect

The level of technology utilized in the manufacturing firms is classified into three main types, namely: technology intensive, labor intensive, and intermediate technology, a mixture of the previous two. Only 4% of the selected firms are technology intensive, 42% applying labor- intensive technology, and 54% apply intermediate technology. The technology-intensive firms relate to the machine shop and food and beverage industries. Other types of industry are those using either intermediate or labor-intensive technology (Fig 2.2). Other factors concerning production are summarized in Table 2.7.

Table 2.7 Surveyed Firms: Production Aspect

Type of Industry	*Machinery*			*Number of Shifts per day*			*Subcontracting*			*Type of Production*						*Raw Materials*		
	Imported	*Domestic*	*Both*	*1*	*2*	*3*	*Offered*	*Received*	*Both*	*Assembly*	*Parts fabrication*	*Feedstock*	*Processing*	*Repairs*	*Services*	*Domestic*	*Imported*	*Both*
Food and beverage	8	11	9	16	8	4						7	21			12	2	14
Plastics	4	8	8	6	14								20			6	10	4
Wood-based	8		5	6	6	1		1				10	3			8		5
Machine shop	4	6	2	10	2		1	1			5	2		5		7	1	4
Textile and garment	10		2	10	1	1	3	2	1			2	10			2	6	4
Electrical products		2	5	3	4		1	2	2	4	1	2				2		5
Pharmaceuticals	3		1	3	1							1	3					4
Paper		3	1		3	1						3	1			4		
Metal	1		3	3	1		1		1			3	1			4		
Construction materials	1	1	1	1	1	1	1		1			3	1					3
Fisheries	2												2			2		
Gems	1		1		2			1				1	1			2		
Printing	1		1	2				1					2					2
Computer software	12			12											12			
Others		6	1	5	2		1	1	2			2	5			3	1	3
Total	**55**	**37**	**40**	**81**	**43**	**8**	**7**	**9**	**6**	**4**	**6**	**33**	**72**	**5**	**12**	**52**	**20**	**48**

Machinery

Regarding machines utilized in the selected firms, the data collected show that 55 firms rely totally on imported machines, 37 on domestic machines, and 40 on both imported and domestic machines. Observation revealed that imported machines are mostly reconditioned ones from various counties, and only few companies can afford brand new ones. Some of the domestic machines resemble foreign-made machines as native technicians imitate them.

Figure 2.2 Type of Technology in Various Enterprises

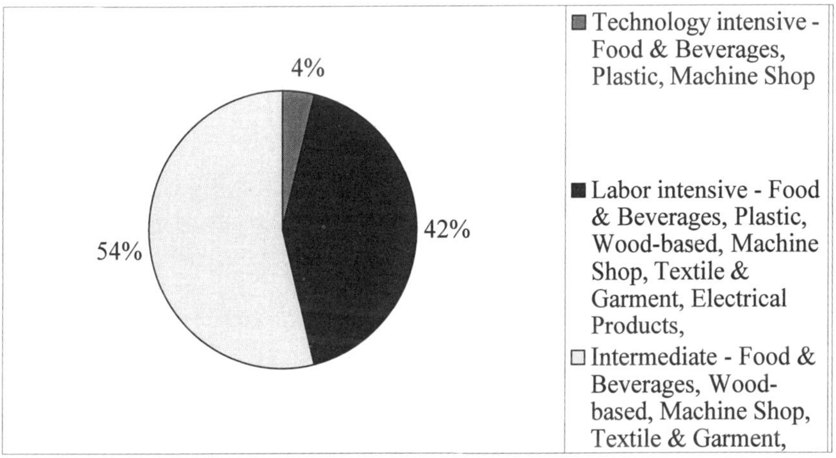

Type of Production

The selected firms are engaged in five types of production: such as assembly of knockdown kits, local fabrication of parts, production based on feedstock, processing, repairs, and services. More than half the firms (72 firms) are of the processing type and a quarter (33 firms) are of the production type based on the feedstock group. Machine shops relate to assembly type, parts fabrication, and repairs. Assembly of imported knockdown kits is executed only in the electrical product industry, and services are provided only by the computer software industry.

Raw Materials

Only 20 out of 132 firms use wholly imported materials. Other firms use either domestic materials or both, except the computer software industry, which does not acquire raw materials.

Shifts per Day

One shift of operation of eight hours is common in every type of industry. Firms operating for one shift only are found in all types of industry except in paper mills, fisheries, and gems factories where two or more shifts will be appropriate in accordance with set up time. Firm size is the determining factor in running of multiple shifts.

Subcontracting

The subcontracting system is not yet much adopted in industrial firms in Myanmar. Only 22 firms are engaged in it. Seven of these offer contracts, nine are receiving, and six are conducting a mix. This situation shows that industrial firms in Myanmar are not linked to each other and are not using the subcontracting system, the strength of industries aiming for a competitive edge.

Marketing Aspect

One hundred and four firms deal solely with the local market (Table 2.8). The group consists of all types of industry except gems and fisheries. The common reason given for not exporting was that there is a huge domestic demand for their products, and that the firms do not yet have plans to export in the future. For distribution, direct sales channels are applied more than the sales agent channel.

Only four types of industries, totaling eleven firms are export-oriented, and they are in wood-based, garment, fisheries, and gems industries. As Table 2.9 illustrates, 17 firms representing seven types of industry have dealt with both the domestic and export markets, using various distribution channels. Based on the data collected, it can be summarized that the products of these industrial firms are mostly import substitutes (Fig. 2.3). Export products are few and are mainly wood-based, or in the garment, fisheries, and gems business.

Personnel Aspect

Table 2.10 shows the characteristics of employees. The status of employees is categorized under six groups such as management level, clerical staff, engineers, technicians, general workers, and others. Based on available information, it can be generalized that job opportunities are meant mostly for general workers. At a high level of expertise, technicians have more job opportunities than engineers. By way of educational background, most employed people have a high school level education, followed by those with a middle school education. It is clear that education is a significant factor in recruiting.

Figure 2.3 Marketing Aspect by Type of Enterprise

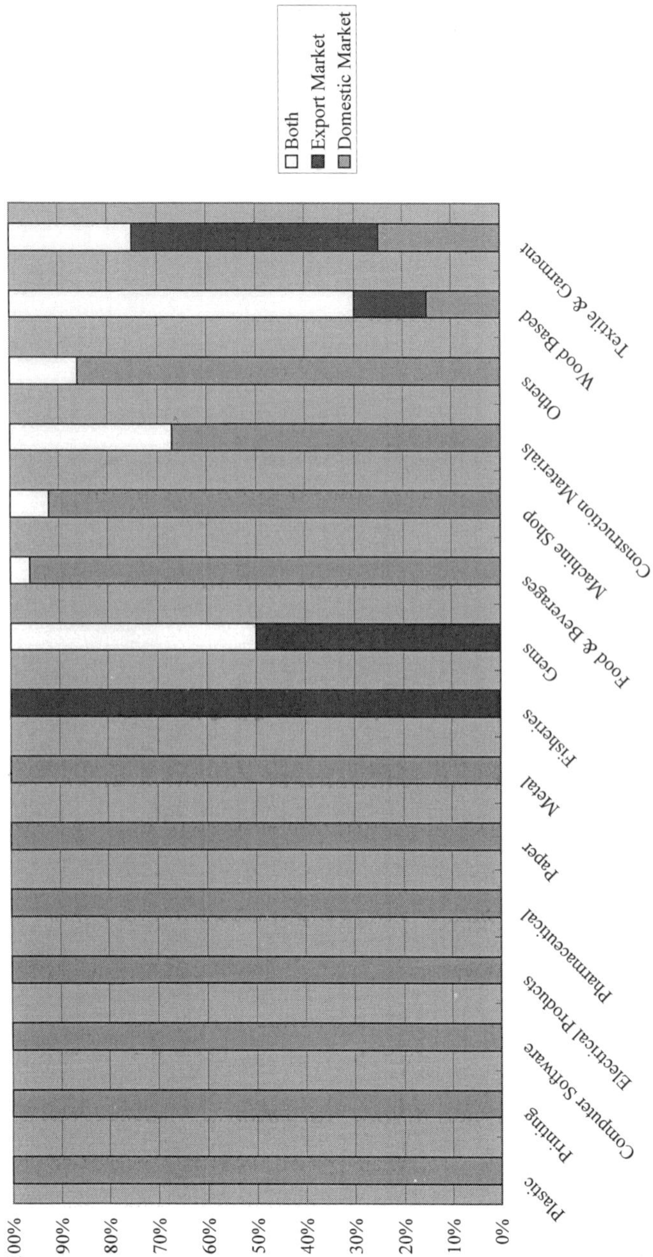

Table 2.8 Surveyed Firms dealing with the Domestic Market

Marketing Channel 100% Domestic

Particular	*Type of Industry*														
	Food and beverage	*Plastics*	*Wood- based*	*Machine shop*	*Textile and garment*	*Electrical products*	*Pharmaceuticals*	*Paper*	*Metal*	*Construction materials*	*Fisheries*	*Gems*	*Printing*	*Computer software*	*Others*
Direct sales	12	8	2	8	2	2		4	1	1			1	12	2
Through agencies	8	3		3	1	1	1		1				1		4
Both	7	7				4	2		2	1#					
Others		2*					1**								
Total	**27**	**20**	**2**	**11**	**3**	**7**	**4**	**4**	**4**	**2**			**2**	**12**	**6**

* on order
** through central army medical store
\# consignment credit system 90%+ Direct sales 10%

Marketing Channel 100% Export

Particular	*Type of Industry*														
	Food and beverage	*Plastics*	*Wood- based*	*Machine shop*	*Textile and garment*	*Electrical products*	*Pharmaceuticals*	*Paper*	*Metal*	*Construction materials*	*Fisheries*	*Gems*	*Printing*	*Computer software*	*Others*
Direct sales			1		1						2				
Through agencies					1										
Both					1							1			
Others			1*		3**										
Total			**2**		**6**						**2**	**1**			

*on order
** CMP, on order

Table 2.9 Surveyed Firms dealing with both Domestic and Export Markets

	Domestic				*Export*				*Total*
Type of Industry	*Direct Sales*	*Through agencies*	*Both direct sales & agencies*	*Others*	*Direct Sales*	*Through agencies*	*Both direct sales & agencies*	*Others*	
Food & beverage			1			1			1
Wood-based products	7	1	1		7		2		9
Machine shop	1					1			1
Textile and garment	2		1			2	1		3
Construction materials			1		1				1
Gems	1							1*	1
Others	1					1			1

*Through Head office abroad (60%) + Direct Sales (40%)

Table 2.10 Surveyed Firms: Characteristics of Personnel

Type of Industry	*Status of Employees*						*Level of Education*					
	Percentage of Employees						*Percentage of Employees*					
	Management level	*Clerical staff*	*Engineers*	*Technicians*	*General*	*Others*	*Graduate*	*High school*	*Middle school*	*Elementary*	*No formal education*	*Others*
Food and beverage	3	8	3	7	71	8	33	25	24	11	3	4
Plastics	7	5	8	2	77	1	16	35	15	26	5	3
Wood-based products	2	10	2	10	73	3	7	26	28	37	1	1
Machine shop	1	7	1	2	69	20	19	19	28	23	11	
Textile and garment	1	3	1	4	90	1	6	37	37	18	1	1
Electrical products	3	3	1	4	89		10	15	43	25	7	
Pharmaceuticals	6	4			90			66	15		19	
Paper	11	2	1	4	82		10	17	24	49		
Metal	8	1	4	6	81		8	38	19	19	16	
Construction materials	6	7	1	15	71		7	28	25	4	36	
Fisheries	1	13	2	1	83		10	80		10		
Gems	2	8	1	2	79	8	33	54	7	3	1	2
Printing	14	5		18	63		9	14	32		45	
Computer software	24	6	1	40	*28	1	66	33	1			
Others	11	3		2	84		6	65	14	14		1

Note: *Operators and trainees

Training

In order to upgrade the skills of the employees, the selected firms have five types of training programs: on-the-job training, off-the-job training, in-house training, training abroad, and the mixed type of in-house training and training abroad. Among these, most firms prefer on-the-job training, followed by in-house training, and training abroad, respectively (Fig. 2.4).

Working Relationship with Employees

Observations were also made on important factors in maintaining good relations with employees. As shown in Figure 2.5, 72 firms prefer to give other incentives, 69 plan to increase wages, 68 would like to add more fringe benefits, 45 want to provide good working facilities, and 43 have decided to have frequent dialogue with their workers so as to attain good relations with their employees. Some firms are trying to use more than one method.

Figure 2.4 Surveyed Firms: Training Programs

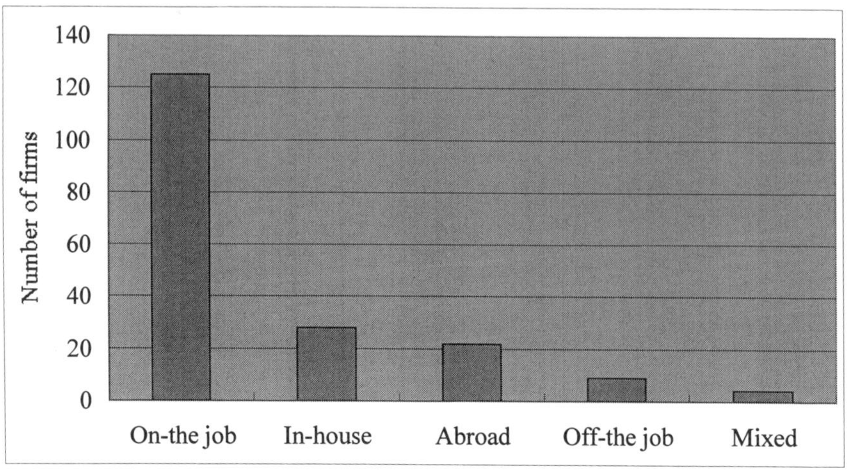

Despite these measures, firms are still faced with problems regarding employees. The most severe problem is job hopping, followed by the difficulty of hiring skilled labor. The firms also face demands for higher wages and consequently have problems with absenteeism. Some firms have problems related to behavior and language barriers. Last but not least is the problem of low productivity. Figure 2.6 shows the composition of problems in the selected firms.

Figure 2.5 Criteria for Good Relationships with Employees

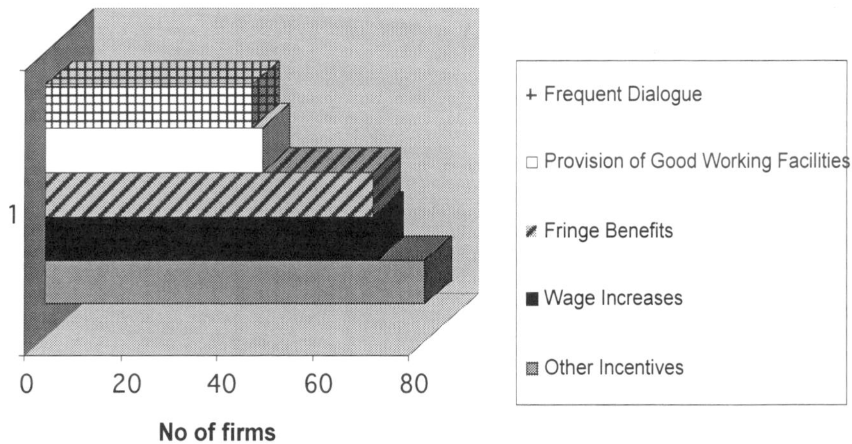

Founders

The profile of the founders can be observed in Table 2.11, which indicates age range, birthplace, nationality, educational level, and previous experience. As regards age, 34% of founders are in their 40s, 24% are in their 30s, and 18% are in their 50s. The majority of founders are Myanmar nationalities, e.g., Bamars, Myanmar-Indians, Myanmar-Chinese. Only

Table 2.11 Surveyed Firms: Profile of Founders

Type of Industry	*Age*					*Birth Place*			*Nationality*				*Education*					
	25-30	*31-40*	*41-50*	*51-60*	*above 60*	*Urban*	*Rural*	*Foreign*	*Myanmar*	*Indian*	*Chinese*	*Others*	*Graduate*	*High School*	*Middle School*	*Elementary*	*No Formal*	*Others*
Food and beverage	1	8	11	1	5	21	2	2	10		11		13	6	3	3		1
Plastics	4	6	7	2	1	17	2		12		9		11	5	1	1		1
Wood-based products	1	2	2	6	1	4	7	1	7		3		5	3		2	1	1
Machine shop	1	3	2	3	1	4	6		10	1			1	3	2	3		
Textile and garment	1	2	6	2		7	1	4	4		1	*4	10	1				
Electrical products		2	2	2		5	2		4		2		1	4		1		
Pharmaceuticals			1		2	1	1		2						2			
Paper		1	1	2		1	2		2		2		4					
Metal		1	2	1		3	1		3		1		1	2		1		
Construction materials				1			1		2				2					**1
Fisheries			1			1	1				1	*1	2					
Gems	1	1						2				*2	2					
Printing			1	1		2			2				2					
Computer software	8	2	2			12			10		1	*1	12					
Others		1	3	1	2	6	1		7				2	2	2		1	
Total	**17**	**29**	**41**	**22**	**12**	**84**	**27**	**9**	**75**	**1**	**31**	**8**	**68**	**26**	**10**	**11**	**2**	**4**
%	**14**	**25**	**34**	**18**	**10**	**70**	**23**	**7**	**65**	**1**	**27**	**7**	**56**	**21**	**8**	**9**	**2**	**4**

*British, Korean, Singaporean, Thai
** Post graduate

7% are foreigners, most being partners in foreign joint ventures. More than 75% of the founders have a high school education or above, and among them 56% are graduates. Only about 2% of the founders have no formal education. Exceptionally, one founder was a postgraduate, and three others had attended various training courses.

Figure 2.6 Problems concerning Employees

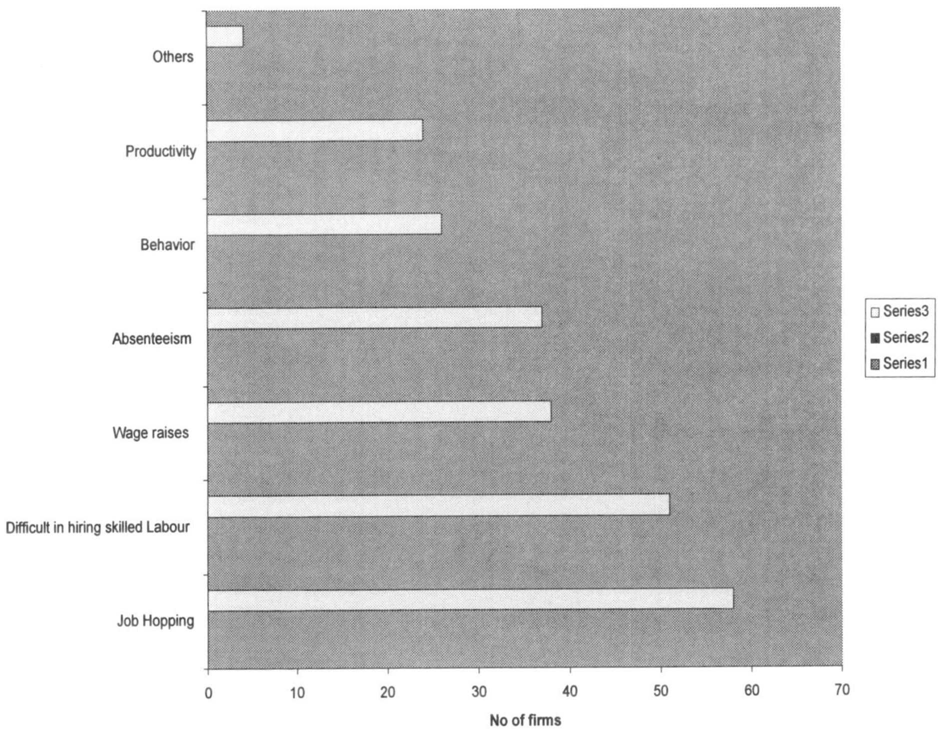

In conducting interviews, founders were requested to give their reasons for going into business. Their responses fell into five categories: (1) their own interest; (2) advice from others; (3) in order to improve their standard of living; (4) acquaintances; and (5) inheritance. More than half conduct the business from their own interest (Fig. 2.7). Others are in business because of family inheritance or from tradition, i.e. 18%, and to improve their standard of living, i .e., 17%.

Figure 2.7 Surveyed Firms: Reasons for Entering Business

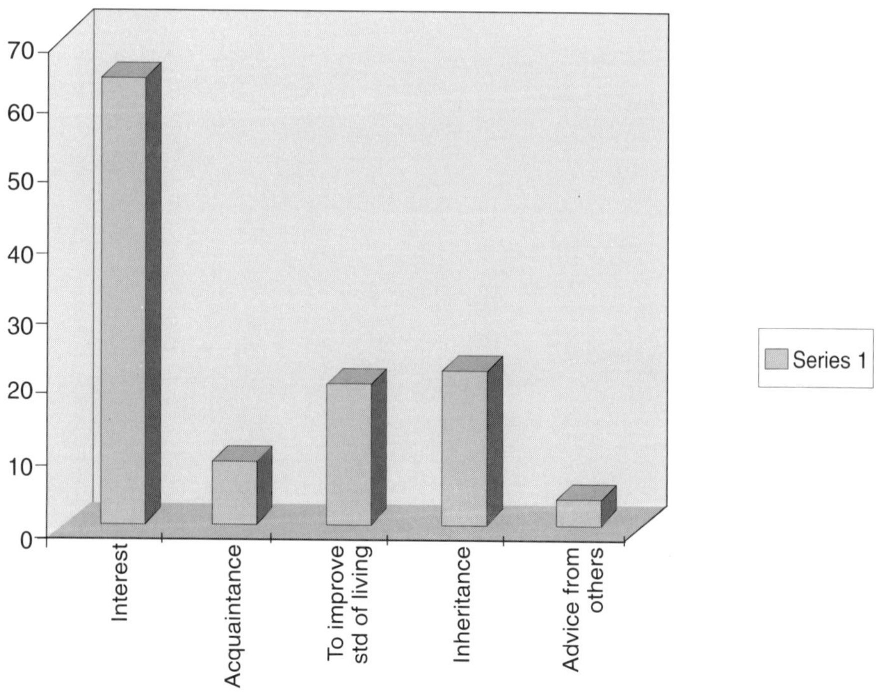

General Problems

The shortage of electricity seems to be the greatest obstacle to productivity for almost all firms. Other constraints concern infrastructure, and other factors mentioned in responses consist of difficulties in transportation and telecommunications, weak drainage and sewage systems, and limited space. Barriers directly related to production processes include the shortage of spare parts and raw materials, a low level of technology, and insufficient machines and equipment. Lack of capital and a shortage of foreign currency are cited as financial barriers.

Conclusion

As a developing country, Myanmar is no different from others in following the stages of the industrial development process, from a subsistence economy to the export of manufactured goods. Developing countries naturally face several problems in their endeavors to develop, major ones being incompleteness of infrastructure, inadequacy of technical knowledge, and shortages of foreign exchange or of required equipment and raw materials. Country try to overcome these barriers in their own way, and the impact of their efforts can be positioned on the development path. In particular, Myanmar adopted a market-oriented economy in 1988 and has taken appropriate reform measures. Since then, the private sector has been given the right to participate extensively in every facet of economic activity. Moreover, the government has promulgated various laws and prescribed related rules and regulations to improve the performance of state enterprises and to encourage the development of private enterprises. Nearly a decade has passed since Myanmar adopted a market-oriented economy, and the impact of endeavors made during these years should be evaluated and appreciated. This was the main objective of the survey described above.

Despite the technical difficulties that firms face on a daily basis, what is really lacking in the country's industries is "inter-firm relationships." It is clear that manufacturing firms have hardly any relationships among them, i.e., linkages between state-owned and private firms and also among private firms themselves. The number of firms engaged in subcontracting shows this. Only 17% of the selected firms, particularly, machine shops and firms engaged in producing electrical products, construction materials, metalwork, and garments are involved in subcontracting, either offering or receiving subcontracts, as the case may be.

With all the weaknesses and difficulties in the manufacturing sector no firm cannot survive alone. It is therefore necessary to encourage and construct inter-firm relationships so as to obtain the strength and ability to move forward. Not only inter-firm relationships within the country but also inter-firm linkages with other countries are needed. Since Myanmar has joined ASEAN, its economy should be considered in the context of the ASEAN economic region. The country's firms should be linked with the industries of ASEAN through subcontracting. If the country's small and medium-sized firms can provide manufacturing parts for the large firms in those countries, the assurance of their survival is promising.

Like all developing countries, Myanmar will have to face new challenges in the twenty-first century. Therefore steps should be taken to build inter-firm relationships locally as well as internationally in order to achieve competitive advantages in the global market. For this, the proper formulation of industrial development plans, appropriate strategies, and adequate public investment policies to accelerate industrialization in Myanmar are urgently needed.

Note

[1] J. M. Juran, *Juran's Quality Control Handbook* (New York: McGraw Hill, 1988), p. 35B-5.

Appendix 1: Profile of Selected Firms by Type of Industry

Food and Beverage Industry

Sr. No	*Name*	*Owner-ship*	*Year of Oper-ation*	*Estimated Capital (million kyat)*	*No. of Employ-ees*	*Main Products*	*Annual Production Volume*
1	Diamond Soft Drinks & Ice Factory	Joint Venture	1926	118	248	Sparkling, fruito, Fantasy (orange, cola)	9.6 million dozens
2	Dagon Dairy Products Co., Ltd.	Joint Venture	1997	253	150	Condensed milk	1.2 million cartons
3	Myanmar Yaung Chi Oo Co, Ltd.	Joint Venture	1994	106.26	95	Mandalay Beer	1.87 million dozens
4	Myanmar Brewery, Ltd.	Joint Venture	1997	US$40 million	233	Tiger Beer, ABC Stout, Myanmar Beer, Anchor Beer	124.8 million cans, 53.04 million bottles, 187,200 kegs
5	Rothmans of Pall Mall, Myanmar, Ltd.	Joint Venture	1995	38.745	217	Cigarettes	187,200 cases (50 cartons per case)
6	Star Diamond Soft Drink	Private	1976	20	24	Sparkling, orange, and cream soda, frutio, lychee, tonics, soda	6,33,600 dozens
7	Joker (Boon & Co.)	Private	1978	1	4	Concentrated juice	1,200 gallons
8	Myanmar Golden Star Beverage Co., Ltd.	Private	1996	10	1440	Crushes (orange, strawberry), Quench (lemon), Star cola	10 million cases
9	Myanmar Winery Distillery Co., Ltd.	Private	1996	3,000	80	Grand Royal Whisky, Royal Dry Gin	300,000 gallons
10	Top (1) Liquor Production Factory	Private	1995	100	30	Concentrated liquor	30,000 gallons
11	Pinya Manufacturin g Co., Ltd.(Max Soft Drink)	Private	1997	280+ Loan US$1.2 million	210	Max Cola, Max Lychee, Max Orange	45,00,000 shells
12	Golden Horse Coconut Oil Manufact.	Private	1977	1.5	11	Coconut oil	100,800 viss

13	Great Wall Sugar Mill	Private	1995	65	141	Sugar	10,000 tons
14	Polar Enterprise	Private	1996	60	28	Ice cream, ice lollipops	1.62 million units
15	Pyola Min Ice Lollipop Industry	Private	1970	0.04	30	Ice lollipops, ice cream, juice bars	1.8 million units
16	Ice Brother Factory (Fipdon Co.)	Private	1997	20	37	Poki, 2 Fun, Scoopa	850 cups (80 mm per cup) 20 cups (6 litres per cup)
17	Shwe Nager (Sunflower seeds)	Private	1984	10	30	Dried sunflower seeds	3,600 bags
18	Boke Son Ma Powder Machine	Private	1995	3	40	Turmeric powder, chili powder, spices	180,000 viss
19	Shwin Shwin Pyone Bakery	Private	1997	0.1	10	Bread	72,000 pieces
20	T. K. Bakery	Private	1969	30	30	Cookies	216,000 packets
21	B. One Enterprise	Private	1994	9	7	Rusk (long), rusk (medium), sugar-coated rusk	280,000 packets
22	Shwe Min Thamee (Wafer)	Private	1989	10	24	Wafers	260,000 packets
23	Myanmar May Sun, Co. Ltd.	Private	1996	60	217	Sandwich bread, cream rolls (4 types), sponge cake, butter cake	5.25 million breads, 1.20 lakhs cakes
24	Double Hatchet Firm	Private	1984	20	18	Pillow crackers, biscuits, wafers	240, 240 lbs
25	Ocean Confectionery	Private	1993	2	13	Dried bread	720,000 packets
26	Shwe Linn Yone Biscuit Factory	Private	1987	1.5	17	Cream crackers, maries	1,440,000 packets
27	Bean Curd Cake Enterprise	Private	1975	2	13	Bean curd cakes	2,520,000 pieces
28	Zaw Pyan Rice Noodle Enterprise	Private	1991	4	8	Rice noodles	365,000 viss

Plastic Industry

Sr. No.	*Name*	*Ownership*	*Year of Operation*	*Estimated Capital (million kyats)*	*No of Employees*	*Main Products*	*Annual Production Volume*
1	Zabu Poly Pack Factory	Joint Venture	1996	26.4 +US$ 0.3 million	260	Jumbo bags, PP woven bags	12.12 million bags
2	Lacky Bag	Private	1993	20	80	Plastic bags	32 lakhs of bags
3	Golden Rabbit Plastic	Private	1985	350	60	Plastic bags	1.02 million packets
4	Lucky Seven Plastic Bags Production Factory	Private	1995	5	12	Plastic bags	12 million bags
5	Dae Wi Plastic Industry	Private	1978	2	6	Plastic bottles	9 million pieces
6	Five Star Plastic Industry	Private	1985	6	20	Plastic containers	11,000 lbs
7	Naing Win Plastic	Private	1970	5	3	Inner hard plastic for caps, plastic sheet for slipper floor covers	2 million pieces
8	Popular Plastic	Private	1995	30	41	Plastic wares	Order basis
9	US Plastic Manufacturing	Private	1992	8	7	Plastic bowls, plastic caps, plastic baskets, plastic plates	30 million pieces
10	U Kyaw Thuya Thet's Plastic Enterprise	Private	1991	N.A	17	Plastic products ordered by UNDP	Order basis
11	Deodar Part	Private	1994	200	40	Plastic chairs, stools, plates, dishes	3.6 million units
12	Dollar Plastic Manufacturing	Private	1991	10	30	Plastic tanks, plastic bottles, plastic baskets	470,000 pieces
13	Peace Industry	Private	1995	4	15	Plastic bags	330,000 lbs

14	Daw Mya Thein & Sons Plastic Industry	Private	1964	30	20	Plastic bags, plastic sheets	400 metric tons
15	Yeong Fwa Industry Co., Ltd.	Private	1996	100	30	Plastic round baskets, chairs (spot) (plain), step stools, handy pails, mini stools, ABC cups, 3 - tiers racks, joint boxes, seedling trays	150 tons
16	Daw Myint Kyi Plastic Industry	Private	1995	3.5	15	PP bags	8.5 million lbs
17	Asia Star Technologies	Private	1992	0.6	12	Plastic baskets, plastic containers, order products	1.02 million packets
18	Thabarwa Co., Ltd.	Private	1990	2.8	14	PVC pipe	2,000 tons
19	Rainbow Industry Co., Ltd.	Private	1996	15	30	Melamine plates, other melamine products	150,000 pieces
20	Shwe Mi Industrial Co., Ltd.	Private	1997	20 + US$ 0.5 million	67	PVC pipe, rato gravure printing & packaging	kyats 240 million

Wood-Based Industry

Sr. No.	*Name*	*Owner-ship*	*Year of Oper-ation*	*Estimated Capital (million kyat)*	*No. of Employ-ees*	*Main Products*
1	No. 1 Plywood Factory, Myanmar Timber Enterprise	State-owned	1962	3.209	334	Timber plywood, veneer
2	No. 2 Plywood Factory, Myanmar Timber Enterprise	State-owned	1968	26.6	443	Timber plywood, veneer
3	No. 4 Sawmill, Myanmar Timber Enterprise	State-owned	1955	500	780	Teak-converted timber
4	Myanmar NC Woodwork Co., Ltd.	Joint Venture	1990	10	178	Doors, doors frames, architrave, parquet, tongue and groove, wall and ceiling paneling and molding, skirting, solid panels, louvres and glass doors, cabinet doors
5	Chin-Su Myanmar Co., Ltd.	Joint Venture	1995	50	577	Plywood (3 and 5 ply), formica sheets, veneer
6	Door and Parquet Enterprise	Private	1987	15	32	Doors, parquet, door frames
7	Scansia Myanmar, Ltd.	Private	1994	US$1.17 million	281	Garden furniture, tables, Queen Mary chairs, benches, butler trays, square folding tables, club cenches
8	Century Development Co., Ltd.	Private	1995	50	117	Rattan furniture, rattan-related home products
9	Khit San Yin	Private	1990	30	75	Door frames, glass frames, window frames, skirting
10	Pioneer Venture, Ltd.	Private	1995	30	92	Parquet, lam parquet, tongue and groove, skirting, sawn timber, four-side planes
11	Packaging Factory No. 1 (Myitmakha)	Private	1994	20	195	Parquet, tongue and groove, lam parquet, finger jointed, flooring board, ceiling board, skirting board, handrails, mosaic panels, furniture components, table tops, teak veneer

12	Hi-Tech Forest Industries Co., Ltd.	Private	1993	50	168	Furniture components, T & G flooring
13	Kyaw Kyaw Aung Co., Ltd.	Private	1993	100	300	Cane (semi- finished), rattan, cane (flatted), cane furniture

Machine-Shop Industry

Sr. No	*Name*	*Owner-ship*	*Year of Oper-ation*	*Estimated Capital (million kyat)*	*No. of Employ-ees*	*Main Products*	*Annual Production Volume*
1	No. 3 Factory, Myanmar Heavy Industry	State-owned	1969	577	2,283	Pumps and diesel engines, power tillers, generators, fan motors, hand tools, welding electrodes	Pumps 4,600 units, hand tools 200,000 units, motors 2,000 units, welding 1,000 tons
2	Tun Industry	Private	1967	5	6	Machine parts and components, tableting machine	4 machines
3	Industrial Workshop	Private	1967	1.5	5	Repairs (motor car engine parts)	Order basis
4	U Tin Win's Enterprise	Private	1997	1.5	12	Bicycles for children (single), (double)	1,280 units
5	U Hlaing Win's Enterprise	Private	1987	15	26	Geer pinions, chain sockets, hand pumps, lathe machines	12,000 chains, 1,200 hand pumps, 24 lathe machines, 12 plastic machines
6	Than Production	Private	1997	4.5	28	Copper conductors, nozzle heads, plastic paddle plates	360,000 pairs
7	Hine Min Home Industry	Private	1967	0.01	14	Grinding machines and machines, hammer mill machines, centrifuging machines	202 units
8	Htay Industrial Firm	Private	1976	30	9	Gear and pinions, machine components by order	Order basis
9	U Kyaw Than & Bros Industrial Firm	Private	1973	50	45	Repairs (car body)	Order basis
10	Nyan Shin & Bros Industrial Firm	Private	1977	30	17	Pumps, motors, air compressors, agricultural machines	300 units

11	Thein Zaw & Bros Car Body	Private	1986	10	11	Repairs (car body)	Order basis
12	Universal Diesel (U Khin Mg Win)	Private	1991	20	15	Engine repairs	Order basis

Textile and Garment Industry

Sr. No.	*Name*	*Owner-ship*	*Year of Oper-ation*	*Estimated Capital (million kyat)*	*No. of Employ-ees*	*Main Products*	*Annual Production Volume*
1	Tatmadaw Canvas Wearing and Water Proofing Factory	State-owned	1989	342	1,092	Cotton gray canvas, waterproofed canvas, tarpaulin sheets, canopy, drill (olive green), web equipment, ribbons	Web equipment 2 million units, cotton canvas 2 million yards
2	Myanmar Segye International, Ltd.	Joint Venture	1990	US$1.25 million	1,873	Pants and skirts, jackets, coats, jogging suits	1.5 million units
3	Myanmar Knitwear Manufact. Co., Ltd.	Joint Venture	1995	12	816	Men's wear, women's wear, children's wear	2 million pieces
4	Myanmar Daewoo International, Ltd. (Factory No.1)	Joint Venture	1991	US$1.25 million	2072	Men's shirts, blouses, pajamas, jackets	240,000 dozens
5	Myanmar Euroworld International Ltd.	Joint Venture	1994	15.86	1837	Knit shirts, jackets, hosiery	72,000 pieces
6	Htoo Htet Co.	Joint Venture	1998	NA	300	Garments, knitting, woven sweaters, sportswear	48,000 dozens
7	Myanmar Daewoo International, Ltd. (Factory No.2)	Joint Venture	1997	9	526	Shirts, blouses, jackets, knit garments, pajamas	360,000 dozens
8	Myo Tint Swe's Sportswear	Private	1994	10	28	Sportswear	120,000 units
9	Pauk-Si Knitting Factory	Private	1995	2.5	200	Gloves, hats	Gloves 5,000 dozen, hats 5,000 dozen
10	Myanmar Wah-Fuh International, Ltd.	Private	1995	US$4.5 million	1,726	Ladies suits, outerwear, trousers and pants, uniforms	383,352 pieces

11	Kyin Yee Garment Factory	Private	1996	NA	91	Hats and caps, sports shirts, boxer shorts	6,600 dozens
12	Mandalay Textile	Private	1997	80	350	Cotton yarn (brown)	48,000 lbs

Electrical Products Industry

Sr No	*Name*	*Ownership*	*Year of Operation*	*Estimated Capital (million kyat)*	*No. of Employees*	*Main Products*	*Annual Production Volume*
1	Soe Electronics Machinery Co., Ltd. (SEM)	Private	1991	300	82	Transformers, dynamos, repairs and servicing	120 transformers, 1,800 dynamos
2	Puzundaung Soe Tint's Dynamo Manufacturing Firm	Private	1980	40	55	Dynamos, combined generators, spare parts for dynamos	8,400 dynamos
3	In Ywat Na Battery Box Enterprise	Private	1998	4	4	Battery boxes	NA (on order)
4	GX Sein Battery	Private	1960	35	65	Batteries	60,000 units
5	U Than Naing XCL Battery	Private	1986	20	64	Battery plates, batteries	70,000 units
6	Dollar Battery Production	Private	1978	5.34	64	Batteries	50,000 units
7	Lwin Battery	Private	1966	0.02	52	Battery plates, batteries	68,000 viss of lead

Pharmaceutical Industry

Sr No	*Name*	*Owner-ship*	*Year of Oper-ation*	*Estimated Capital (million kyat)*	*No. of Em-ployees*	*Main Products*	*Annual Production Volume*
1	Myanmar Pharmaceuti-cal Factory	State Owned	1957	420	2,362	Tablets and capsules, powders, liquids, ointments, sterile products, biological products, alcohol and allied products	840 million tablets, 70,000 litres (liquid), 24 million bottles (injection)
2	Pharmacists Cooperative, Ltd.	Coope-rative	1996	2.2	18	Germitol, methylated spirit, Benediets' Solution	1,152 gallons
3	Myat Chan Thar Myanmar Pharmaceutica ls Enterprise (Kay Thi Pan)	Private	1985	6	10	Herbal tonic, blood tonic	360,000,000 tablets
4	Wa-Na-Theik Di Ointment	Private	1979	NA	4	Ointments for skin diseases	626,000 units

Paper Industry

Sr. No	*Name*	*Ownership*	*Year of Operation*	*Estimated Capital (million kyat)*	*No. of Employees*	*Main Products*	*Annual Production Volume*
1	La Pyi Wunn Paper Mill	Private	1986	14	82	Voucher paper	24,000 packages
2	Golden Rose Paper Mill	Private	1995	21	55	Paper and cards	300 tons
3	Lin Paper Mill	Private	1996	15	4	Waterproof, harder cards	500 tons
4	Hteik Tan Paper Mill	Private	1993	50	65	News print, offset paper, exercise book paper, cards	750 tons

Printing Industry

Sr. No	*Name*	*Ownership*	*Year of Operation*	*Estimated Capital (million kyat)*	*No of Employees*	*Main Products*	*Annual Production Volume*
1	Pan Kyar Khine Printing Industry	Private	1983	3	5	Magazines, invitation cards	96,000 sheets
2	Mingalar Thaung Printing Press	Private	1990	20	17	Color print	9 million pieces

Metal Industry

Sr No	*Name*	*Ownership*	*Year of Operation*	*Estimated Capital (million kyat)*	*No. of Employees*	*Main Products*	*Annual Production Volume*
1	Hla Hla and Sons Industry	Private	1967	15	28	Chinese shutter frames, regulator parts, antenna	120,000 pieces
2	Thein Industry	Private	1980	3	13	Nail, barbed wire	280 tons
3	U Kyaw Win Home Industry	Private	1978	10	8	Bolts & nuts	750,000 pieces
4	Mg Kyi Oo Industry	Private	1975	20	22	3/8" diameter screw, 5/16" diameter screw	3100 dozens

Construction Materials Industry

Sr No	*Name*	*Owner-ship*	*Year of Oper-ation*	*Estimated Capital (million kyat)*	*No. of Employ-ees*	*Main Products*	*Annual Production Volume*
1	Myanmar Ace Metal Industries	Joint Venture	1990	1.6	173	Alu-zinc roofing sheets, enamelware, aluminum ware	3,504.232 metric tons
2	Sin Phyu Taw Concrete Ware	Private	1997	50	100	Concrete poles, concrete pipes	12,000 poles
3	Gypsum Ceiling Board Enterprise	Private	1997	30	10	Ceiling board	30,000 pieces

Fisheries Industry

Sr. No	*Name*	*Owner-ship*	*Year of Oper-ation*	*Estimated Capital (million kyat)*	*No. of Employ-ees*	*Main Products*	*Annual Production Volume*
1	Myanmar Seafoods, Ltd.	Joint Venture	1996	27.5	563	Deep frozen prawns	US$1.6 million
2	T.T International, Ltd.	Joint Venture	1996	200	234	Deep frozen prawns	1,050 tons

Gems Industry

Sr No	*Name*	*Owner-ship*	*Year of Oper-ation*	*Estimated Capital (million kyat)*	*No. of Employ-ees*	*Main Products*	*Annual Production Volume*
1	Myanmar VES Joint Venture Co., Ltd.	Joint Venture	1993	US$2.6 million	375	Jewellery, gem stones	5,334 pieces
2	Myanmar Nouveau Co., Ltd.	Joint Venture	1996	22.8	406	Rubies, sapphires	30,049.6 carats

Computer Industry

Sr. No	*Name*	*Owner-ship*	*Year of Oper-ation*	*No. of Em-ployees*	*Software*
1	ACE Data Systems Co., Ltd.	Private	1992	103	Accounting, banking, hotel, integrated manufacturing, staff & payroll, supermarket
2	CE Technology	Private	1992	14	Government
3	Hledan	Private	1996	6	Other customized projects
4	Geocomp Myanmar Ltd.,	Private	1989	41	Government, civil engineering
5	Integra Systems Co., Ltd.	Private	1998	9	Banking, sales points
6	Myanmar Comper Co., Ltd.	Private	1988	68	Accouting, government
7	Myanmar Information Technology Pte., Ltd.	Private	1996	25	Accounting, hotel, sales points, other customized projects
8	Miracle Co., Ltd.	Private	1995	16	Supermarket, travel & tours
9	Pro Co., Ltd.	Private	1997	20	Hotel sales points, travel & tours, HR (Executive job)
10	Tell Technology Co., Ltd.	Private	1995	16	Other customized projects
11	Way Forward Technologies	Private	1998	70	Hotel
12	Winner Co., Ltd.	Private	1988	75	Government, manufacturing, hospital

Miscellaneous

Sr. No	*Name*	*Owner-ship*	*Year of Oper-ation*	*Estimated Capital (million kyats)*	*No of Employ-ees*	*Main Products*	*Annual Production Volume*
1	Yawma Slipper Industry	Private	1990	5	20	Slippers	1,50,000 pairs
2	Shwe Myitta Industry (Coya Beauty Product)	Private	1964	10	43	Coya snow, Coya make-up, Coya Thanutkhar	40,000 dozens
3	Sin Minn Soap Factory	Private	1975	300	50	Washing soap	60 lakhs bars
4	U Than Sein Industry	Private	1994	3	9	Rubber sole	3,00,000 sheets
5	La Yon Rubber Sole Manufacturing	Private	1997	15	7	Rubber sole shut	30,000 sheets
6	Maha Business	Private	1990	1	80	Candles	2304 lakhs pieces
7	Aung Sein Powdering Machine	Private	1962	4	3	Raw material for incense sticks	Order basis

Appendix 2

Questionnaire for a Survey of Manufacturing Firms in Myanmar

Nu Nu Yin

Department of Management Studies
Institute of Economics, Yangon

Questionnaire for Manufacturing Firms

PART A

PROFILE

(1) Firm Name: ______________________

(2) Location: ____________________ Street ____________________ Township
____________________ State / Division

Are you located in an industrial zone? Yes = 1 No = 2 ☐

(3) Type of Organization: Sole proprietorship = 1 Company = 2
Joint Venture = 3 Cooperative = 4
Other (specify ______________) = 5 ☐

If joint venture, who is your partner?

(a) Partner's name: ____________________ Nationality: ______________

(b) Distribution of Capital	US$	Kyat
Your company's portion:	________	________
Your partner's portion:	________	________
(c) Share of profits:	________	________

(d) Period of contract: ____________ (From ________ To ________)

(4) Year of firm's establishment: 19_____
First year of operation: 19_____

(5) Type of industry: ______________________________

(6) Main products: ______________ ______________
______________ ______________
______________ ______________
______________ ______________

(New Products = 1 Upgraded Products = 2) ☐

(7) How much capital are you required to hold? __________
How much capital do you currently hold? __________

(8) Total number of employees __________

PART B

PROFILE OF FIRM'S FOUNDER

(1) Name _________________ Age______ Title___________________________
Nationality ______________________
(2) Birthplace: Township __________________ State / Division ________________
(urban area = 1 rural area = 2 foreign country = 3) ☐
(3) Educational background
(a) college graduate or above = 1
(b) high-school graduate = 2
(c) middle school graduate = 3
(d) elementary school graduate = 4
(e) other (specify__________) = 5 ☐

(4) Involvement / occupation before going into business
(a) student = 1
(b) government servant = 2
(c) employee of a joint venture = 3
(d) employee of a state-owned enterprise = 4
(e) other (specify ______________) = 5 ☐

(5) Reason for going into business
(a) interest in developing business potential = 1
(b) advice from others = 2
(c) desire to improve living standard = 3
(d) acquaintance with business partners = 4
(e) inheritance = 5
(f) other (specify_________________) = 6 ☐

(6) How did you acquire your technical and managerial skills?

	Technical skills	Managerial skills
(a) schooling	________________	________________
(b) former job experience	________________	________________
(c) from parents friends / relatives	________________	________________
(d) self-study	________________	________________
(e) others (specify___________)	________________	________________

PART (C)

FIRM OPERATION

I. PRODUCTION ASPECTS

(1) Operation	1990 (or year of establishment if later	1997
Average numbers of days per year	________	________
Average numbers of hours per week	________	________
Number of shifts per day	________	________
Number of hours per shift	________	________
Number of regular working hours per day	________	________
Number of working hours on Saturday	________	________

(2) Percentage of your total machinery cost by origin
- (a) imported ________%
- (b) domestically made ________%
- (c) other (specify________________) ________%

TOTAL 100 %

(3) Purchase of raw materials
- (a) imported directly ________%
- (b) purchased locally ________%
- (c) sub-contracted ________%

TOTAL 100%

(4) Type of operation

Technology intensive = 1 Labor intensive = 2 Intermediate =3 ☐

(5) Type of production
- Assembly of imported knockdown kits = 1
- Local fabrication of product = 2
- Production based on feedstock = 3
- Other (specify ________________) = 4

(6) Are you making any effort to improve your technology

Yes = 1 No = 2 ☐

If yes, in what way (chose the main one)?
- (a) introduction of new machinery ☐
- (b) technical training ☐
- (c) purchase of know-how or patents ☐
- (d) hiring of technicians ☐
- (e) other (specify________________) ☐

(7) Volume of production (annual average) ____________________________

(8) What are the main problems or obstacles you face in producing your product?

- i. ________________________________
- ii. ________________________________
- iii. ________________________________
- iv. ________________________________
- v. ________________________________

3

II. MARKETING ASPECT

(1) Market breakdown (1997)

(a) domestic	________%
(b) export	________%
TOTAL	100%

(2) Marketing channels

	Domestic	Export
(a) direct sales	________%	________%
(b) through agencies	________%	________%
(c) other (specify ________)	________%	________%
TOTAL	100%	100%

(3) If you do not export your products

(a) What are the main reasons?

i. Products are of a type not well suited for export ☐

ii. Export not necessary due to large domestic demand ☐

iii. Products are of sub-standard quality for export ☐

iv. weak price competitiveness ☐

v. Lack of knowledge about export business ☐

vi. Other (specify________________) ☐

(b) Do you intend to export your products in the future?

Yes = 1 No = 2 ☐

(4) Is your firm involved in subcontracting?

Yes = 1 No = 2 ☐

If yes, do you

(a) offer subcontracts ☐

(b) receive subcontracts ☐

(c) both ☐

(5) To how many companies do you sell your products? ☐

(6) From how many companies do you buy the production materials? ☐

(7) Annual Sales (average) ________________

III. PERSONNEL MANAGEMENT

(1) No. of Employees (on average)

	regular: 1990 (or year of establishment if later)	regular: 1997	temporary: 1990 (or year of establishment if later)	temporary: 1997
(a) management level	____	____	____	____
(b) clerical staff	____	____	____	____
(c) production workers				
I. engineers	____	____	____	____
II. technicians	____	____	____	____
III. general workers	____	____	____	____

4

(d) Other (specify____) _______ _______ _______ _______

(2) Educational levels of employees

	No. of employees
(a) college graduates	______________
(b) high-school graduates	______________
(c) middle school graduates	______________
(d) elementary school graduates	______________
(e) no formal education	______________
(f) other (specify____________)	______________

(3) No. of employees (in 1996)	resigned	hired
(a) engineers	______	______
(b) technicians	______	______
(c) general workers	______	______

(4) What measures do you take in maintaining good labor relations?
(Prioritize responses)

a) frequent dialogue ☐

b) provision of good working facilities ☐

c) wage increases ☐

d) fringe benefits ☐

e) other incentives ☐

f) other (specify________________) ☐

(5) How do you train your employees?
(Prioritize responses)

a) On- the-job training (OTJ) ☐

b) In-house training program ☐

c) Training programs abroad ☐

d) Both b & c ☐

e) No training ☐

f) Other (specify________________) ☐

(6) What problems do you face regarding employees?
(Prioritize responses)

a) difficulties in hiring skilled labor ☐

b) job-hopping ☐

c) demand for wage raise ☐

d) absenteeism ☐

e) behavioral problems ☐

f) low productivity ☐

g) other (specify___________________) ☐

6

3

Investment Opportunities in the Processing and Manufacturing Sector in Myanmar

Aung Myint
The Directorate of Investment and Company Administration, Yangon

Introduction

The industrial development of the developing countries has become one of the great world struggles of our time. By this an effort they hope to find a solution to the problems of poverty, insecurity, and overpopulation and end their newly realized backwardness in the modern world. The reasons for this belief are simply understood. The underdeveloped regions have long been mainly producers of raw materials, and they have observed that there is a strong and positive connection between the wealth and standard of living of a country and the extent of its industrialization. Myrdal described the relationship of industrialization to economic development as follows:

> Manufacturing industry represents, in a sense, a higher stage of production. In advanced countries the development of manufacturing industry has been concomitant with these countries' spectacular economic progress and rise in levels of living; many of its products are indeed almost symbolic of a high living standard. Not least in the underdeveloped countries, the productivity of manpower in industry tends to be considerably greater than in the traditional agricultural pursuits. Industrialization, and the growth of that part of the working population that is engaged in industry,

> is therefore a means of raising national income per capita. In countries like India and Japan, with a high ratio of population to natural resources and, in particular, to land, manufacturing industry represents virtually the only hope of greatly increasing labor productivity and raising levels of living, however much is done to improve agriculture. But even in countries where the population pressure is lower—as, for example, in many Latin American countries—the successful exploitation of a more favorable relation between population and natural resources requires mostly the growth of manufacturing industry.[1]

Manufacturing industries have been a dynamic driving force of economic development and social progress of a country. In this context, the government of the Union of Myanmar has all along been endeavoring to pursue a resource-based industrialization strategy aimed at increasing the domestic value-added industries that are derived from the processing of natural resources in the agriculture, fisheries, forestry, and mining sectors. It serves as a means for providing a wide range of consumer goods and of intermediate and capital goods for other branches of the economy and for various manufacturing industries themselves. Moreover, it is also capable of generating employment, and serving as a focal point for disseminating technological change in the country.

Myanmar's Recent Economic Development

In the development of the national economy, it is evident that Myanmar's comparative advantage lies in its natural and human resources endowments. The effective allocation and utilization of these will result in the sustained growth of production and exports, thereby creating favorable capital formation for further development. In order to achieve the maximum benefits from such endowments effectively, the allocation of natural and human resources will have to be done properly. These resources, together with the influx of capital associated with appropriate technology and managerial skills, can play a vital role in the process of economic development.

On the assumption of state power by the State Law and Order Restoration Council (SLORC) in late 1988,[2] the economy was in extremely bad shape, having suffered severe declines for three consecutive years from 1986-87 to 1988-89. Consequently, the government had no choice but to take urgent reform measures to arrest decline and to spur the economy's immediate recovery and stabilization during the first three years from 1989-92.

With the establishment of the rule of law and order and stability in the country, a short-term Four-Year Plan (1992-96) was formulated. Its principal objectives were furthering the revitalization of the economy in order to achieve economic recovery with stability in the short term, and laying down firm foundations for sustained growth in the long term, targeting at the same time an average annual growth rate of 5.1%. The main thrust of the plan's guidelines was to step up production and exports in order to achieve complete economic recovery as quickly as possible and to speed up development of the economy. Priority was given to the development of productive sectors, such as agriculture, livestock, fishery, mining, oil and gas, and services. Emphasis was also placed on enhancing the production of the processing and manufacturing and mining sectors by promoting the more effective use of existing capacities. Moreover, efforts were made to promote the export not only of traditional items but also new export commodities and to enhance foreign exchange earnings from services.

To give impetus to the plan's implementation, the first and second years of the short-term plan were designated as "economic years" and the third and final year as an "all-round development year." All-out efforts were made right from the beginning of implementation for realizing these targets. Special emphasis was also placed on significant progress in production, the increased mobilization of savings, channeling savings into productive investments, and making a relentless drive for export promotion and foreign exchange earnings from services.

Table 3.1 GDP, Population, and Per Capita GDP, 1985-86 and 1989-97

Particulars	*1985-86*	*1989-90*	*1990-91*	*1992-93*	*1993-94*	*1994-95*	*1995-96*	*1996-97*
Real GDP (million kyat)	55,989	48,883	50,260	54,757	58,064	62,406	66,710	70,586
Population (million)	37.1	40.0	40.8	42.3	43.1	43.9	44.7	45.6
Per Capita GDP (kyat)	1,510	1,221	1,232	1,293	1,347	1,421	1,491	1,549

Source: Ministry of National Planning and Economic Development, *Review of Financial, Economic, and Social Conditions*, 1992-93, 1996-97, and 1997-98

The short-term Four-Year Plan was successfully implemented, achieving an average annual growth of 7.5% as against the target of 5.1% during the plan period (see Table 3.11). This significant achievement was mainly due to relentless efforts of the leadership from the top to the lowest levels, the active participation of the private sector, including foreign direct investment (FDI), in every economic activity following the introduction of the market economic system. Most importantly, it was due to the achievement of tranquility and the rule of law and order throughout the country. This augurs well for the future progress of the economy, as these successes have been achieved almost entirely with the country's own resources without much help from overseas. Much valuable experience and strength has also been gained for the further development of the country.

In addition, the achievement of the remarkably high average annual growth rate of 7.5% during the period of the plan was attributable to the ability to mobilize relatively high levels of investments for financing various development programs, coupled with the ability to more than double the value of exports. For instance, the level of gross investment increased from 27.6 billion kyat in 1991-92 to 71.7 billion kyat in 1995-96, comprising approximately 50% of investment by the private sector, including FDI. Thus, gross investment increased at a relatively high annual average rate of 27% during the period of the plan (Table 3.1).[3]

Current Status of the Processing and Manufacturing Sector

State, cooperative, and private industrial enterprises mainly contribute to the processing and manufacturing sector in the economy. It would be pertinent here to give a brief account of the present status of industrial enterprises in Myanmar, describing various aspects of the institutional framework, ownership pattern, and production performance.

Institutional Framework

The Ministry of Industry No. 1 and Ministry of Industry No. 2 are the two major government organizations responsible for formulating industrial policy and promoting industrial development. The Ministry of Industry

No. 1 controls light industries such as the food, pharmaceuticals, and cosmetic industries, and cement, paper, and spinning and weaving mills, and personal goods. The management and control of the eighty-five light industry enterprises are placed under the respective industrial enterprises, namely, the Myanmar Textile Industries, Myanmar Foodstuff Industries, Myanmar Pharmaceuticals Industries, Myanmar Paper and Chemical Industries, Myanmar Ceramic Industries, and Myanmar General and Maintenance Industries.[4] The Ministry of Industry No. 2 is responsible for the manufacture of heavy industries. This includes tractors, agricultural machinery, equipment, and implements; motor car and diesel engines; diesel injection pumps and nozzles; motor vehicles including trucks, buses; petrol and water bowsers and fire engines; machine tools such as lathes, drilling machines, and hand tools; water pumps and pumping sets; storage and dry cell batteries; electric cables, fluorescent lamps, electric bulbs, transformers, generators, and other electrical appliances and accessories; refrigerators and air conditioners; and rubber tires and tubes of different sizes.[5] Other ministries, such as the Ministries of Commerce, Agriculture and Irrigation, Rail Transportation, Transport, Forestry, Livestock and Fisheries, Mines, Energy, and Information have their own industrial activities.

All cooperative societies are established under the Cooperative Law, which is administered by the Ministry of Cooperatives. These are private limited companies and are permitted to operate independently just like other private companies limited. Some are producer cooperatives running their own industrial units, such as the Condensed Milk Factory in Mandalay; the Milk Factory in Pyin-Oo-Lwin; rice and edible oil mills; mechanical and engineering workshops; the textile industry; plastics and chemical factories; the foundry and metallurgy industry; and an enamelware factory.

The Department of Cooperatives manages all cooperative societies, while the Department of Cottage Industries gives technical assistance to handicraft and cottage industries. With a view to promoting, encouraging, and fostering the development of private industrial enterprises, the Private Industrial Enterprises Law was promulgated in 1990. The Cottage Industries Promotion Law was also enacted by the government in 1991 with the intention of promoting cottage industries or mini-industries.

The Directorate of Regional Industrial Coordination and Industrial Inspection under the Ministry of Industry No.1 control industrial enterprises registered under the Private Industrial Enterprises Law. Cottage and handicrafts industries register with the Department of Cottage Industries under the Ministry of Cooperatives. Private industrial firms required to register compulsorily under the Private Industrial Enterprises Law are classified into three groups (Table 3.2).

Table 3.2 Industries by Size, Investment, Workforce, and Production Factors

Size	*Power Installed (hp)*	*Investment (million kyat)*	*Labor (No.)*	*Annual Production Value (million kyat)*
Small	Up to 25	Up to 1.00	Up to 50	Up to 2.5
Medium	More than 25 up to 50	More than 1.00 up to 5.00	More than 50 up to 100	More than 2.5 up to 10
Large	Over 50	Over 5.00	Over 100	Over 10

Source: Ministry of Industry No. 1, Procedures relating to the Private Industrial Enterprises Law, 1991

According to the above mentioned Private Industrial Enterprises Law, the registered private industrial firms have the right to apply for infrastructural facilities, exemption and relief from taxes, loans for fixed capital and working capital, raw materials for manufacturing and spare parts, technical know-how, etc. from the relevant government departments.

The number of state-owned factories and industrial establishments was 1,737 in 1992-93 but fell to 1,601 in 1996-97 due mainly to the restructuring program of the state-owned factories and to privatization during the period 1992-93 to 1996-97. On the other hand, the total number of private industrial establishments (including 593 industrial units in the cooperative sector) was 37,225 in 1992-93. However, this number increased significantly to 50,672 in 1996-97, of which the cooperative sector accounted for only 637. The position of state-owned factories and industrial establishments along with the factories in cooperative and private sectors is shown in Table 3.3.

Table 3.3 State-Owned, Cooperative, and Private Enterprises (Number)

Particulars	*1992-93 (Actual)*		*1996-97 (Provisional)*	
	State	*Private**	*State*	*Private**
Food and beverages	208	20,933	209	28,627
Clothing and wearing apparel	63	2,404	33	3,819
Construction materials	128	3,417	127	3,562
Personal goods	14	1,241	14	1,355
Household goods	15	168	15	228
Printing and publishing	28	334	28	354
Industrial raw materials	928	1,870	821	1,765
Mineral and petroleum products	23	1,925	22	2,660
Agricultural equipment	3	35	3	82
Machinery and equipment	7	105	7	323
Transport vehicles	5	110	5	191
Workshops and dockyards	305	0	305	0
Miscellaneous	10	4,683	12	7,706
Total	**1,737**	**37,225**	**1601**	**50,672**

Source: Ministry of National Planning and Economic Development, *Review of Financial, Economic, and Social Conditions*, 1993-94, 1995-96, 1996-97, and 1997-98
Note: *Includes industrial establishments managed by the cooperative sector

Ownership Structure and Production Performance

It is interesting to note the ownership structure of manufacturing industries for the industrial development of the country. Table 3.4 indicates that the number of state-owned factories and industrial establishments has decreased while private factories have increased steadily. For example, state-owned factories decreased from 4.5% in 1992-93 to 3.1% in 1996-97, whereas private factories increased from 94% in 1992-93 to 96% in 1996-97.

Table 3.4 Structural Changes of Number of Factories by Ownership, 1992-97 (%)

Ownership	*1992-93*	*1993-94*	*1994-95*	*1995-96*	*1996-97*
State-owned	4.46	3.84	3.39	3.29	3.06
Cooperative	1.52	1.59	1.21	1.30	1.22
Private	94.02	94.57	95.40	95.41	95.72
Total	**100**	**100**	**100**	**100**	**100**

Source: Ministry of National Planning and Economic Development, *Review of Financial, Economic, and Social Conditions*, 1993-94, 1994-95, 1995-96, 1996-97, and 1997-98

It can also be seen from Table 3.5 that not only the private factories and industrial establishments increased in number but also the share of production value of the private factories went up throughout 1992-93 to 1996-97. The production value of 28.45% of state-owned factories in 1992-93 fell to 27% in 1996-97 while that of the private sector increased from 69% to 72% during the same period. This indicates that private industrial enterprises are contributing to industrial production but at a slow pace.

By looking at the production by commodity group (see Table 3.12), the principal activities are related to the processing of natural resources, mostly agricultural and petroleum resources. The composition of gross manufacturing output during 1992-97 indicates that food and beverage production generated more than 84% and that industrial raw materials contributed about 5%. Other commodities contributing about 3% were mineral and petroleum products, construction materials, and clothing and wearing apparel. The total value of production is also increasing steadily.

Table 3.5 Production Share of Private Industrial Enterprises, 1992-97 (at 1985-86 constant producers' prices)

Ownership	*1992-93*	*1993-94*	*1994-95*	*1995-96*	*1996-97*
	(%)	*(%)*	*(%)*	*(%)*	*(%)*
State-owned	28.45	27.21	27.71	27.00	27.10
Cooperative	2.35	1.64	0.92	0.90	0.90
Private	69.20	71.15	71.37	72.10	72.00
Total	**100**	**100**	**100**	**100**	**100**

Source: Ministry of National Planning and Economic Development, *Review of Financial, Economic, and Social Conditions*, 1993-94, 1994-95, 1995-96, 1996-97, and 1997-98

Note: Number of state-owned factories and establishments during 1996-97 included related mills that were amalgamated.

Reform measures undertaken by the government since late 1988 revitalized the processing and manufacturing sector to achieve higher positive growth rates in the past four years, namely, 10.8% in 1992-93, 9.4% in 1993-94, 8.5% in 1994-95, and 7.5% in 1995-96, respectively. These figures were actually higher than the GDP growth rates in the corresponding years. It will also be observed that the structure of production, services, and trade in the GDP has been in the order of approximately 61%, 17%, and 22%, respectively, since 1989-90. A comparative schedule of the structural changes is shown in Table 3.11.

According to data for the structural changes in Myanmar's GDP during the Four-Year Plan Period (1992-96), the agricultural sector contributes approximately 38%, while the manufacturing sector's share remains about 9% of total GDP at 1985-86 constant prices. This situation has not changed much for quite a number of years. Actually, for a country to enjoy the gains of industrialization, the manufacturing sector and other industrial activities should also appreciably increase. The reason why the processing and manufacturing sector fell behind the primary sectors was partly due to the heavy burden of processing of natural resources in manufacturing activities, with food and beverage production generating more than 84% of gross manufacturing output. Infrastructural constraints and insufficient industrial services were also a factor.

Investment Environment and Potential

Nowadays, governments need to make it not only attractive for foreign investors to come to their shores but also increasingly need to create attractive conditions for domestic investors to stay on shore. In other words, governments have to create an environment in which investment, whether domestic or foreign, can prosper. Moreover, they have to do this under conditions in which all governments are competing to do the same thing, namely, to entice their own as well as foreign firms to local production facilities in their territories.[6]

After pursuing a centrally planned economy emphasizing an inward-looking policy of self-reliance and self-sufficiency for more than two-and-a half decades, Myanmar discarded the political and economic system with a view to building up a new, developed, and modern state. It embraced a market-oriented economic system under which the private sector could engage in most economic activities especially in the areas of trade and investment. New and more liberal economic policies and reform measures were introduced to promote and foster all-round development of the national economy.

It is widely accepted that Myanmar is endowed with natural resources that are still fully untapped. The country's resource base constitutes vast cultivable land, a large continental shelf with an exclusive economic zone for fishing, properly conserved forests, abundant minerals and gems, and proven reserves of oil and gas. A fairly well trained and literate labor force also constitutes one of the primary resources of the economy. In short, Myanmar is rich in natural and human resources. What is really needed in order to reap the highest benefits of this endowment is an influx of capital, state-of-the art technology, and access to international markets.

Reform Measures

In the latter part of 1988, a series of reform measures were initiated to lay the foundations for a market-oriented economic system. Salient reform measures introduced included: decentralizing central control, encouraging private sector development, abolishing price controls and reducing subsidies, allowing FDI, initiating institutional changes, initiating a new financial management system, streamlining taxes and duties, promoting exports by streamlining export and import procedures, diversifying exports through the introduction of new products and emphasizing semi-processed and processed goods, improving infrastructure support, restructuring wages and prices, and allowing farmers to cultivate crops of their choice and to process, transport, and trade freely.

The State Law and Order Restoration Council since it assumed responsibility for the state made legal reforms in line with a liberalized economic policy. A series of legislative measures were taken, new laws were promulgated, and existing laws no longer appropriate to the new system were amended to be compatible with the changing economic environment. The underlying purpose of these changes was to strengthen the institutional framework for facilitating a market-oriented system. Twenty-seven new economic laws were enacted, and nine old laws were amended from 1988 to 1997. Included in this list are three significant laws, namely, the Union of Myanmar Foreign Investment Law of 1988, the State-Owned Economic Enterprises Law of 1989, and the Myanmar Citizens Investment Law of 1994. By terms of the last mentioned, private entrepreneurs can enjoy privileges relating to tariffs and taxes comparable to those given under the Foreign Investment Law. As a result, a significant increase in the area of trade and investment is expected to help accelerate the country's economic development.

The Foreign Investment Law enacted in November 1988 is intended to allow and encourage foreign direct investment with its prime objectives as export promotion and the expansion and acquisition of high technology. The main objective of the State-Owned Economic Enterprises Law of 1989 is to enable the private sector to invest in all economic activities, with the exception of twelve economic activities reserved for the state sector. Even so, those twelve activities can be disclosed to the private sector if beneficial for the state.

Myanmar's overall restructuring and development policy is based on three main components, namely: (1) the adoption of a market-oriented system for the allocation of resources; (2) the encouragement of private investment and entrepreneurial activities; and (3) the opening of the economy to foreign trade and investment.

The objectives of the Foreign Investment Law are as follows: (1) the promotion and expansion of exports; (2) the exploration of natural resources that require heavy investment; (3) the acquisition of high technology; (4) supporting and assisting production and services involving large capital; (5) the creation of more employment opportunities; (6) the development of works that would save energy consumption; and (7) regional development.

The Myanmar Investment Commission

The Myanmar Investment Commission (MIC) was formed to oversee and administer the Foreign Investment Law and the Myanmar Citizens Investment Law. It is an initial approving authority for investment proposals made by foreigners or by nationals. The Directorate of Investment and Company Administration (DICA) serves as the secretariat of the MIC. The duties and powers of the MIC are to:

- scrutinize proposals to see that they conform with the rules and regulations set out in the Foreign Investment Law
- ensure that proposals are financially credible and economically justifiable, and that the proposed technology is appropriate

- ensure that the proposed projects are environmentally friendly
- grant approval by issuance of a permit with stated terms and conditions
- monitor and evaluate foreign investment after approval has been granted
- relax and amend the terms and conditions previously defined, if necessary
- make suggestions and recommendations, where necessary
- facilitate and promote foreign investment
- take necessary and prompt action in respect to issues regarding the promotion of foreign investment.

Types of Economic Activities Allowed for Foreign Direct Investment

In order to provide more specific guidance to foreign investors, a notification listing the types of economic activities allowed for foreign investment has been issued. It covers most activities with the exception of those reserved under the State-Owned Economic Enterprises Law. However, if a foreign investor is interested in an activity not specified in the notification or an activity defined in the law, he can apply to the Myanmar Investment Commission stating his interest and the reasons why it will be mutually beneficial to the state and to himself. If the Myanmar Investment Commission is satisfied that the proposed activity will be in the interest of the state, it may approve the application.

Form of Organization and Minimum Amount of Foreign Capital

Under the Foreign Investment Law, foreign investment activities can be undertaken either in the form of a wholly foreign owned company or a joint venture with a Myanmar partner, either an individual, private company, cooperative society, or state-owned enterprise. If a joint venture, the foreign capital will not be less than 35%. Where the incorporation of a joint venture company does not involve the interest of the state, incorporation will be regulated under the Burma Companies Act of 1914.

If there is state interest in the joint venture, then the incorporation must be regulated under the Special Companies Act of 1950.

Minimum foreign capital to be brought into Myanmar has been notified by the Myanmar Investment Commission. This is US$500,000 for manufacturing and US$300,000 for services. Foreign capital can be brought into the country under the following categories:

- any foreign currency acceptable to the Myanmar Foreign Trade Bank
- machinery, equipment, machinery components, spare parts, instruments, etc. required for use in the business but unavailable in the country
- license, trademarks, patent rights, and other rights that can be evaluated
- technical know-how and re-investment out of profits accrued to the enterprise from the above or out of a share of profits.

Incentives and Guarantees

As the Foreign Investment Law is aimed at bringing more foreign capital into the country, it offers investment incentives and guarantees to foreign investors. An enterprise permitted by the Foreign Investment Law will enjoy a tax holiday of three years inclusive of the year the enterprise commences commercial operations and also to a reasonable period upon application, provided that the MIC, in the interest of the state, considers this appropriate. In addition, the MIC may grant one or all of the following exemptions or reliefs:

- exemption or relief from income tax on reinvested profits within one year
  accelerated depreciation rates approved by the Commission
- 50% relief from income tax on profits accrued from exports
- employers' right to pay income tax on behalf of foreign experts and technicians employed in their business and the right to deduct such payment from assessable income
- foreign employees' right to payment of income tax at a rate applicable to Myanmar nationals

- the right to deduct research and development expenditures from assessable income
- the right to carry forward and set off losses up to three consecutive years from the year in which the loss is sustained
- exemption or relief from customs duties or other internal taxes, or both, on the import of machinery, equipment, instruments, machinery components, spare parts, and materials used in the business during the period of construction
- exemption or relief on customs duties or other internal taxes, or both, on imported raw materials for the first three years of commercial operation after the completion of construction.

In the case of export-oriented commodities, commercial taxes levied on such commodities may be exempted upon application. Relief of commercial tax on locally distributed commodities is also considered on a case by case basis. The Foreign Investment Law provides an irrevocable state guarantee that an enterprise permitted by MIC under the law will not be nationalized during the permitted period or the extended period, if any. It also provides repatriation of profits after the deduction of all taxes and prescribed funds as well as the legitimate balance of salary and lawful income of foreign personnel, after the payment of living expenses and taxes. In the case of the termination or dissolution of the business, repatriation of foreign capital may also be allowed.

Inducement of Foreign Direct Investment

Since the enactment of the Foreign Investment Law, the MIC has approved 303 projects from twenty-three countries to the end of March 1998, amounting to total foreign direct investment of US$7.06 billion (Table 3.6).

In terms of the number of projects, the largest sector for foreign investment approval has been in the processing and manufacturing sector, with a total number of 113 projects, followed by oil and gas, mining, and the hotel and tourism sectors. Unlike other Southeast Asian countries, such as Thailand and Vietnam, Myanmar allows a foreign company to enjoy 100%

ownership. Joint ventures may also be undertaken with either a private company or a state-owned enterprise.

Table 3.6 Foreign Direct Investment by Sector (as of 31March 1998) (US$ million)

Sector	*Number of Projects*	*Approved Amount*
Oil and gas	46	2,303.12
Manufacturing	113	1,436.31
Hotel and tourism	40	1,037.45
Real estate	18	997.14
Mining	43	501.36
Transport and communications	13	275.39
Livestock and fisheries	18	275.35
Industrial estates	3	193.11
Construction	1	17.27
Agriculture	3	14.35
Other services	5	13.69
Total	**303**	**7,064.54**

Source: Ministry of National Planning and Economic Development, Directorate of Investment and Company Administration

Foreign Direct Investment by Country

As shown in Table 3.7, in terms of the volume of investment, the largest foreign investment in Myanmar comes from Singapore (US$1,485.76 million), followed by the United Kingdom (US$1,352.29 million) and Thailand (US$1,237.16 million).

The government attracted FDI with incentives to supplement the lack of domestic savings and technology. Combined with a relatively favorable incentive system for foreign capital, investment flowed not only for export-promotion industries but also for import-substitution industries to meet domestic demand. Products in apparel, food processing, home appliances, and plastics were a few examples. As income grew, the domestic market gradually expanded, and this attracted more foreign investment. Low wages as well as a diligent and dexterous labor force were other important factors inducing the inflow of FDI.

Table 3.7 Foreign Direct Investment by Country (as of 31 March 1998) (US$ million)

Sr. No.	*Country*	*Number of Projects*	*Approved Amount*
1	Singapore	66	1,485.76
2	United Kingdom*	32	1,352.29
3	Thailand	42	1,237.16
4	Malaysia	25	587.17
5	USA	16	582.06
6	France	3	470.37
7	Netherlands	5	237.84
8	Indonesia	8	236.37
9	Japan	19	218.87
10	Philippines	2	146.67
11	Hong Kong	20	121.32
12	South Korea	20	99.33
13	Australia	14	82.08
14	Austria	2	72.50
15	Canada	12	37.83
16	Panama	1	30.53
17	China	9	29.26
18	Germany	1	15.00
19	Denmark	1	13.37
20	Bangladesh	2	2.96
21	Israel	1	2.40
22	Macau	1	2.40
23	Sri Lanka	1	1.00
Total		**303**	**7,064.54**

Source: Ministry of National Planning and Economic Development, Directorate of Investment and Company Administration

Note: *Inclusive of enterprises incorporated in the British Virgin Islands, Bermuda, and the Cayman Islands

Investment by Myanmar Nationals

The Myanmar Investment Commission already permitted 129 projects of Myanmar nationals, amounting to a total investment of 2,3349.32 million kyat to the end of March 1998. Of this, the manufacturing sector accounted for 3,973.77 million kyat investing in 81 projects during the same period. This investment is shown by sector in Table 3.8.

Table 3.8 Investment by Myanmar Nationals by Sector (as of 31 March 1998)

Sector	*Number of Projects*	*Total Investment (million kyat)*
Agriculture	1	251.20
Livestock and fisheries	6	289.87
Manufacturing	81	3,973.77
Transport	4	2,034.93
Hotel and tourism	13	1,103.89
Construction	2	2,262.00
Real estate development	16	1,917.87
Industrial estates	1	1,012.79
Others	5	503.00
Total	**129**	**23,349.32**

Source: Ministry of National Planning and Economic Development, Directorate of Investment and Company Administration

Analyzing the investment by sector by Myanmar nationals indicates that the manufacturing sector is at the top of the list in terms of the number of the projects. The sector, however, falls to the second position if measured by the volume of investment, registering 17% of the total. It is observed that Myanmar investors are more interested in real estate development by putting in 11,917.87 million kyat, amounting to 51% of total investment in all sectors of the economy. The volume of investment in the manufacturing sector is considerably low compared to that of the real estate sector because of the capital-intensive nature of the real estate business. It appears, however, that industrialization in Myanmar is starting to take shape because of the government's endeavor to develop infrastructure, creating an environment that enables local industrialists to establish factories in the industrial zones across the country and because local industrialists enjoy incentives and privileges relating to tariffs and taxes comparable to those given under the Foreign Investment Law.

Investment Potential of the Processing and Manufacturing Sector

With abundant natural and human resources, Myanmar is trying to accelerate its industrial development. This sector is witnessing steady improvement with reforms initiated in accord with the new economic policy. According to the recent investment and development situation, the processing and manufacturing sector registered 5.2% growth in 1996-97 over the previous year. An industrial growth rate of 10.7% is projected during the second year of the Five-Year Plan.

Environment Conducive to Local and Foreign Investors

Prior to 1988, the Ministry of Industry No. 1 and Ministry of Industry No. 2 established state-owned factories in such industrial areas as Hmawbi, located about thirty-five miles from Yangon, and Daik-Oo, twenty-five miles north of Bago. They also set up Bago and Sagaing Industrial Estates in their respective regions. In addition, the Ministry of Industry No. 2 had its own industrial area in Padaung Township, on the west bank of the Ayeyarwaddy River. The construction of industrial parks and economic processing zones is considered an important element in the industrial development of the country. Furthermore, on 18 July 1995, the Myanmar Industrial Development Committee (MIDC) was formed in place of the National Industrial Promotion Committee in order to give greater impetus to the rapid industrialization. The MIDC has the following objectives: (1) the development of industries with agriculture as the base; (2) the enhancement of quantity and quality of industrial products; (3) the increased production of new types of machinery and equipment; (4) the production of machinery and equipment for industrial use; and (5) the creation of suitable conditions for transformation into an industrialized nation.

Since its formation, the MIDC has taken steps to: (1) create an environment that will enable foreign and local industrialists to establish their factories on the plots of land where basic infrastructure such as power, water supply, and telecommunication networks have already been set up; (2) establish seventeen industrial zone supervision committees in those states and divisions where a sizeable number of private industrial establishments exist to facilitate measures for the promotion of these small firms; (3) set up the Myanmar Industrial Development Bank (MIDB) for industrial financing; and (4) form the Myanmar Industrial Trading Corporation.

With a view to promoting industries, production and creation of jobs for citizens, the Department of Human Settlement and Housing Development (DHSHD) was assigned to establish industrial zones as part of its overall comprehensive development plans. The first industrial zone was established in Shwepyitha, a new satellite town twenty-four kilometers from Yangon. Three hundred hectares of land were developed to accommodate light industries for local private industrialists. The second was in Dagon South, a new satellite town sixteen kilometers from Yangon, for accommodating small-scale and light industries. The third zone was developed in Hlaingthayar, about eighteen kilometers from Yangon on the western side of the Hlaing River. The zone, developed in four phases, covers a land area of 600 hectares. Details of the zones are shown in Table 3.9.

All plots of land in these zones have already been sold as leasehold land to private industrialists. There is still a very high demand for industrial land, and to cope with this, the DHSHD is now expanding its industrial zone activities by developing more zones around Yangon (Table 3.10).

Foreign Joint Venture Industrial Parks

Industrialization is investment-intensive infrastructure for national development. The government has made judicious and crucial decisions promoting private investment in the industrial sector to accelerate the pace of industrialization. In addition to the industrial zones specifically meant for local industrialists, the DHSHD signed a joint venture agreement with Mitsui & Co. of Japan to establish an industrial zone in Mingaladon, twenty

Table 3.9 Industrial Zones Owned and Developed by DHSHD

Industrial Zone	*Designated Year*	*Size (hectares)*
Shwepyitha 1	1989	300
Dagon South		
Zone 1	1992	110
Zone 2	1996	225
Hlaingthayar		
Zones 1 and 2	1994	350
Zones 3 and 4	1996	250
Zone 5	1997	90

Source: Ministry of Construction, Department of Human Settlement and Housing Development

Table 3.10 Industrial Zones under Construction by DHSHD

Industrial Zone	*Targeted Completion Year*	*Size (hectares)*
Dagon Port	1998	370
Shwepyitha 2	1998	80
Shwepaukkan	1998	45
Dagon Port 2	1999	150
Hlaingtharyar	2000	400
Shwepyitha 3	2000	100

Source: Ministry of Construction, Department of Human Settlement and Housing Development

kilometers south of Yangon. The first phase of 89 hectares was implemented in February 1996, and the first phase was completed according to the original schedule. It provides infrastructure, such as power, water supply, an industrial waste treatment facility, and a telecommunications network. The second phase of the park of approximately 90 hectares, commenced in early 1998, is scheduled for completion at the end of 1999. The park's target is for export-oriented light industries.

The second international standard industrial zone is the Thanlyin Kyauktan Industrial Zone, close to the new Thilawa Port development area, about eighteen kilometers south of Yangon. The DHSHD signed a joint venture agreement with Sinmardev of Singapore to establish a joint venture industrial zone covering 12.3 kilometers, targeting medium and heavy industries. The first phase was completed in 1998.

Hlaingthayar Industrial Zone to the northwest of Yangon is the third foreign joint venture zone. Rojana Industrial Park Company of Thailand has signed an agreement with DHSHD to set up the zone, injecting US$14 million into the project. The first phase of 100 hectares will be ready for occupation by the end of 1999.

Apart from the above three joint venture industrial parks and zones, the DHSHD is negotiating with other foreign companies to develop additional industrial parks in Insein, Htauk-kyat, and Dagon Port Townships and also in Thanlyin Kyauktan regional development zone to respond to the influx of potential foreign investors in the manufacturing sector.

The industrial zones in Hlaingthayar, Shwepyitha, Mingaladon, and Dagon Myothit Seikkan Townships are being set up mainly for domestic industrialists, while the Thanlyin-Kyauktan Industrial Zone is targeted only for foreign companies. Local industrial zones are being implemented for boosting domestic products to have a proper export and import ratio and to generate more employment for nationals. Some of the factories in local industrial zones have begun operation, and some are starting to export their products. Of the existing industrial zones, the Hlaingthayar Zone is at present the most successful.[7]

Investment Opportunities in the Processing and Manufacturing Sector

The State Peace and Development Council is striving hard to develop Myanmar into a modern and developed state. As the country is an agro-based one, development of the agriculture sector is being brought about with all-out efforts and impressive success is being achieved. Likewise, earnest efforts are being made to enhance the development of the industrial sector. The state has laid down four economic objectives. One is "the development of the economy inviting participation in terms of technical know-how and investments from sources inside the country and abroad." Consequently, foreign investment and technical cooperation are invited and joint ventures with foreign firms from various countries have been emerging.

The objectives of the processing and manufacturing sector during the present Five-Year Plan (1996-2001) are laid down as follows: (1) to setup agro-based industries for building a new, modern and developed nation; (2) to take measures for the establishment of heavy industries; (3) to promote the agro-supportive industries in support of the agricultural sector; and (4) to make efforts for self-sufficiency and export promotion. Measures adopted for achieving the government's industrial development objectives include improving the efficiency of the state enterprises by effective use of capacities; privatizing state-owned factories that are losing concerns; establishing and giving effective support to regional resource-based zones (regional industrial zones) to promote regional development; giving effective encouragement and support to the development of private industrial enterprises; and setting up industries that manufacture new types of machinery, tools, and equipment for industry.

Some of the above measures are now being implemented. Under the Privatization Scheme some state-owned industrial establishments were transferred to private ownership. In addition, foreign and local private enterprises entered into agreements with state-owned enterprises in one of the following ways: (1) the formation of joint ventures; (2) production on a consignment basis (contract manufacturing); (3) the buy-back system; (4) the build, operate, and transfer system (BOT); and (5) the leasing of buildings and land. For example, some textile industries, pharmaceuticals and household goods industries, and general and maintenance industries under the Ministry of Industry No. 1 were operated on a consignment basis for export promotion or import substitution.

Light Industries

The Ministry of Industry No.1 has been taking steps to collaborate with foreign and local partners to run the existing factories on a joint venture basis, consignment arrangement, or buy-back system in the fields of textiles and apparel, foodstuffs and beverages, pharmaceuticals, ceramics, pulp and paper, packaging, rubber, and leather for the mutual benefit of both parties. The potential for investment in the area of light industries is:[8]

- in textiles, such as spinning, weaving, bleaching, dyeing, printing, knitting, and garment manufacturing, with Myanmar Textile Industries
- processing and manufacturing mainly concerned with beverages, alcohol, monosodium glutamate, biscuits, noodles, and soy sauce, with Myanmar Foodstuff Industries
- manufacturing of pharmaceuticals and related products, soap, toothpaste, and toiletry goods, plastic goods, and refined oil, with Myanmar Pharmaceuticals Industries
- manufacturing of pottery, marble, glass, and asbestos cement sheeting, with Myanmar Ceramic Industries
- manufacturing of footwear, rubber goods, leather and leather goods, packaging materials, thermos flasks, fountain pens and ink, with Myanmar General and Maintenance Industries
- manufacturing of matches, paint, gases, and chemicals, with Myanmar Paper and Chemical Industries.

Thus far the Ministry has signed joint venture agreements with foreign and local enterprises to form eleven joint venture enterprises to manufacture garments, tobacco, beer, and wood-based and metal materials. It has also been operating garment factories and textile mills with foreign enterprises on a consignment basis.

Heavy Industries

Myanmar Heavy Industries under the Ministry of Industry No. 2 own production facilities such as injection pump and nozzle plant, piston and piston ring plant, tire plant (automobile, farm machinery, and bicycles), cast iron foundries, forging plants, press shops, tractor plants, truck assembly lines, and light vehicle assembly line for cooperation with foreign partners.[9] Local and foreign entrepreneurs are welcome to invest in the manufacturing of vehicles, agricultural machinery, equipment and implements, motors, dynamos, generators, fluorescent lamps and electrical appliances in collaboration with the Ministry of Industry No. 2 in one of the ways mentioned above for the mutual benefit of the investor and the state. The Ministry has already established three joint ventures with the Daewoo Group and Fritz Werner Industries Co., Ltd to manufacture television sets, refrigerators, electrical appliances, and machine tools and parts.

Agro-Based Industries

In the area of agro-based industries, setting up of new industries or upgrading the existing industries is also given priority by the Ministry of Agriculture and Irrigation for cooperation with foreign or local investors either in the form of joint ventures or 100% foreign-owned firms.

Agricultural Machinery and Implements. As the sown area of cereals, edible oil crops, and pulses and beans is being increased, more farm machinery is in high demand. Investments by foreign or local companies are welcome by the Ministry in assembling and manufacturing of the machinery and farm implements such as power tillers, walking tractors, water pumps, sprinklers, threshers, seeders, weeders, and dryers.

Sugar Industry. Myanmar exports sugar produced by the eight existing sugar mills of the Ministry of Agriculture and Irrigation. In addition, a joint venture agreement was recently signed by the Myanmar Sugarcane Enterprise of the Ministry of Agriculture and Irrigation and Sutech Engineering & Associates, Co., Ltd of Thailand in June 1997 for building a 2,000-ton sugar mill in Pyay, Bago Division, with the leasing of land. This joint venture has been implemented with financial support from the Export-Import Bank of Thailand. At the signing ceremony, the Minister for Agriculture and Irrigation said that the development of the industrial sector, particularly agro-based industries, in parallel with the agriculture sector, is required to boost the national economy. He observed that increased production of sugarcane along with other economically important crops such as cotton, rubber, and coffee, is a priority area in diversifying the agriculture sector.[10] Apart from this joint venture sugar mill project, the Ministry has already signed contracts for two 1,500 TCD (tons of sugarcane crushed per day) sugar mills with Guang Dong Zhuhai Corp. of China.

Cotton Industry. Most cotton ginning and bailing mills in Myanmar are in need of innovation. The modernization of these mills with the cooperation of foreign and local investors is on the priority list of the Ministry's planning board. Cotton seeds, oil refining, cocoon production, silk production, and weaving are other options for foreign and local investors.

Other Agro-Based Industries. Factories for the production of jute, rubber, pesticide, edible oils, food processing and canning, animal feed plants, and other industries such as PVC pipes and hoses, containers and packing materials for finished agricultural products, cold storage, and transport facilities are also being given priority for cooperation.

Wood-Based Industries

Until recently, logs and sawn timber were the main export product of the Myanmar Timber Enterprise of the Ministry of Forestry. Currently, the Myanmar Timber Enterprise is promoting downstream processing to maximize earnings and minimize waste. The export of logs will be reduced and value-added processing will be increased accordingly. On recent visits to private furniture manufacturers, the then Minister for Forestry Lieut.-Gen. Chit Swe cited benefits that will accrue from the establishment of furniture factories–first, job opportunities due to the labor intensiveness in manufacturing wood-based products, and second, profits that can be made from using scantling as raw wood, which will in turn contribute to the conservation of forests. Another important benefit is minimization and cessation of exports of teak and other precious hardwood logs if value-added finished wood products are manufactured extensively. Teak, other kinds of hardwood, and lesser-known species will be effectively used in manufacturing finished products.[11]

Up to the end of December 1997, a total of nine wood-based factories were operating in this sector. They included five joint ventures between foreign investors and state-owned economic enterprises for the manufacturing and marketing of value-added wood products, plywood, sawn timber, furniture, etc., and four other 100% foreign-owned enterprises to produce value-added timber products and veneer.

The country's forest resources are so abundant that forests cover about 50% of the total land area. The forest area, with significant teak resources, covers about 6.1 million hectares. Teak is highly reputable in the world market, and Myanmar enjoys the largest share of the world teak trade. This sector is an essential source of raw materials for value-added woodwork both at home and abroad.

Fishery

Myanmar has the advantage of a 2,832 km long coast line that is ideal for developing marine resources. The total area of swamps along the coast is about 0.5 million hectares, which provide very good bases for the development of shrimp and prawn culture. According to surveys and research undertaken in marine fisheries, the country's maximum sustainable yield is estimated at about 1.05 million metric tons per year, out of which 0.59 million metric tons were used during the previous year, leaving a large potential for inland fishing and processing industries such as fish meal plants, canning plants, and industries related to fisheries, such as the construction of fishing vessels, fishing nets, etc.

Conclusion

It is envisaged that the circumstances and the analytical description mentioned above provide a rich venue for investment in the processing and manufacturing sector. The government has laid down four economic objectives, one of which is the "development of the economy inviting participation in terms of technical know-how and investments from sources inside the country and abroad" to play a vital role in development. With proper infrastructure and assistance provided by the state, more investors and industrialists are expected to take part in developing the country's processing and manufacturing sector. However, it is worthwhile to note that market forces alone are not likely to lead to the social and economic gains that are generally anticipated by the governments of developing countries. Myanmar should learn from some of the best achievements from the experience of the four Asian newly-industrialized economies (NIEs) of Hong Kong, Singapore, South Korea, and Taiwan, and the ASEAN 4 (Indonesia, Malaysia, the Philippines, and Thailand) that have already achieved the status of newly industrialized economies and high economic growth.

Macroeconomic stability is a requisite base for carrying out business activities and offers a basis for sound progress in trade and investment. To this end, suitable government decisions in macroeconomic policy are essential. It is a fact that investment in the manufacturing sector is the key to economic growth. It should also be noted that export-oriented strategies encourage investment, and this investment contributes to the building up of export earnings that, in turn, are re-invested for further export. If this virtuous cycle between investment and exports can be generated, following an outward-oriented line, the economy will be on a sustained path to growth.

In addition, technology plays an important role in determining product quality and costs in modern trade. Efforts from both the state and private sector to catch up with new technology are indispensable. The government should emphasize basic research, while the private sector should accumulate knowledge through research and development. In this context, foreign direct investment is one of the vital sources for promoting technology transfer. The development of supporting industries, namely, small-scale enterprises, is crucial for developing modern industries. The creation of small-scale enterprises and supporting industries and their integration with large- and medium-scale enterprises, that is, the formation of industrial networks, is also necessary for efficient production.

Notes

[1] Gunnar Myrdal, *An International Economy* (New York: Harper, 1956), p. 226.

[2] The State Law and Order Restoration Council was dissolved in November 1997, and the State Peace and Development Council (SPDC) was formed simultaneously.

[3] Ministry of National Planning and Economic Development, Union of Myanmar, *Review of the Financial, Economic, and Social Conditions for 1995-96*, p. 31, Table 4.

[4] For details, see Tin Hlaing, "Manufacturing Sector: Making it in Light Industry Sector." Paper presented at the Golden Opportunities in Myanmar 96 Conference, Yangon, 7–8 March 1996.

[5] The Third Workshop on Economic Development Plan: Implementation and Prospects in Myanmar, 16-17 November 1994, International Business Center, Yangon, pp. 48-52.

[6] Karl P. Sauvant, "Trends in Foreign Direct Investment and Implications for Host Countries." Paper presented at the International Conference on "SMEs—FDI—DEVELOPMENT: Attracting SMEs and Promoting Development in Developing Asia," Kunming, China, 29-31 October 1997.

[7] *The New Light of Myanmar*, 16 July 1997.

[8] Hlaing, *op. cit.*
[9] The Third Workshop, *op cit.*
[10] *The New Light of Myanmar*, 3 August 1997.
[11] *The New Light of Myanmar*, 14 September 1997.

References

Ministry of Industry No.1. Private Industrial Enterprises Law, 1991.

———. Notification No. 23/91: Procedures relating to the Private Industrial Enterprises Law, 1991.

Ministry of National Planning and Economic Development. *Economic Development of Myanmar*, June 1996.

———. *Review of Financial, Economic, and Social Conditions*, 1993-94, 1994-95, 1995-96, and 1996-97.

*Myanmar Business, Trade & Investment Digest (*Manila), November 1997.

Myanmar Watch. Monthly Information Briefs published by the Singapore Trade Development Board, October 1997.

Myint, Win. "Industrial Parks and Free Zones." Paper presented at the Technology Myanmar 1997 Conference, Yangon, 28-29 October 1997.

The New Light of Myanmar. 16 July, 3 August, and 14 September 1997.

Union of Myanmar. "Foreign Investment Law," 1988.

———. "Myanmar Citizens Investment Law and Procedures," 1994.

———. "Procedures relating to the Union of Myanmar Foreign Investment Law: Notification No. 11/88," 7-8 December 1988.

———. "State-Owned Economic Enterprises Law and Procedures," 1989.

———. "Types of Economic Activities Allowed for Foreign Investment: FIC Notification No. 1/89," May 1989.

United Nations Conference on Trade and Development. *World Investment Report, 1997 (Overview)*. New York and Geneva, 1997.

Appendix

Table 3.11 Structural Changes and Growth Rates of GDP, 1989-96 (at 1985-86 constant prices, %)

Economic Sectors	*Structure*					*Growth Rates*				
	1989-90	*1992-93*	*1993-94*	*1994-95*	*1995-96*	*1989-90*	*1992-93*	*1993-94*	*1994-95*	*1995-96*
1 Goods	61.0	61.1	61.0	60.7	60.6	6.5	11.0	6.0	6.9	6.7
1 Agriculture	39.0	38.4	37.9	37.6	37.1	5.2	12.4	4.7	6.7	5.5
2 Livestock and fishery	7.4	7.3	7.2	7.1	6.8	-4.0	4.5	4.8	6.0	3.0
3 Forestry	1.8	1.6	1.6	1.2	1.1	28.4	-3.3	1.0	-14.3	-3.9
4 Mining	0.9	1.1	1.1	1.2	1.3	30.6	20.0	11.0	14.9	15.0
5 Processing and manufacturing	9.3	8.9	9.1	9.2	9.3	11.3	10.8	9.4	8.5	7.5
6 Power	0.7	0.9	1.0	1.0	1.0	14.1	31.1	24.4	4.8	6.6
7 Construction	1.9	2.9	3.1	3.4	4.0	32.7	11.2	11.7	15.7	27.2
2 Services	16.2	16.8	17.2	17.6	18.0	-7.5	6.1	8.0	10.0	9.2
1 Transportation	3.7	4.0	4.1	4.3	4.3	9.7	9.1	9.2	11.2	7.3
2 Communications	0.7	1.0	1.0	1.1	1.3	11.6	26.0	8.5	20.4	22.1
3 Financial institutions	0.5	0.6	0.9	1.2	1.5	-85.7	15.1	38.4	47.3	34.8
4 Social and administrative services	6.7	6.7	6.8	6.8	6.7	17.9	2.9	7.2	6.8	5.5
5 Rentals and other services	4.6	4.5	4.4	4.2	4.2	1.5	3.6	3.5	4.0	6.3
3 Trade	22.8	22.1	21.8	21.7	21.4	5.3	8.9	4.6	7.0	5.6
4 GDP (1+2+3)	**100.0**	**100.0**	**100.0**	**100.0**	**100.0**	**3.7**	**9.7**	**6.0**	**7.5**	**6.9**

Source: Ministry of National Planning and Economic Development, *Review of Financial, Economic, and Social Conditions for 1996-97*

Table 3.12 Production by Commodity Group, 1992-97 (at current prices) (%)

Sr No	*Commodity Group*	*1992-93*	*1993-94*	*1994-95*	*1995-96 (Provisional actual)*	*1996-97 (Provisional)*
1	Food and beverages	81.25	86.56	83.88	84.42	84.4
2	Clothing and wearing apparel	3.61	2.48	2.76	2.66	2.32
3	Construction materials	3.28	2.60	2.26	1.86	1.76
4	Personal goods	1.29	0.86	1.19	1.17	0.94
5	Household goods	0.42	0.31	0.32	0.27	0.27
6	Printing and publishing	0.53	0.41	0.33	0.32	0.35
7	Industrial raw materials	4.39	2.95	4.41	5.62	5.37
8	Mineral and petroleum products	3.05	2.11	2.68	1.86	2.51
9	Agricultural equipment	0.07	0.40	0.40	0.35	0.51
10	Machinery and equipment	0.02	0.05	0.05	0.05	0.05
11	Transport vehicles	0.51	0.28	0.60	0.61	0.66
12	Electrical goods	0.36	0.08	0.14	0.14	0.15
13	Miscellaneous	1.22	0.91	1.00	0.68	0.70
Total (%)		100	100	100	100	100
Total current value (million kyat)		**102,961**	**151,866**	**183,283**	**256,498**	**299,299**

Source: Ministry of National Planning and Economic Development, *Review of Financial, Economic, and Social Conditions for 1996-97*

4

Industrial Development and Reforms in Myanmar

Chit So
Itochu Corporation, Yangon

Introduction

A few decades ago economic development was viewed as requiring a rapid structural transformation of an economy from one predominantly focused on agricultural activity to one founded on a more complex modern industrial and service society. This view was based on and developed out of the Western experience of industrialization. Agriculture's primary role was to provide adequate low-priced food and manpower to an expanding industrial economy. Recently, this concept has been challenged, and today development economists believe that the agriculture sector in particular and the rural economy in general must be dynamic and leading elements in any overall development strategy.

In retrospect, the agriculture sector in many developing countries stagnated during the 1960s. As Third World countries have turned their attention to raising agricultural productivity, the situation has improved. For example, from 1970 to 1980, per capita food production grew at an annual rate of 0.5%.[1] Myanmar is a Third World country of this type. Its government believes that a development program cannot afford to emphasize industrialization at the expense of agricultural development and that mutually supportive interactions between agriculture and industry should receive primary attention. Agriculture, it believes, should be the basis for the all-round development of other sectors in the economy.

The old dispute as to whether industry or agriculture should receive priority is no longer a real issue, and the focus now is on how to achieve agricultural and industrial development concurrently. Structural transformation over time from a low-income, agrarian, rural economy to an industrial, urban economy with higher per capita income involves the phenomena of industrialization, agricultural change, migration, and urbanization. Agricultural transformation involves a relative decline in the agriculture sector, but absolute levels of agricultural output and employment will rise throughout much of the process of structural transformation. During this process, the rural labor force will gradually dwindle. Industrialization offers substantial dynamic benefits that are essential for changing the traditional structure of a less developed economy. Hence, Myanmar is determined to strive for industrialization but not at the expense of its agriculture sector.

This paper attempts to analyze the evolution of Myanmar's industrial sector and the industrial policies of its successive post-independence governments following a brief outline of the country's economy during colonial rule.

Historical Background

Myanmar's industrialization has deep roots in the King Mindon era with industrialization being initiated by Prince Kanaung, the King's younger brother, around the middle of the nineteenth century. Prince Kanaung, who is regarded as the father of the country's industrialization, established a cannon factory, arms and weapons factories, a shipbuilding industry, foundries, sawmills, a silver coin mill, and so forth. Technicians were sent to England, France, Italy, and India, to study industrial development. Prince Kanaung made Mandalay or "Yadanabon," the former national capital, into an industrial area, which is still much visited today by tourists interested in studying the country's traditional handicrafts, art, and garment industries.

Furnivall comments that "Although Burman industries had made little progress under Burmese rule, they have gone backwards under the British government."[2] When the country was fully colonized by Great Britain in 1885-86, the Industrial Revolution in Europe was at its culmination and the capitalist system was gaining momentum. Burma (now Myanmar) was then a mediaeval economy relying on subsistence agriculture, handicrafts, and cottage industries to fulfill its basic domestic needs. The country's indigenous pre-colonial industries were confined to cotton spinning and weaving, salt exploitation, pottery, brick making, cart making, boat making, carpentry, iron smelting, blacksmithery, and the like.[3] The colonial ruler favored a policy of free trade that encouraged agricultural production and hindered industry, given the country's advantages in certain forms of agricultural production and disadvantages in respect to industrial production.[4] However, as the agricultural sector showed impressive growth, an industrialization process also gradually took shape.

Under the British system of the division of labor and the localization of industry, the country became an agricultural rather than an industrial state. The British transformed the country's subsistence agriculture into a commercial scale and cottage industries became large-scale factories, i.e., processing and manufacturing industries. The British brought foreign direct investment (FDI) and limited technology such as steam engines or food processing mills soon after colonization. During the 1920s technology for manufacturing consumer goods and food-processing such as sugar, oil, textile, and flour mills, and coffee, soft drinks, rubber, and match factories were introduced. Under the laissez-faire system, foreign companies were free to bring in their own skilled personnel, whether British, Indian, or Chinese, to manage their businesses while the indigenous population was employed as laborers.

The country's industrialization, in effect, began with the arrival of printing machines in 1830 in the Tenassarim area under British colonial dominance. The first operation of a sugar mill can be traced in the 1840s in lower Burma, and the first rice mill was established in 1860 near Rangoon (now Yangon). After full colonization by the British in 1859, the country became the world's largest rice basket, and rice production grew substantially year after year. This factor contributed to the multiplication of rice mills in vital rice production areas throughout the country, and it seems natural that rice mills have played an important role in the country's industrial sector. Teak was the export item next in demand to rice during the colonial period and numerous sawmills were thus built. These along with rice mills were the forerunners of the industrial sector. Next were petroleum refinery plants, metal and mineral refinery plants, and power generators. After rice and timber, crude oil, minerals, metals, rubber, and cement were important export items. The shipbuilding and cotton industries also thrived.

The country supplied 45% of the world's food demand during the prewar period with rice exports reaching their culmination in 1934-35 when 3.36 million tons were shipped. Until 1940, Myanmar exported an average of 3.1 million tons per year, a figure that can be compared with Thailand's 1.5 and Indochina's 1.4 million tons. Until the end of the colonial rule in 1948, Myanmar remained a monocultural economy relying chiefly on the export of rice.

The laissez-faire policy practiced by the British encouraged large private enterprises like Bombay Burma, Steel Brothers, the British Oil Company, and the Irrawaddy Flotilla to secure a strong foothold in the country. Foreign companies developed simple processing industries to export raw materials. The production of industrial raw materials needed for domestic consumption was almost neglected and thus these had to be imported. The exploration and development of minerals were limited to gems and jewelry that were in high demand in the world market. Thus, exploration of gems and jewelry as well as oil refinery, mineral exploration and refinery, and the construction of rice mills and sawmills were given priority. The colonial industrial policy aimed at expanding the base for producing export commodities but targeted short- rather than long-term benefits and therefore focused on processing of raw materials for export. The policy did not lead to the building of factories or training of people to manufacture basic consumer goods or machinery, either for export or domestic consumption. Hence, few industries produced food, clothing, or consumer commodities. In 1940, 1,027 factories were in operation, including 673 rice mills and 116 sawmills. Of these, nationals owned a third while the rest belonged to foreigners.

During the colonial period, industrialization was almost neglected. Most consumer goods, including food and clothing, had to be imported from industrialized countries. The British did not favor establishing industries for manufacturing consumer commodities, wearing apparel, and food processing, and under the laissez-faire policy domestic industries were not protected. In assessing imports, it can be discerned that wearing apparel occupied the largest share while machinery and parts remained low. Regarding industrial imports, the volume of raw materials, coke, iron, steel, and fuel remained higher than that of machinery and parts. The annual growth rate for the import of machinery or parts was lower than that for consumer commodities.

The industrial facilities built during the colonial period were destroyed during the Second World War under a scorched-earth policy when British troops fled to escape the Japanese invasion in 1942. The Japanese military did the same on its retreat in 1945. In 1942, large rice mills located in Rangoon and Mawlamyine were ruined by war, and only some small mills in remote areas remained intact. However, the invading Japanese army renovated the rice mills with domestic-made machinery and parts, and by the end of 1944, managed to operate half the mills located in Rangoon.[5] Nearly 60% of the sawmills were destroyed by war. The Japanese did not make much effort to repair these mills and instead used manpower for domestic purposes. During the Japanese Occupation, the shipbuilding industry using teak was revamped and oil wells located in Yenangyaung and Chauk were renovated. Between 1943 and 1945, the wells were producing 2.68 million barrels of crude oil. Daily production increased to 3,133.59 barrels per day in 1945 from 2,694.88 barrels per day in 1942. The Japanese military attempted to develop cottage industries and sent young people to Japan for technical training. Factories destroyed by the war were also repaired and renovated including oil refinery plants and those processing minerals.

In 1946-47, overall production was only 57% of the pre-war period. In 1946, 345 private industries and 10 state-owned industries were registered under the Factories Act of Burma 1934. Of these, 279 were involved in food and beverage production, including 272 rice mills. Annual rice exports declined to 1.2 million tons in the aftermath of the war. This may be attributed to the destruction of 411 rice mills in addition to dwindling acreage of paddy during the war. When the British returned in 1945, they planned to implement industrial development in accordance with the "New Industries for Burma" report embodied in the Simla Plan. Projects to rehabilitate various industries were launched with financial assistance from the Government of Burma. During this period, most private industries that had existed prior to the war were reluctant to resume business solely with their own finances and requested financial support from the government.

After the country gained independence in 1948, the Anti-Fascist People's Freedom League (AFPFL) government conducted land and tenancy reforms while nationalizing certain vital industries. The Agricultural Project, Timber Project, Electricity Supply, and Inland Water Transport Boards were established following the nationalization of these industries. The government, however, welcomed foreign investment in the private sector and established joint ventures (JVs) with both domestic and foreign businesses.

The AFPFL government implemented a two-year industrial development plan to establish a steel rolling mill, brick and tile factories, jute and textile mills, and like enterprises as state-owned industries. Most private industries that had flourished during colonial rule continued operations in the period from 1948 to 1962. While the government set up state-owned industries under the long-term industrial plan, the Pyidawtha Plan, private industries were allowed to run in parallel with factories operated by public entities. In 1959-60, there were 2,468 factories, comprised of 1,294 foodstuff factories, 529 clothing and apparel factories, and consumer goods manufacturing factories.[6] Of these, 87.44% were owned by nationals,

4.54% were fully foreign owned, and 8.02% were joint ventures with foreign and local involvement. As large-scale industries, the state sector operated cotton and garment factories, and steel, jute, and sugar mills. Small-scale industries run by the state sector comprised sericulture mills and condensed milk, tea, and chinaware factories. Thanks to government incentives and encouragement, small and medium-sized industries in the private sector had achieved considerable progress by the early 1960s. Government incentives included extending industrial loans to private industrialists and supplying raw materials. The private sector established food, garment, and consumer goods enterprises, including factories producing noodles, vermicelli, biscuits, ice, weaving, blankets, towels, men's underwear, nylon, rayon, plastic, soap, umbrellas, slippers, dry batteries, batteries, and cosmetics. As the number of factories in the private sector annually increased, production of some consumer goods such as soap and men's underwear came to exceed domestic demand, and by 1960 the government had to limit the issuance of licenses to construct new factories. Since then state-owned factories have run at a loss.[7] During the period 1952-62, the Industrial Development Corporation managed eight projects, namely, steel, jute, and textile mills; an engineering industry project; sugar, cement, and silk-reeling factories; and a pottery works.[8]

Private sector involvement in industrial development operated under the free market economy was greatly hampered after the military takeover in 1962 as the new government opted for a socialist economic system and nationalized all sizable private industries. The vital means of production and distribution such as large-scale industries, businesses, and banks were nationalized, and the state monopolized foreign trade. The number of factories owned by the private sector nonetheless remained far greater than those owned by the state. More than two-thirds of private enterprises remained small, with fewer than ten workers to a factory. The majority of these were engaged in food and beverage processing. Of the15,453 factories and industrial establishments registered in 1970-71, 1,048 were state owned, 159 were cooperatives, and 14,246 were private.

During the first decade of socialist rule, the industrial sector was given priority over agriculture under an import-substitution strategy. Only in the early 1970s after the failure of industrialization due to overemphasis on the manufacturing sector while neglecting the importance of agriculture did the government reset its priorities. Industrialization thus received a low profile in the second decade of socialist rule, that is, from 1974 to 1986. In the Second Four-Year Plan, which commenced in 1974, the agriculture sector came to the forefront with the government attempting to increase output in order to obtain greater export earnings. Nonetheless, the government continued to maintain an import-substitution strategy, placing emphasis on the consumer goods manufacturing and foodstuff processing industries.

During the twenty-six years of socialist rule, public sector investment remained the main driving force for industrial development. Private investment was confined to small-scale activities concentrating on processing natural resources. The government's import substitution strategy aimed at fulfilling basic domestic needs within the framework of a virtually closed-door and self-reliant economic system. Ironically, some of the factories built under bilateral and multilateral aid programs were later found to be unmatched by the prevailing weak industrial infrastructure. Industry was shielded from international competition and remained at a low productivity level. By the end of socialist rule in 1986-87, the contribution to GNP of the manufacturing and processing sector was 10.7%, and the sector's labor force constituted 8.7%. During those years, the output of food industries shared 71.5% of the overall output of the manufacturing and processing sector whereas the garment and textile industries shared 6.3%, industrial raw materials production 5.6%, mineral and oil production 3.8%, and construction materials production 3.5%, respectively.[9]

Industrial Reforms under a Market-Oriented System

After it took power in 1988, the State Law and Order Restoration Council (SLORC) government abolished the socialist economic system and adopted a market-oriented one. It continued, however to pursue a resource-based industrialization strategy aimed at improving the quantity and quality of domestic value-added products derived from processing natural resources in the agriculture, fisheries, forestry, and mining sectors.

Various reform measures were taken to stimulate active participation by the private sector. These measures included the decentralization of central control, the abolition of price controls and the reduction of subsidies, streamlining taxes and duties, the initiation of institutional changes, the privatization of some inefficient state enterprises, the diversification of exports, the establishment of industrial zones, the opening of border trade, and the improvement of infrastructure, including, the construction of new sea and air ports. Between 1988 and 1997, twenty-seven new business-related laws were promulgated, including the Foreign Investment Law (1988) and the Myanmar Citizens Investment Law (1989), and nine existing laws were amended.

As a traditional agricultural country endowed with rich natural resources, Myanmar's industrial structure is centered on processing agricultural, forestry, mining, and fisheries resources. Food and beverages production enjoys the lion's share of this activity, amounting to 85% of gross manufacturing output. Recently, the processing of marine products has been gaining momentum.

Promoting the status of traditional agro-based enterprises from serving local to national and thence export market remains high on the policy agenda. Myanmar needs to develop its agro-based industry given the agriculture sector's contribution of nearly 40% to overall output. Over 60% of the labor force are engaged in this sector, and the government deems that industrialization should be based on the sector's development. At the same time, elevating light industries to medium- and large-scale ones capable of manufacturing specialized parts, components, and tools has been envisaged. Rendering associated services for better structural integration of the industrial sector with other economic sectors is also assuming importance since a lack of substantial industrial linkages is regarded as a drawback of the present structure.

The main difference in the mode of acquisition of foreign technology between the former socialist government and the current market-oriented government is the latter's total reliance on FDI while the former was dependent on overseas development assistance (ODA). The Foreign Investment Law aims for the acquisition of high technology as well as for supporting and assisting production and services involving large capital.[10]

Given the termination of large-scale ODA from bilateral donors as well as multilateral institutions such as the World Bank, the International Monetary Fund, and the Asian Development Bank, the country, since 1988, has had no choice but to rely on FDI and commercial credits from foreign multinational corporations to establish factories or import capital goods and machinery to speed up industrialization. The only aid that Myanmar currently enjoys comes in the form of Basic Human Needs (BHN), whether bi- or multi-lateral. The amount of grant-aid for BHN is small, and its contribution to technological progress is minimal. Unless the nation acquiesces in changing its polity, the Western community, led by the United States, is unwilling to lift the current ODA ban and concomitant economic sanctions.

It is costly for a developing country like Myanmar to carry out infrastructure development projects without foreign assistance. Delays in inflows of ODA for multi-million dollar projects like the construction of international airports or deep-sea ports hamper the nation's overall economic progress. Financial and technical assistance in the form of ODA would greatly facilitate the rapid construction of such projects; however, over the past ten years, the government has built roads, bridges, dams, and irrigation facilities using its own budgetary resources.

In the FDI era, the government assigned a consortium of Singaporean companies for the construction of a new Yangon port in Thanlyin under the BOT system. The new port has already commenced operations. The expansion of Yangon International Airport eagerly awaits the full resumption of ODA yen loans by Japan. The Japanese government approved this as an ODA project in the 1980s, but the suspension of aid by DAC countries since 1988 has delayed implementation. The construction of an international airport in Mandalay, the country's second largest city (with a population of 1.5 million), appears, however, ready for early completion, with plans for commercial operations to commence in mid-1999. Once this airport becomes operational, it will significantly change the industrial structure of Mandalay, located at the country's geographic center, and the tourism industry will receive a boost at the same time. The ancient capital may replace Yangon as the center of tourist attraction and the focal entry point for foreign tourists.

Myanmar's industrial base remains weak despite continuous inflows of FDI in the aftermath of the transition from a socialist to a market-oriented economy in 1988, with the amount of FDI totaling US$7,064.54 million by 31 March 1998 on an approval basis. While the share of manufactured goods in the country's total exports in 1996-97 constituted less than 9%, agricultural goods occupied more than 35%. Similarly, the number of industrial workers in the total labor force constituted some 8.76%, against agricultural workers at 63.35%. The processing and manufacturing sector accounted for 9.2% of GDP in the same year, while the agriculture and livestock and fisheries sectors shared 36.4% and 7.1%, respectively. The services and trade sectors accounted for 18% and 21.2%, respectively. This structure has virtually remained unchanged over the past two decades.

Industrial production has continued to decrease in real terms, as do capacity utilization rates, which lie in the 30-50% range. During the period from 1985-86 to 1992-93, the quantum index of production for each year dropped below the 1985-86 level.[11] Only in 1993-94 and 1994-95, did it exceed the 1985-86 level. This cannot, in fact, be claimed as a real increment if annual population growth of approximately 1.8% is taken into account. The production of some personal goods, printing and publishing materials, mineral and petroleum products, electrical appliances, and miscellaneous goods have yet to reach their 1985-86 level. After 1988, it hence became a challenge for the new government to improve the economy's industrial competitiveness while promoting and diversifying manufactured or processed commodities for export. Given a long history of public sector dominance in the industrial sector and the narrow base of domestic private entrepreneurship, the road to rapid industrialization with wide private sector participation does not promise to be a smooth one.

In terms of the number of establishments, private factories accounted for 95%, state-owned factories 4%, and cooperative factories 1%, while in terms of net output value the ratio among private, state-owned, and cooperative enterprises remained at 75: 23: 2 in 1996-97. Most private industrial units are engaged in manufacturing simple consumer commodities to supply the domestic market. Almost all industrial concerns of considerable size are concentrated in state-owned enterprises, which account for 60% of the total in the agriculture sector, and 70% in the case of machinery and equipment.

State Guidelines for Industrialization

With regard to industrialization, Senior General Than Shwe, Chairman of the State Peace and Development Council, emphasized the following points when delivering speeches on several occasions during 1992-95:

(1) In the industrial sector, the government should be responsible only for those industries that the private sector cannot handle while the private sector should manage the rest.

(2) To compete with the private sector, industrial cooperative associations should be formed.

(3) To become a modernized state, investments from agriculture will be sought and these should be proportionately utilized in the industrial sector with gradual transformation into an industrial state. Lacking an industrial base, one cannot build an industrial state. Based on agriculture, an industrial state can gradually be built.

(4) Various ways and means should be sought in order for factories to operate at full capacity utilization.

(5) There should be standardization for manufacturing machinery and parts, and linkages should be established between producers and consumers.

(6) Factories should make efforts to produce their own required machinery and parts instead of ordering from abroad.

(7) Research should be conducted for upgrading the quality of export commodities.

(8) Reliance on the import of capital goods and agricultural implements should be reduced.

(9) The quantity and variety of agricultural implements should be boosted as required.

(10) Foreign technicians should be recruited.

(11) The productivity of other industries should increase while agro-based industries should be promoted.

(12) Products should be diversified.[12]

Role of the Myanmar Industrial Development Council

The Myanmar Industrial Development Council (MIDC), composed of cabinet ministers and deputy ministers, is responsible for coordinating, overseeing, and supervising the state sector's industrial performance as well as that of the private and cooperative sectors. The MIDC replaced the National Industrial Promotion Committee (NIPC), formed on 27 November 1992, on 18 July 1995 by SLORC Notification No. 37/95. Its objectives are as follows: (1) development of industries with agriculture as a base; (2) enhancement of the quantity and quality of industrial products; (3) increased production of new types of machinery and equipment; (4) production of machinery and equipment for industrial use; and (5) creation of suitable conditions for transformation into an industrialized state.

The Minister for Science and Technology, U Thaung is the chairman of the MIDC and the Deputy Minister of the Ministry of Industry No. 2, U Thein Tun, is its secretary. Of the twelve MIDC members, nine are ministers. The Minister for Industry No. 2 chairs the Working Committee formed under the MIDC. Composed of forty members, the Working Committee includes the deputy ministers and heads of department and state-owned enterprises. The Committee is divided into the following sub-committees: (1) Production of Agricultural Machinery and Equipment; (2) Technology Transfer and Industrial Information; (3) Innovation, Production, and Distribution of Fuel other than Firewood; (4) Promotion of Private Industries; (5) Supervision of Regional Industries; (6) Standardization; (7) Drafting of Industrial Laws; (8) Industrial Research and Development; and (9) Propagation of Industrial Information.

The MIDC has also laid down plans and programs for the successful operation of regional industrial zones. Since 1988, fourteen industrial zones have been established in various states and divisions to speed up the development of private industries.[13] The objectives of the regional industrial zones are to:

- develop agro-based industries
- enhance the quantity and quality of industrial products
- increase raw industrial products
- produce machinery and equipment
- create suitable conditions for transformation into an industrialized state.

In addition, the MIDC has formulated plans to create industrial parks that will accommodate industries using modern technology as well as those industries that have export potential. The Department of Human Settlement and Housing Development (DHSHD) of the Ministry of Construction has thus far developed four industrial parks in Yangon. This has been done jointly with foreign investors or single-handedly and aims to accommodate factories established under joint-ventureship with foreign firms or with 100% foreign investment. The Hlaingthayar Industrial Zone, covering an area of 1,119 acres located in the northwest of Yangon, is regarded as the most successful.[14] A total of 142 factories are under construction, and 32 including those owned by foreign firms have already begun operations in Hlaingthayar. Shwepyitha Industrial Zone situated in

Table 4.1 Industrial Parks with Joint Venture Partnerships in Yangon

Name	JV Partners	Investment (US$ million)
Mingaladon Industrial Park	DHSHD/Mitsui and Co., Ltd.	14
Thanlyin-Kyauktan	DHSHD/Sinmardev Industrial Zone International Pte, Ltd	166.1
Hlaingthayar Industrial Zone	DHSHD/Rojana Industrial Park	14
Shwepyitha Industrial Zone	DHSHD	-
Dagon Myothit Industrial Zone	DHSHD	-

the northern part of Yangon is also showing good progress. These two industrial zones accept both local and foreign industries, and some of the factories are even exporting their products. However, Mingladon and Thalyin-Kyuaktan Industrial Parks, jointly developed by foreign firms, have not yet completed land and infrastructure preparations to establish foreign factories. Mingladon and Thalyin-Kyuaktan Industrial Parks are reserved for 100% foreign-owned or joint venture industries under the Foreign Investment Law. The list of industrial parks/zones in Yangon is shown in Table 4.1

In addition, the MIDC is responsible for organizing industrial exhibitions or technology fairs inviting domestic and/or foreign industrialists. The first international industrial exhibition sponsored by the government, entitled "The Myanmar Industrial Exhibition," was held in Yangon from 24 to 31 May 1996. Its main purpose was to create an opportunity for local public and private industries to establish contact with foreign firms. It also afforded local industrialists operating in various regions to meet and consult with one another for future cooperation and industrial linkages among regions. In fact, the first industrial exhibition for local industries was held in Monywa in 1995. The following year, two industrial exhibitions were held in Mandalay and Bago, on 18-27 January and 4-12 March, respectively.

In order to extend industrial loans to promising private industries and help with financing problems, the MIDC established the Myanmar Industrial Development Bank on 15 February 1996 with an authorized share capital of 2 billion kyat (composed of 4,000 shares). Interest rate of loans financed in local currency range between 16.5-18.5% per annum, and the interest rate of loans financed in foreign currency is 8.5% per annum.

Industrial Policy

The government plans to transform the current low-productivity agricultural economy into a high productivity agro-based industrial economy. To achieve this objective, the following measures are to be taken:

(1) to develop industries by inviting participation in terms of technical know-how and investment from sources within the country and abroad; (2) to produce value-added manufactured products based as far as possible on local natural resources and to create local sales as well as overseas markets; (3) to raise the efficiency of private, cooperative, and state-owned industrial enterprises as well as labor productivity; (4) to raise capacity utilization of existing factories by economic collaboration with private firms on a joint-venture basis, consignment arrangement, or buy-back system as well as leasing out the factories, buildings, lands, or liquidations; and (5) to coordinate the production of spare parts, components, and tools and die.

The Ministry of Industry No. 1 and the Ministry of Industry No. 2 share major responsibility for formulating strategies and policies for effective and rapid industrialization. While the domain of Ministry of Industry No. 1 ranges from the production of a large variety of consumer commodities and to manufacturing light industrial goods, the Ministry of Industry No. 2 concentrates on developing heavy industry. The Myanmar Investment Commission needs to consult these ministries and related ministries when it receives applications from foreign firms wishing to invest in the manufacturing or processing industry.

Other ministries of direct relevance to industrial development comprise the Ministries of Cooperatives, Trade, National Planning and Economic Development, and Finance and Revenue. In addition to the Ministry of Industry No. 1 and Ministry of Industry No. 2, other ministries directly involved in manufacturing and processing include the Ministries of Trade, Agriculture and Irrigation, Railways, Livestock and Fisheries, Forestry, Mines, Energy, and Information.

Industries Managed by the State, Cooperative, and Private Sectors

Table 4.2 shows the number of state-owned, cooperative, and private factories and establishments in operation by 1997-98.

State-Owned Industries: State-owned industries operated by each ministry include the following:

Table 4.2 State-Owned, Cooperative, and Private Enterprises (million kyat)

Particular	*State*	*Cooperative*	*Private*	*Total*
Food and beverages	209	220	28,816	29,245
Clothing /Wearing apparel	33	183	3,733	3,949
Construction materials	126	79	3,535	3,740
Personal goods	14	23	1,358	1,395
Household goods	15	29	198	242
Printing and publishing	28	13	354	395
Industrial raw materials	821	7	1,803	2,631
Mineral and petroleum products	22	12	2,708	2,742
Agricultural equipment	3	-	3	6
Machinery and equipment	-	7	331	338
Transport vehicles	7	-	194	201
Workshops and dockyards	305	-	-	305
Miscellaneous	12	64	7,988	8,064
Total	**1,600**	**637**	**51,101**	**53,338**

Source: Ministry of National Planning and Economic Development, *Review of Financial, Economic, and Social Conditions for 1997-98*

Ministry of Agriculture and Irrigation: cotton gins, cotton seed oil mills, sugar mills, jute mills, jute carpet factory, palm oil and vegetable oil mills, fruit and vegetable canning factory, and silk yarn factory.

Ministry of Commerce: rice mills, rice bran oil mills, cotton mills, 87 industrial units including vehicle repair workshops and rice-milling machinery and spare parts production factories.

Ministry of Industry No. 1: 85 light industries managed by Myanmar Textile Industries, Myanmar Foodstuff Industries, Myanmar Pharmaceuticals Industries, Myanmar Paper and Chemical Industries, Myanmar Ceramic Industries, and Myanmar General and Maintenance Industries.

Ministry of Industry No. 2: agricultural machinery, equipment and implements, tractors, car engines, diesel engines, diesel injection pumps and nozzles, motor vehicles including trucks, buses, petrol and water bowers, and fire engines, machine tools such as lathes, drilling machines and hand tools, water pumps, pumping sets, storage and dry cell batteries, electric cables, fluorescent lamps, electric bulbs, transformers, generators, electrical appliances and accessories, refrigerators, air conditioners, and rubber tires and tubes.

Ministry of Railways: five large maintenance and repair shops, workshops, oxygen gas plant, spare parts manufacturing factories, and dockyards.

Ministry of Livestock and Fisheries: twelve factories including a milk plant, fish and meat canning factories, and an animal feed mill.

Ministry of Forestry: sawmills, plywood factories, wood furniture factories, wood-based products factories.

Ministry of Mines: metallic lead and zinc concentrate production (Namtu Bawdwin Mines), copper production (Monywa Mines), tin smelting plant (Thanlyin), iron and steel mills (Insein, Pyin-Oo-Lwin), salt production.

Ministry of Energy: hydro and thermal electricity generation plants, petroleum refineries, fertilizer plants, methanol plant.

Ministry of Information: printing presses.

A major portion of light industrial manufacturing industries are engaged in the production of consumer goods that constitute about 85% of all manufacturing establishments and 90% of total manufacturing output. Yet, the current production level of consumer goods is insufficient to meet overall domestic demand, and thus consumer goods valued at approximately US$500 million must be imported annually. The value of consumer goods share is 40% of total imports.

A recent major goal of the government's industrial reforms and restructuring programs is to improve performance levels in state-owned industries while encouraging the development of private industries. The regular evaluation and assessment of the efficiency of state-owned factories thus assumes importance. Based on the results of this review, certain state-owned factories have either been restructured or privatized. For instance, the number of factories owned by the Ministry of Industry No. 1 was reduced to 86 factories in 1995 from 142 factories in 1988. The restructuring and reform process to strengthen industrial competitiveness and promote productivity involves the following measures:

- integrating some factories either on the utilization of raw materials or on the basis of production capacity in the total production at the industry and enterprise levels while phasing out some uneconomic sections of factories
- handing over the factory to a ministry capable of running it efficiently
- leasing the factory to a private entrepreneur
- collaborating with foreign and/or local enterprises to run an existing or renovated factory on a joint-venture basis, consignment arrangement, or buy-back system.

The Ministry of Industry No. 1 has taken the lead with respect to establishing joint ventures with foreign enterprises, arranging with eleven firms to manufacture garments, tobacco, beer, wood-based products, and metal materials. Some of these JV firms achieved success in securing export markets. Between 1990-91 and 1994-95, the value of exports rose from 54 million to 81 million kyat. The same Ministry has also been operating three garment factories and two textile mills with foreign firms on a consignment basis. Likewise, the Ministry of Industry No. 2 has established three joint-venture companies with the Daewoo Group and Fritz Werner Industries Co., Ltd, to manufacture televisions, video cassette recorders, refrigerators, electrical appliances, and machine tools and parts aimed at the export market, and importing and marketing Korean new motor vehicles for domestic consumption.

Cooperative Industries: Industries registered under the Promotion of Cottage Industries Law (PCIL) of 1991 perform their activities in accordance with the regulations prescribed by the Ministry of Cooperatives. Producer cooperatives are eligible to apply for industrial loans from the Ministry. After SLORC took power in 1988, a new Cooperative Societies Law was promulgated in 1992, and cooperative societies have been reformed in accord with it. Thus far, 21,617 cooperative societies, with 2.8 million members, are in operation throughout the country. Among the productive sectors, agriculture production is given top priority. Hence, 6,682 co-op societies belong to agriculture producers societies. Under its farm mechanization programs, the Ministry of Cooperatives has provided farm implements and agricultural inputs to co-op farmers. Co-op societies have also taken part in the industrial, livestock breeding, fisheries, mining, construction, and electric power sectors.[15] The Ministry of Cooperatives organizes co-op market festivals, trade fairs, packaging exhibitions, and the like from time to time. Cooperative societies are currently operating condensed milk and milk factories, rice, edible oil, and textile mills, mechanical and engineering workshops, plastics and chemical factories, foundry, metallurgy, and enamelware factories, agricultural machinery and equipment manufacturing factories, water pump factories, and handicraft factories.[16]

Private Industries: Private industries though different in scale and size are scattered throughout the country. Table 4.3 shows factories and industrial establishments categorized by number of employees in 1997-98.

Most private industries are concentrated in the Mandalay and Yangon areas, the nation's two largest cities, where infrastructure facilities such as the electric power supply, water systems, gas availability, and road conditions are more developed than in other cities. With a view to regulating the orderly growth of private industries that have been annually increasing, the government enacted the Private Industrial Enterprise Law (PIEL) and the Promotion of Cottage Industries Law in 1990 and 1991, respectively. While the private industries registered in accordance with the PIEL are controlled by the Directorate of Regional Industrial Coordination and Industrial Inspection of the Ministry of Industry No. 1, the handicraft and cottage industries set up under the PCIL are administered by the Department of Cottage Industries of the Ministry of Cooperatives.

Table 4.3 Factories and Industrial Establishments by Number of Employees, 1997-98

Particulars	*State*	*Cooperative*	*Private*	*Total*
Fewer than 10 workers	811	324	48,898	50,033
10-50 workers	251	231	1,978	2,456
51-100 workers	144	75	124	343
Over 100 workers	398	7	101	506
Total	**1,600**	**637**	**51,101**	**53,338**

Source: Ministry of National Planning and Economic Development, *Review of Financial, Economic, and Social Conditions for 1997-98*

Of the 51,101 private industries registered in 1997-98, 56.4%, or 28,816, were engaged in the production of food and beverages. The second largest industry appeared to be involved in making clothing and wearing apparel followed by the production of construction materials. Recent strains in the relations between Myanmar and Western countries thwarted the progress of a booming wearing apparel industry. Reflecting growing domestic demand, the production of plastic bags, basins, containers, shopping baskets, PVC pipes, foam mattresses, and similar products has shown a sharp rise. Cottage industries engaged in manufacturing plasticware have spread throughout the cities, and some medium-size factories have already secured export markets.

The number of small enterprises occupies 86% of the industrial sector. Mandalay has the potential to become the center for small and medium-sized enterprises. Currently, Mandalay Division accommodates over 7,000 enterprises while Yangon Division has 6,000. In terms of production value, Mandalay Division produced 3.8 billion kyat compared to Yangon Division's 8 billion kyat in 1996-97. By contrast, production for the whole country amounted to 8 billion kyat.[17]

To encourage private sector participation in economic development and industrialization, the government lifted restrictions on the activities of the Union of Myanmar Chamber of Commerce and Industry (UMCCI) on 6 January 1989. During the twenty-six years of socialist rule, the UMCCI had remained dormant. After its reactivation, it soon established an ad hoc committee to encourage private sector participation in industrial development.

The Processing and Manufacturing Sector

In 1997-98, the production of agro-based industrial goods showed a decline, but the output of agro-supportive products and other manufactures increased. The quantum index of the production of processing and manufacturing sector with 1985-86 as the base year rose to 130.1 in 1997-98 from 123.7 in 1996-97.

The government's major industrial development objectives during 1997-98 were to: develop heavy industries, extend agro-based and agro-supportive industries, ensure self-sufficiency, promote exports, and enhance the production of value-added goods. Measures to achieve these objectives included: giving more autonomy in the managerial and financial aspects to state economic enterprises; undertaking various ways and means for effective production and export promotion; giving emphasis to the effective utilization of production capacity; reducing wastage and loss: minimizing production costs and producing equipment and spare parts; supervising private industries in accord with the PIEL; disbursing loans to private entrepreneurs by state and private banks; and establishing industrial zones in cooperation with foreign and local private entrepreneurs.

Wood-based factories under the State Timber Enterprise were operated under the buy-back system. Textile, pharmaceuticals, and household goods factories, and general and maintenance factories under the Ministry of Industry No. 1 and heavy industries under the Ministry of Industry No. 2 were operated on a consignment basis for either export promotion or import substitution.

According to government statistics, the value of export for manufacturing and processing products amounted to 1,805 million kyat or 30% of the overall export of 602 million kyat in 1997-98. The share of agricultural products in overall export value remained 30.2%, livestock and fishery products 15.7%, forestry products 21.6%, and minerals and gems 2.8%, respectively.[18]

State investment in the processing and manufacturing sector amounted to 2,458 million kyat or 3.8% (573 million kyat or 0.9% in the agro-supportive and agro-based industries) of overall state investment in 1997-98. This figure can be compared with the state investment of 7,750 million kyat or 11.9% in the agricultural sector.[19]

Of total employment of 18.36 million in 1997-98, the largest work force, amounting to 11.51 million, or 62.68%, was engaged in the agriculture sector while the manufacturing and processing sector employed 1.66 million, or 9.07%, in 1997-98. The share of this sector in GDP in the same year showed 7.4% or 79,822.1 million kyat at current producers' prices. The contribution of the agriculture sector to GDP remained the largest among all productive sectors with 52%, or 555,531.7 million kyat. GDP in 1997-98 remained 1,067,521.9 million kyat at 1985-86 producers' prices. The manufacturing and processing sector realized a growth rate of 5.3% in 1997-98 over the previous year at 1985-86 constant producers' prices, while the agriculture sector registered a growth rate of 2.9%.

Table 4.4 Production by Commodity Group, 1997-98
(at current prices)

Commodity Group	*Value (million kyat)*
Food and beverage	405,542
Clothing and wearing apparel	8,500
Construction materials	6,553
Personal goods	4,800
Household goods	995
Printing and publishing	871
Industrial raw materials	24,737
Mineral and petroleum products	32,797
Agricultural equipment	2,362
Machinery and equipment	209
Transport vehicles	2,869
Electrical goods	590
Miscellaneous	3,050
Total	**493,875**

Source: Ministry of National Planning and Economic Development, *Review of Financial, Economic and Social Conditions for 1997-98*

Table 4.5 shows FDI inflows between 1988 and the end of December 1997. The oil and gas sector, which proves to have the highest potential, secured the largest share of FDI with a total of US$2295.92. The manufacturing sector was the second largest in terms of attracting FDI, with 107 projects in this sector, or 36.5% of the overall FDI projects received between 1988 and 1997. Most investors in the manufacturing and processing sector are from ASEAN countries. Among the NIES, apart from

Hong Kong and Singapore, South Korea also showed an interest in investing in Myanmar's manufacturing and processing sector. South Korean companiesoccupied about 1 of the total number of JVs or 100% foreign-owned enterprises that are currently operating factories either for export promotion (e.g., the garment industry) or import substitution (e.g., an automobile assembly plant).

Table 4.5 Foreign Direct Investment Inflows by Sector, 1997-98

Sector	*No. of Projects*	*Amount Approved (US$ million)*
Oil and gas	45	2,295.92
Manufacturing and processing	107	1,269.90
Real estate	18	997.15
Hotel and tourism	39	770.56
Mining	42	498.66
Transport and communications	13	275.39
Livestock and fisheries	17	269.54
Industrial estate	3	193.11
Construction	1	17.27
Agriculture	3	14.35
Other services	5	13.68
Total	**293**	**6,615.53**

Source: Ministry of National Planning and Economic Development, Directorate of Investment and Company Administration

Myanmar's oil and gas sector appears to be attracting the most foreign investors due to new discoveries of offshore natural gas deposits with large potential. The manufacturing and processing sector remains weak and has not yet attracted large-scale investors. This shows that the country is still not sufficiently attractive as regards long-term investment in medium- or large-scale industries. Thus far most foreign investors are interested in the small-scale, labor-intensive, or low technology manufacturing or processing sector. Similarly, by analyzing Myanmar citizens' investments by sector, it appears that the manufacturing and processing sector is not a top priority (Table 4.6). While investors are more interested in real estate development, industrialization is taking shape, and more government incentives and infrastructure development could divert investments to this sector.

Table 4.6 Investment of Myanmar Nationals by Sector
(as of 31 July 1997)

Particulars	*Number of Projects*	*Total Investment (million kyat)*
Livestock and fisheries	5	250.27
Manufacturing	48	2,330.33
Transport	4	2,034.93
Hotel and tourism	10	759.10
Construction	2	2,262.00
Real estate development	7	2,607.20
Others	5	503.00
Total	**81**	**10,746.83**

Source: Ministry of National Planning and Economic Development, Directorate of Investment and Company Administration

Problems currently encountered by the industrial sector include the following:

- a small range of products and weaknesses in industrial linkages
- weakness in research and development and a low level of technology and technical know-how
- insufficient production of basic industrial raw materials and chemicals to supply factories manufacturing basic consumer commodities

- weak infrastructure, including insufficient supplies of electricity, gas, and water
- insufficient foreign exchange to invest in new technologies and import plants, machinery, or parts
- lack of international entrepreneurship and access to overseas market information
- lack of full capacity utilization of state-owned factories
- overvalued exchange rate problem
- high reliance on imported raw materials in producing consumer commodities.

Conclusion

While the "flying geese" pattern has been referred to with respect to the success stories of the economic development and industrialization of Asian NIEs (Hong Kong, Singapore, South Korea, Taiwan) or ASEAN countries like Indonesia, Malaysia, the Philippines, and Thailand, Myanmar remains a case apart. Japan was the first country in the Asian region to industrialize. Some years later, the Asian NIEs successfully imitated its industrialization pattern. The ASEAN countries followed the steps taken by the NIEs. Myanmar should study this formula for industrialization and take advantage of the globalization of technology. Technology transfer has sped up, and globalization has advanced the diffusion of technologies. Globalization has also generated a relocation of industries from industrialized countries to developing countries. The economic structures of industrialized countries are turning toward services due to the gradual erosion of their international competitiveness in manufacturing. Even human-capital-intensive industries in industrialized countries, such as transport equipment, electrical machinery, and scientific goods have begun to lose some ground to developing countries.[20] Yet, the strategy Myanmar should adopt to speed up its industrialization is a subject of debate.

The Industrial Revolution in Europe proved that the quality of life could change. Through the mass production of goods and the rise in productivity, income, and employment, the quality of life of ordinary people improved. Developing countries are dependent on industrialized countries technologically and economically. Industrialization is regarded as essential to overcome technological dependence and to break away from a colonial pattern of production whereby a country relies on the production of a few primary commodities for its export earnings and has to import most of its necessary manufactures.

In reviewing Myanmar's past economic performance, it is evident that the share of the industrial and agriculture sectors in GDP has remained nearly stagnant for the past sixty years. Between 1988-89 and 1997-98, while the contribution of the manufacturing and processing sector in GDP remained around 9%, the share of the agriculture sector was approximately 38%.[21] If Myanmar becomes industrialized, these figures will be reversed.

To become an industrial estate, the share of manufacturing value added (MVA) should occupy at 30% of GDP. Myanmar's current MVA is approximately 7-8%.[22] At present, the share of industry in GDP remains the lowest in Southeast Asia.[23] In Thailand's case, the share of agriculture in GDP fell to 11.1% from 30.2% over the past quarter century, while that of industry rose to over 40%. In Indonesia as well, the contribution of agriculture in GDP declined to 16.6% from 35% while the share of industry increased to more than 40%.[24]

A lack of structural shift in production means little change in the commodity composition of exports. Although there was diversification in export of commodity products, the share of manufactured goods in total exports has remained nearly stagnant. A significant change in Myanmar's primary commodity exports is that the importance of rice has declined in recent years as pulses and beans have replaced it. However, the share of traditional items in total exports accounted for nearly 70% between 1991-96.[25]

High reliance on primary commodity exports shows that Myanmar has had only limited success in producing non-traditional and manufactured exports. In terms of the Burma Standard International Trade Classification (BSITC), manufactured exports accounted for an average of 11.3% of total exports during the period 1992-95.[26] In the 1990s, the share of manufactured products in exports remained lower than the average of the least developed countries or the average of all developing countries. Even neighboring countries like Bangladesh or Nepal fared better, achieving some success in producing non-traditional exports although engaged in labor-intensive industries. Garments share more than 50% of total exports in Bangladesh and 30% in Nepal.[27]

Myanmar should learn from the Japanese success story or that of the NIEs that its most valuable resource is not cultivable land or minerals or forests but it human resources. It should make its utmost efforts to develop these with human capital formation figuring high on its policy agenda. However, given the country's low productivity industrial sector and abundant and cheap labor force, it should still pursue industrialization through the initial production of technologically simple products in a comparative labor-intensive way.

As a strategy to sustain growth, Myanmar should strive for rapid industrialization. Technology plays an undisputed role in economic growth by increasing the productivity potential of all production factors. In a globalized world, technology emerges as a decisive factor in determining international competitiveness and hence growth prospects. Technology can foster growth through improved export performance by shifting the composition of exports from primary commodities to manufactured goods.[28]

Myanmar believes that its potential lies in the agricultural sector and that a key element in its growth strategy is to strengthen its agricultural base. This, in turn, would contribute to the growth of other sectors, and its industrialization should therefore be based on its agriculture sector. The agricultural sector is the main source of export earnings and has strong links with the rest of the economy by providing industrial raw materials. It acts as a market for goods and services produced by other sectors. Another advantage is that by raising farm productivity by means of agricultural mechanization, incomes will increase, given that 63.35% of the total workforce is engaged in this sector. A rise in agricultural productivity will release workers from food production for employment in other sectors. The Asian Development Bank considers that prospects for boosting Myanmar's manufactured exports are linked to the processing of agricultural and natural resources.[29]

A rapid expansion of government expenditure on public works projects such as constructing bridges, roads, and buildings, has led to a widening budget deficit.[30] This is viewed as unbalanced growth. Substantial budgetary disbursements should also be devoted to developing local industries. The process for industrialization will require investment and time. The government should provide incentives to the private sector for more active participation and strive for importing and diffusing technology. However, the development of major infrastructure projects such as ports, airports, highways, electric power supply stations, and the like, will attract foreign manufacturing firms to invest more and will contribute to rapid industrialization.

While Myanmar takes pride in its abundant natural resources, it should realize that the development of its human resources is also a prerequisite for industrialization and modernization. People must acquire a certain level of education and technical training to absorb technology transferred from abroad.[31] Equally important are macroeconomic stability and the creation of an environment that would encourage domestic industries as well as foreign companies to invest more in the manufacturing and processing sector.

Some Myanmar economists suggest that the country should take short-cut measures to catch up with ASEAN front runners like Malaysia or Thailand instead of treading the traditional process. One such measure is to specialize in information technology for the mass production of computer software and hardware with the aid of foreign multinationals. The government should provide incentives such as offering land at suitable prices, arranging for an electricity supply, tax reductions, and protection against importers to this sector in order to induce foreign investment. Manufacturing computer software mainly requires human resources and is less concerned with high-grade infrastructure facilities that can be provided by industrialized countries. A recent report in a Japanese newspaper claimed that Fujitsu Corporation, one of Japan's major computer manufacturers, has decided to establish a foothold in Myanmar beginning with a semi-knockdown assembly plant. In the initial stage, the plant will depend on parts directly imported from Japan, but, in the final stage, it will become a manufacturing plant producing software and hardware. Fujitsu aims at exporting a major portion of the products manufactured in Myanmar.

The quickest way to promote the industrial sector is to create a favorable environment for the migration of FDI. Attractive foreign investment laws, government incentives, a good political climate, business-oriented institutions, a transparent legal framework, streamlined bureaucratic regulations and procedures, and developed infrastructure facilities seem to be requirements for achieving this objective. Myanmar is already endowed with rich natural resources, a large land areas, an educated population, an English-speaking entrepreneurial class and labor force, comparatively low labor costs, and a British-based legal framework. Hence, it depends on both the state and private sectors to strive for rapid industrial growth. The government should encourage the private sector to take the leading role while the state plays a facilitating and support role for this end.

Notes

[1] Michael P. Todaro, *Economic Development* (London: Longmans, 1997), pp. 295-329. See also Gerald M. Meir, *Leading Issues in Economic Development* (Oxford: Oxford University Press, 1995).

[2] J. S. Furnivall, *An Introduction to the Political Economy of Burma* (Rangoon: Burma Book Club, 1938), pp. 195-208.

[3] Ministry of Industry No. 1, *Burma's Industrial History: Volume I: Industrial History during the Rule of the Burmese Kings* (Rangoon: 1988), pp. 11-46.

[4] *Ibid.* p. 178.

[5] Andrus J. Russell, *Burmese Economic Life* (Bombay: Oxford University Press, 1947), p. 159.

[6] *Burma's Industrial History*, Vol. III: 164-65.

[7] *Ibid.*, pp. 350-53.

[8] Directorate of Information, *Burma: National Economy* (Rangoon: Central Press, 1964), pp. 35-59.

[9] *Burma's Industrial History*, VI: 21-22.

[10] Other objectives are the promotion and expansion of exports, the exploitation of natural resources that require heavy investment, the opening up of more employment opportunities, the development of works that would save energy consumption, and regional development.

[11] If 1985-86 is kept as the base year, the quantum index of production was 99.0 in 1986-87, 94.2 in 1987-88, 77.5 in 1988-89, 86.1 in 1989-90, 86.6 in 1990-91, 83.8 in 1991-92, 93.7 in 1992-93, 102.1 in 1993-94, and 111.0 in 1994-95.

[12] State Guidelines: Excerpts, 1992-95.

[13] The zones are located as follows: Mandalay, Taunggyi, Yangon, Mawlamyine, Myeik, Myaunmya, Hinthada, Pyay, Bago, Chauk, Yenangyaung, Monywa, Myingyan, and Meiktila.

[14] *The New Light of Myanmar*, 17 July 1997.

[15] *The New Light of Myanmar*, 8 February 1998.

[16] Myanmar Industrial Development Committee, *A Guide to Industrial Investment in Myanmar: Myanmar Industrial Exhibition Committee, 24-31 May 1996*, pp. 13-14.

[17] *Myanmar Dana*, "1997 Private Enterprises Part 2," 8.4 (January 1998): 124-25.

[18] Ministry of National Planning and Economic Development, *Review of Financial, Economic, and Social Conditions for 1997-98* (Yangon: Printing and Publications Distribution Enterprise, 1998), p. 4.

[19] *Ibid.*, p. 225.

[20] UNIDO, Industrial Development Global Report, 1996 (New York: Oxford University Press, 1996), pp. 14-16.

[21] *Review of Financial, Economic, and Social Conditions for 1996-97*, pp. 27-28.

[22] This was defined by U Zaw Win Myat, Deputy Director, Regional Industrial Supervision and Inspection, Ministry of Industry No. 1. See "Interview with U Zaw Myat" in *Dana Economic Magazine*, 8.4 (January 1998).

[23] See Asian Development Bank, *Asian Development Outlook 1995 and 1996* (Hong Kong: Oxford University Press, 1995), p. 244, Table 16. In 1994, among nineteen Asian countries Myanmar remained the lowest, with 14.4% of industrial share in GDP. The countries included Bangladesh (18.9%), Bhutan (24.8%), Cambodia (19.6%), Laos (17.9%), and Nepal (19.0%).

[24] See Danny M. Leipziger and Vinod Thomas, *The Lessons of East Asia: An Overview of Country Experience* (Washington, DC: World Bank, 1993).

[25] IMF, *Myanmar: Recent Economic Development* (Washington, DC: IMF, May 1997), p. 100, Table 41).

[26] Central Statistical Organization, *Statistical Yearbook, 1995* (Yangon: Central Statistical Organization, 1995), p. 197, Table 10.06.

[27] See UNCTAD, *The Least Developed Countries 1995 Report* (New York: United Nations, 1995), Table A-18.

[28] UNIDO, *Ibid.*, p. 54.

[29] Asian Development Bank, *Asian Development Outlook 1997* (Hong Kong: Oxford University Press, 1997), pp. 93-94.

[30] Commercial Section, Embassy of the United Kingdom, Yangon, "Burma: Economic and Trading Brief," July 1996.

[31] See Daniele Archibugi & Jonathan Michie, eds., *Technology, Globalization, and Economic Performance* (Cambridge: Cambridge University Press, 1997), and G. N. von Tun Tunzelmann, *Technology and Industrial Progress: Foundations of Economic Growth* (Cheltenham: Edward Elgar, 1997).

5

Industry in Yangon

Tun Aye
The Yadana Rice Milling Company, Yangon

The National Economy from 1948 to 1962

After gaining independence from Britain in 1948, economic plans were formulated and implemented for the rehabilitation and economic development of the Union of Burma (now the Union of Myanmar). The capitalist economic/market economic system was practiced allowing three types of ownership known as the "three pillar system" of state (public), cooperative, and private ownership. The state sector took responsibility for large projects essential for the country but requiring large amounts of capital to implement, while the private sector undertook small- and medium-scale projects, with short recoupment periods and earning quick profits.

In the state sector, large industries such as steel rolling mills, brick and tile factories, jute and textile mills were established in hopes of rebuilding a country suffering the ravages of war. At the same time, a large private sector developed in almost all processing and manufacturing activities such as food processing, synthetic and cotton textile manufacturing, and the production of rubber, plastics, chemicals, and some personal goods. Some consumer goods were exported to neighboring countries. Private sector participation in the free market economy was at the time very promising. In 1962, however, the main driving force of industrial and economic development came to a halt with a drastic change of economic systems from a market to a centrally planned economy. The number of private industries consequently began to decrease and gradually declined to a small-scale level with heavy emphasis on the processing of raw materials into consumer goods.

The National Economy from 1962 to 1988

With the introduction of a centrally planned economic system in 1962, the state sector was made the government's first priority followed by the cooperative and private sectors as second and third priorities. Almost all privately owned industries were nationalized within the short period of six years from 1962 to 1968. As a result, the number of industries in the state sector increased significantly. Being of top priority, state sector enterprises had all opportunities of financial and technical support from the state, as well as from foreign sources in the form of bilateral and multilateral loans and aid from donor countries and the United Nations.

In addition to having local raw materials available in line with requirements set out in national economic plans, state enterprises could import foreign raw materials, machinery, and spare parts according to the availability of foreign exchange. Private enterprises, on the other hand, received nothing substantial in terms of raw materials, spare parts, or financial and technical support, and the scope of the private industrial sector thus became narrower and narrower.

While state sector industries were growing quantitatively, they were not developing qualitatively mainly because of foreign exchange shortages, organizational inefficiency, managerial weakness, and low capacity utilization. Consequently, the processing and manufacturing (P&M) sector as a whole showed little progress or negative growth rates (Table 5.1).

From the figures shown in Table 5.1, we can observe that the contribution of the P&M sector to total GDP, one of the main indicators of industrial development, fluctuated downward from 9.9% in 1985-86 to 8.7% in

1988-89. Moreover, sectoral growth rates decreased from -7.9% in 1985-86 to -15.9% in 1988-89.

Table 5.1 Ratio and Growth Rate of Processing and Manufacturing, 1985-89

Sector	*1985-86*	*1986-87*	*1987-88*	*1988-89*
Ratio of P&M sector to GDP (%)	9.9	9.3	9.2	8.7
Growth rate of P&M sector (%)	-7.9	-6.1	-5.0	-15.9

Source: Ministry of National Planning and Economic Development, *Review of Financial, Economic, and Social Conditions*, 1985-86 and 1988-89

Present Status of Industries in Myanmar

Industries by Ownership

There are three industrial sectors in the country: namely state-owned, cooperative, and private. According to the *Report on Financial, Economic, and Social Conditions 1996-97*, as of 31 March 1997 there were 49,201 industrial enterprises under the processing and manufacturing sector, of which 1,609 (3.3%) are state owned, 637 (1.3%) are cooperatives, and 46,955 (95.4%) are under private ownership. According to 1996-97 provisional data for as of 31 March 1997, the value of exports in the processing and manufacturing sector was 519 million kyat, 9.9% of total exports. Of the total GDP in 1996-97, the share of the manufacturing industries was 9.2%. A review of the contribution of the three industrial sectors to the GDP gives the figures shown in Table 5.2.

From these figures, it can be deduced that private industries play a major role in national industrial production. However, from 1994 to 1996 the contributions of the state-owned, cooperative, and private sectors remained constant at approximately 28%, 1%, and 71%, respectively.

Table 5.2 Industrial Sector Contribution to GDP, 1994-97
(at 1985-86 constant prices) (kyat million)

Sector	*1994-95*	*%*	*1995-96*	*%*	*1996-97*	*%*
State-owned	1,595.3	27.7	1,674.6	27.1	1,869.5	28.7
Cooperative	52.7	0.9	55.6	0.9	56.7	0.9
Private	4,108.9	71.4	4,458.1	72.0	4,583.6	70.4
Total	**5,956.9**	**100**	**6,188.3**	**100**	**6,509.8**	**100**

State-Owned Industries

The control and management of state-owned industries is placed under various ministries with the intention of selecting the most appropriate ministry to operate the industry concerned. The work allocation of the various ministries is listed below.

Ministry of Commerce: Rice mills and oil mills, rice-milling machinery, and spare parts production factories.

Ministry of Agriculture and Irrigation: Cotton ginning, cottonseed oil, palm and other vegetable oil mills, sugar mills, jute factories, jute carpet factories, fruit and vegetable canning factories, coffee production, and silk yarn factories.

Ministry of Industry No.1: *Myanmar Textile Enterprise:* Textile spinning, weaving, dyeing and finishing mills, blanket and towel weaving factories, knitting mills, and garment factories.

Myanmar Foodstuffs Enterprise: Soft drinks, beverage and pure drinking water plants, ice plants, noodle factories, biscuit and sweets manufacturing, tapioca starch plants, monosodium glutamate plants, oil hydrogenation plants, cigarette factories, and breweries and distilleries.

Myanmar Pharmaceuticals Enterprise: Pharmaceuticals factories, soap and detergent factories, plastics industry, and toilet goods manufacturing.

Myanmar Ceramics Enterprise: Brick and tile factories, pottery plants, glass bottle and plate glass factories, cement factories, asbestos factories, and marble factories.

Myanmar General and Maintenance Enterprise: Shoe and leather factories, rubber industry, packing materials factories, and building construction and maintenance work.

Myanmar Paper and Chemical Enterprise: Pulp and paper factories, chlorine and caustic soda plants, oxygen and acetylene plants, match factories, lead acid battery factories, rubber processing, and paint factories.

Ministry of Industry No. 2: *Heavy Industries Corporation:* Agricultural machinery, equipment and implements, motor car engines, diesel engines, diesel injection pumps and nozzles, motor vehicles, trucks, buses, water dowsers, fire engines, machine tools, lathes, drilling machines, hand tools, water pumps, pumping sets, storage and dry cell batteries, electric cables, fluorescent lamps, electric bulbs, transformers, generators and electrical appliances and accessories, refrigerators, air conditioners, and rubber tires and tubes.

Ministry of Livestock and Fisheries: Milk, vegetable, fish and meat canning factories, and animal feed mills.

Ministry of Forestry: Sawmills, plywood, wooden furniture factories, parquet and wood-based industries.

Ministry of Mines: No. 1 Mining Industry: lead, zinc, and copper; No. 2 Mining Industry: tin smelting; No. 3 Mining Industry: iron and steel mills, gold, and salt.

Ministry of Energy: Petroleum refinery, fertilizer plants, and methanol.

Cooperative Sector

The Ministry of Cooperatives, through the Department of Cooperatives, looks after the affairs of all cooperative societies, including producer cooperatives. Some industries run by the cooperatives are (1) condensed milk factories in Mandalay; (2) milk factories in Pyin-Oo-Lwin; (3) rice mills and edible oil mills; (4) mechanical and engineering workshops; (5) the textile industry; (6) plastics and chemicals production; and (7) foundry and metallurgy industry and enamelware factories. Some prominent producer cooperatives are the Sein Pan Cooperative, Ltd, Mandalay, which produces a wide range of machinery and equipment including oil mills, agricultural machinery and equipment, water pumps, motor car spare parts, and the Meiktila Cooperative Engineering and Naungyo Engineering Workshop, Yenangyaung, which is well known for innovative machinery and spare parts production. The Cottage Industries Department under the Cooperative Ministry registers and gives assistance to handicraft and cottage industries.

Private Sector

Private industries, especially the rural and handicraft industries, are scattered all over the country. To supervise and regulate the orderly growth of private industries, the Private Industrial Enterprise Law was promulgated in 1990, followed by the Promotion of Cottage Industries Law in 1990. The second act was meant only for the promotion of cottage industries that operate at a level of under three horsepower. The registration of cottage industries is voluntary, unlike the larger private industries that come under the Private Industries Law.

The Regional Industrial Coordination and Industrial Inspection Directorate of thc Ministry of Industry No. 1 control those industries registered under the Private Industries Enterprise Law. The handicraft and cottage industries register with the Department of Cottage Industries under the Cooperative Ministry. Private industries, which are required to register compulsorily under the Private Industries Law, are classified into three groups.

Table 5.3 Classification of Private Industries

Size	*Power Installed (HP)*	*Investment (kyat million)*	*Number of Employees*	*Annual Production Value (kyat million)*
Small	1-25	1.00	50	2.5
Medium	26-50	More than 1.00, up to 5.00	51-100	more than up to 1.00
Large	over 50	over 5.00	over 100	over 10

Registered private industries can apply for the following privileges if they comply with the requirements under the law: (1) land, power, raw materials, machinery, etc., from the government departments concerned; (2) tax and duties relief and exemption for a limited period; (3) bank loans; and (4) hiring of foreign experts and technicians.

The total registration of private industries as of 31 July 1997 was 3,555,560. The food industries group, totaling 22,492, was the most numerous of all registered private industries. Motor vehicle workshops and spare parts manufacturing establishments stood second at 2,873. Wood-based industries, numbering 2,685, stood at third, followed by textile industries with 2,361 registrants. Seventeen other types of industries such as rubber, plastics, etc., each totaled less than 1,000 registrants.

Although the number of small industries registered at 86% of the total, their investments equaled only 54%. The average investment in each unit was only 0.11 million kyat. On the other hand, medium-sized industries, although only 10% of the total registrants contributed approximately 21% of total investment, meaning that the investment per unit was three times that of the small industries. Investments for each medium-sized industry were on the average approximately 0.39 million kyat. The industries in the large category, totaling 1,194 registrants, were only 4% of the total number, but the investment per unit was about four times (that of the small industries) with 0.49 million kyat per unit on average. Private large-scale industries in Myanmar can be considered medium-scale from the point of view of more developed countries like China, Japan, and South Korea.

The State Law and Order Restoration Council (SLORC), now the State Peace and Development Council, after assuming power in 1988, promulgated two significant laws that have played a major role in building up a market-oriented system. The first law was the Union of Myanmar Foreign Investment Law, enacted in November 1988, allowing and encouraging foreign direct investment with the prime objectives of, among others, export promotion and the expansion and acquisition of high technology. The second law was the State-Owned Economic Enterprises Law enacted in March 1989 to provide the private sector with opportunities to invest in all economic activities with the exception of twelve reserved for the state sector. Nonetheless, these twelve activities can be opened to the private sector if doing so is beneficial to the state.

Myanmar's overall restructuring and development policy is based on three main components, namely: (1) the adoption of a market-oriented system for the allocation of resources; (2) the encouragement of private investment and entrepreneurial activities; and (3) the opening of the economy to foreign trade and investment. The facts mentioned above show that Myanmar was trying for what it aimed at and did well with respect to its investment goals.

Foreign Investment Law and Myanmar Citizen Investment Law

Since the Union of Myanmar Foreign Investment Law (FIL) was promulgated in November 1988 and its procedures prescribed in December 1988, Myanmar has opened its doors to foreign investors to participate actively in taking advantage of its natural resources, thereby enhancing long-term, mutually beneficial economic cooperation. The policy on foreign investment can be seen as an important component of the state's overall economic restructuring and development policy. The policy objectives underlying foreign investment are: (1) the promotion and expansion of exports; (2) the exploration of natural resources requiring heavy investment; (3) the acquisition of high technology; (4) supporting and assisting production and services involving large capital; (5) the opening up of more employment opportunities; (6) development of works that would save energy consumption; and (7) regional development.

fter enacting FIL, the Myanmar Investment Commission permitted 297 projects from twenty-three countries in eleven sectors of economic activity, amounting to US$6,641 million from which approximately 30% was invested in the P&M sector. The government also enacted the Myanmar Citizen Investment Law in line with FIL, giving incentives and guarantees to local investors. To the present, 113 projects have been invested in eight sectors, amounting to 16 million kyat.

Industries in Yangon

Yangon, the capital city of Myanmar, has a population of about 4.9 million and entry ports by air and sea. According to official statistics, as of 30 November 1997 there were 7,730 registered industries in Mandalay, 5,514 in Yangon, and 4,514 in the Bago Division. While Mandalay had the largest number of industries, Yangon has a greater industrial production value than any other division or state in Myanmar (Table 5.4).

Table 5.4 Investment and Production by Region

Region	*Investment (%)*	*Production (%)*
Yangon	34.55	27.92
Ayeyarwaddy	6.29	19.12
Mandalay	26.66	12.97
Bago	13.23	14.53

Yangon, a seaport, has infrastructure and other facilities, and industrialists prefer it to other divisions or states, and most state economics enterprises are also located in the capital. Successive governments have encouraged industries in Yangon, providing industrial sites and locations in industrial zones at South Okklapa and Hlaing Townships.

Yangon and Mandalay Division Industrial Zones

Statistical figures for the Yangon and Mandalay industrial zones during 1988-98 indicate that there are 382 enterprises with 8,948 workers in Yangon and 1,000 enterprises with 4,939 workers in Mandalay (Table 5.5). During the period the number of industries and industrial workers was greater in Mandalay Division.

Table 5.5 Comparison of Yangon and Mandalay Industrial Zones by Industry

	Yangon Division		*Mandalay Division*	
Type of Industry	*No. of Enterprises*	*No. of Workers*	*No. of Enterprises*	*No. of Workers*
Textile	14	3,716	1	87
Engineering	23	296	141	651
Mineral	75	682	48	225
Foodstuffs	60	964	62	738
Chemical	17	208	7	45
Paper and Printing	24	299	7	43
Wood-based	25	676	31	319
Weaving and Packaging	2	224	7	47
General	142	1,883	696	2,784
Total	**382**	**8,948**	**1,000**	**4,938**

In 1990, the government engaged in programs to upgrade the country's physical infrastructure to accommodate increased investment. The Department of Human Settlement and Housing Development (DHSHD) has incorporated industrial zones in and around Yangon (Tables 5.6 and 5.7).

Table 5.6 Industrial Zones Owned and Developed by DHSHD

Industrial Zone	*Designated Year*	*Size (Ha)*
Shwepyitha 1	1989	300
Dagon South		
Zone 1	1992	110
Zone 2	1996	225
Hlaingthayar		
Zone 1/2	1994	350
Zone 3/4	1996	250
Zone 5	1997	90

Table 5.7 Industrial Zones under Construction by DHSHD

Industrial Zone	*Targeted Completion Year*	*Size (Ha)*
Dagon Port	1998	370
Shwepyitha 2	1998	80
Shwepaukkan	1998	45
Dagon Port 2	1999	150
Hlaingthayar 6	2000	400
Shwepyitha 3	2000	100

Under the Privatization Scheme introduced in January 1995, some state-owned industries were transferred to private ownership. Private companies or individuals, whether local or foreign, could enter into agreements with state enterprises in one of the following ways: (1) formation of a joint venture; (2) production on a consignment basis (contract manufacturing); (3) payback arrangement; (4) leasing of buildings and land.

The following laws and notifications were issued by the government to regulate the systematic growth of industries.

- Union of Myanmar Foreign Investment Law of November 1998
- Sate Enterprises Law of March 1989
- Notification No. 11/98 of 30 May 1989: Types of Economic Activities Allowed for Foreign Investment
- Private Industrial Enterprise Law of 1990
- Promotion of Cottage Industries Law of 1991
- Myanmar Citizen Investment Law of 1994

The State and Order Restoration Council constituted the Myanmar Industrial Development Committee (MIDC) on 18 July 1995 by Notification No. 37/95 to replace the National Industrial Promotion Committee (NIPC) formed in 1992 in order to give greater impetus to the industrialization process. The MIDC is a high-level committee comprised of respective ministers of industrial and economic matters. The Minister of Science and Technology acted as chairman and two deputy ministers from the Ministries of Industry No. 1 and 2 acted as secretary and additional secretary, respectively.

The Objectives of MIDC are:

- Development of industries with agriculture as the base
- Enhancement of quantity and quality of industrial products
- Increased production of new types of machinery and equipment
- Production of machinery and equipment for industrial use
- Creation of suitable conditions for changing over to an industrialized economy.

Almost all the activities of the MIDC were devoted to promoting private industries, whether local or foreign. The MIDC conducted industrial exhibitions, seminars, and conferences on industrial promotion and technology matters and dealt with problems facing private industries in industrial zones. These zones were formed where there were sizable numbers of private small- and medium-sized industries (SMEs) in the hope of assisting them in their smooth operation and advancement.

To promote the development of private industrial enterprises, some factories have been leased to joint venture companies, and state and private banks have been disbursing loans to private entrepreneurs. The Myanmar Industrial Development Bank was opened to provide financial aid for the development of industrial enterprises and industrial exhibitions, and private entrepreneurs of cottage industries have held cooperative market festivals with the aim of enhancing domestic and external markets for industrial products.

State economic enterprises in cooperation with foreign organizations and some local private entrepreneurs have produced and exported industrial products such as beer, cigarettes, ready-made garments, carious wooden door leaves, door frames, parquet, furniture, sawn timber, plywood, iron bars, Aluzinc roofing sheets, machinery for rice mills, television receivers, refrigerators, reconditioned motor vehicles, jewelry, plastic water pipes, and cement.

Since the State Law and Order Restoration Council adopted a market economy in 1988, private sector enterprises have increased significantly. Private industries, which were insignificant in the socialist period, have been revitalized and with government encouragement are now growing substantially.

From the above, it will be evident that the government has been striving very hard and giving full encouragement to the development process of national industry in terms of firm support, a strong legal framework, a commercial system, and investment opportunities. Many foreign firms are thus coming into Myanmar with capital investment and technology, and approximately 1,000 foreign companies, branches, and joint venture enterprises are currently doing business in Myanmar (Tables 5.8 and 5.9). The citizens of the country have also responded positively to these initiatives and to an improving economic climate (see Table 5.10).

Table 5.8 Foreign Investment in Permitted Enterprises by Sector (as of 31 January 1998) (US$ million)

	Permitted Enterprise	
Particulars	*No.*	*Approved Amount*
Oil and gas	46	2,303.12
Manufacturing	109	1,283.27
Real estate	18	997.14
Hotel and tourism	39	770.56
Mining	42	498.66
Transport and communications	13	275.39
Livestock and fisheries	18	275.36
Industrial estate	3	193.11
Construction	1	17.27
Agriculture	3	14.35
Other services	5	13.69
Total	**297**	**6,641.92**

As the government of Myanmar has made significant progress toward a market-oriented economy, efforts have also been made to promote all-round development of national economy to upgrade living standards. Results that have been achieved thus far are quite favorable for the general well being of the population. What is still needed for further development is an influx of capital and appropriate technology, managerial skills, and access to international markets in order to reap the most effective benefits from the country's natural and human resources endowments. The government has taken, and will continue to take, necessary actions to encourage participation by both the public and private sectors in the country's economic development. This is the most opportune time for foreign investors to do business in Myanmar, and to make the best use of its abundant resources for mutual benefit.

Table 5.9 Foreign Investment in Permitted Enterprises by Country (as of 31 January 1998) (US$ million)

	Permitted Enterprises	
Particulars	*No.*	*Approved Amount*
United Kingdom*	31	1,329.75
Singapore	65	1,312.89
Thailand	42	1,165.16
Malaysia	25	587.17
United States	16	582.07
France	3	470.37
Netherlands	5	237.84
Indonesia	8	236.37
Japan	18	209.36
Hong Kong	20	121.32
South Korea	19	96.33
Australia	14	82.08
Austria	2	72.50
Canada	11	35.13
Panama	1	30.53
China	9	29.26
Germany	1	15.00
Denmark	1	13.37
Philippines	1	6.67
Bangladesh	2	2.96
Israel	1	2.40
Macau	1	2.40
Sri Lanka	1	1.00
Total	**297**	**6,641.92**

*Inclusive of enterprises incorporated in the British Virgin Islands, Bermuda Islands, and Cayman Islands

Table 5.10 Investment by Myanmar Nationals by Sector (as of 31 January 1998) (kyat million)

	Permitted Enterprises	
Particulars	*Number*	*Total (kyat)*
Real estate development	14	6,934.04
Manufacturing	69	3,187.59
Construction	2	2,262.00
Transport	4	2,034.93
Hotel and tourism	12	1,003.89
Others	5	503.00
Livestock and fisheries	6	289.87
Total	**113**	**16,466.52**

Close cooperation between the Union of Myanmar Chamber of Commerce and Industry, the Myanmar Industries Association, and organizations in Japan is most desirable at the present moment to obtain the successful development of an economic, trade, and investment atmosphere that will ultimately lead to the greater prosperity of both countries. As Japan is the leading industrially developed country in Asia, it is hoped that more trade, industrial, and socio-cultural cooperation will take place between Japan and Myanmar. With the official slogan, "Leap Decades, Industrial State," Myanmar is moving toward becoming an industrialized state. Japan's small- and medium-sized enterprises can, therefore contribute much to this process. Finally, I hope that Japan will help us greatly with its capital and technical know-how. We have high hopes in this because Japan is an Asian country, of Asian people and Asian blood.

6

Direct Investment in Asia by Japanese Corporations: A Message from Vietnam to Myanmar

Yoshiaki Ueda
University of Marketing and Distribution Sciences, Hanoi
and
Hanoi National Economics University

1 Direct Investment in Vietnam: Local Political Implications

In 1986, Vietnam began implementing its "Doi Moi" reform measures, introducing market-oriented economic principles into its socialist system. Vietnam joined ASEAN in July 1995, and diplomatic relations with the United States were normalized in August the same year. In July 1997, Myanmar joined ASEAN. Looking at the GDP levels of both countries in 1996, Myanmar (US$109.9 billion) was five times higher than Vietnam (US$20.2 billion). By contrast, in the same year Vietnam's trading volume was more than five times higher than Myanmar's. Its product exports were 8.3 times higher and product imports 5.7 times higher.[1]

Lifting of US Economic Sanctions

The total lifting of economic sanctions by the United States in February 1994 unleashed brisk economic activity with the outside world. For example, direct (authorized) Japanese investment into Vietnam in 1993 was US$76.2 million. This grew to US$332.6 million (4.4 times) in 1994, and US$1,129.9 million (14.8 times) in 1995. Direct US investment was a mere US$200,000 in 1993 but jumped to US$219.9 million in 1994, and to US$531.3 million in 1995.[2]

Orderly Investment Approvals

In a market-oriented economic system, freedom to invest is a natural right of companies. In Vietnam, however, a flood of applications for short-term investments would, if all were approved, lead to subsequent excess supply, and the market would languish in the face of price competition and demand deficiency. Two prominent examples are automobiles and tourism. Currently, eleven companies are assembling cars in Vietnam. Meanwhile, hotels and tourist facilities have conspicuously high vacancy rates. In such a difficult economic climate perhaps only large companies can survive.

Of course, companies are solely responsible for their decisions to enter the market, and it would thus be a mistake to blame the Vietnamese government for subsequent disappointments. However, if the government had a consistent industrial policy and granted investment approvals based on it, the subsequent potential for companies that entered the market to achieve healthy growth would significantly expand.

Nurturing Successful Companies to Serve as Models

In addition, the government can also benefit investment promotion and economic growth by actively supporting companies that have received investment approval, and by nurturing such companies until they become successful role models. This in turn would foster trust in the government and have the benefit of attracting other investments. Sony, for example, struggled with the problem of contraband products until 1997, but a crackdown by the Vietnamese government allowed Sony to achieve rapidly improved results.

This is not limited to large corporations. If the government gives special treatment to small and medium-sized companies that have accepted the risk to make investments, this would be taken to mean that the government is showing its appreciation for such risk-taking. Such forward-looking small and medium-sized companies would then play leadership and advisory roles. Thus, a meticulous response by the government to such companies is crucial.

Official Bodies as "Intermediaries"

A desirable concrete measure for the government to take on behalf of small and medium-sized companies would be to establish, for example, an "Investment and Trade Promotion Center." In order for the government to respond quickly to the demands and problems of foreign companies, it should set up an official permanent institution to act as an "intermediary." Large companies can negotiate directly with the government, but small and medium-sized companies have difficulty doing so. In particular, such companies need accurate information about taxation and the legal system. By using such an official institution, companies would be able to avoid unhealthy "bonds" between government and certain companies.

To cite an example. In September 1998, the Ministry of Commerce of Vietnam began considering the establishment of a bureau specifically to promote exports.[3] In contrast, Japan acted to allay criticism of the "closed nature" of its markets by promoting a number of deregulation measures and by treating import promotion and inducements for foreign companies as government issues. In 1993, this led to the establishment, with government support, of the Japan Investment Support Service Company, Ltd (known as FIND).

Lessons from the Asian Financial Crisis

It is claimed that Vietnam's establishment of an "Export Promotion Bureau" was one of the lessons learned from the Asian financial crisis. It has been said that "An export-oriented development strategy, based on labor-intensive product exports, is thought to be the best strategy for Vietnam."[4] This underscores the conclusion that actively fostering export industries instead of import-substitute industries will alleviate international financial risks. Similarly, an issue facing Myanmar is to study how to nurture industries that can demonstrate the greatest competitive edge in the country and to promote direct investments toward this end.

2 Practical Research in Vietnam: Successes and Failures

Having discussed political implications in Vietnam, I will now explain specific experiences of companies. Letters have replaced company names, but the content reflects research conducted via interviews.

Collapse of Company A: Ample FS

Company A, a joint venture food manufacturer, was unable to stem losses incurred since it commenced operations. Its Japanese parent company decided to withdraw, and the company went bankrupt in September 1998. The fundamental reason for Company A's collapse was that its products did not reflect consumer tastes. In general, Vietnamese prefer spicier food than do the Japanese, but the company continued to adhere to its "Japanese taste" policy. Although Japanese residents in Vietnam welcomed this policy, the company failed to attract the support of the Vietnamese consumer masses.

The same company is successful in Japan. However, it was either over-confident or did not conduct preliminary market research with "trial products" before its entry into Vietnam. Moreover, its initial capital investment outlays were large, incurring a huge depreciation expense burden. Its production system only handled one product, and that product's failure led to the failure of the entire firm. What we can learn from the experience of Company A is that conducting ample corporate research before entering overseas markets is crucial.

Company B's Ups and Downs: Supervisory System for Managers

Company B developed a diversity of businesses in Vietnam, becoming the envy of other companies. It was considered a potential master of "success stories" for small and medium-sized companies. However, it was affected by Japan's prolonged economic slump, and funding for its large investment plans deteriorated.

A more serious problem, however, was that the company's business plan was the result of arbitrary actions by decision-makers in the field. Due to human resource shortages and personnel cost reductions, the company had very few Japanese managers posted to Vietnam. Each was given broad authority, and there was no way to monitor their behavior. With the changeover to the Vietnamese government's Guidance Bureau in the latter half of 1997, the company lost its "connections," and this proved a decisive setback to its business. "Verbal promises" made to former managers naturally cannot have validity in the business world. Company B's experience teaches us about the importance of monitoring overseas managers of small and medium-sized companies.

Company C's Withdrawal: Concern about Economic Trends in Japan

A medium-sized trading company, Company C, was mainly involved in the import of consignment-processed textiles and daily-use items from China and South Korea, for sale to large retailers. The company turned its attention to Vietnam's "investment boom" that began in 1994, and obtained approval to set up a representative office in 1995. Subsequently, it began importing wooden items, ornamental pottery, jewelry, and textiles, and also tried its hand at providing consulting services for investment into Vietnam. No matter what the company imported, its products continually failed to sell well in Japan. In August 1998, it sold its representative office and decided to continue its business by dealing with a state-owned trading company on a business- trip basis.

The following comment from the manager of the representative office left an impression: "Our withdrawal was not Vietnam's fault. It was totally a consequence of Japan's economic slump." A potential measure to deal with this situation is to compensate for sluggish sales in Japan by cultivating the US market, which has remained healthy. However, as a medium-sized trading company, Company C did not have sufficient managerial resources to make this possible. The performances of small and medium-sized companies are dictated by economic trends in Japan, more so than the economies or operating environments of other foreign countries. A decision on direct overseas investment that took Japanese domestic consumption trends into consideration would have been desirable.

Company D's Success in the Domestic Market: Close Attachment to Japan

Company D, a mid-size manufacturer of cakes, was a forward-looking entrant into the Vietnamese market, and in 1993 established a joint venture with one of the largest state-owned cake makers. By using its partner's existing sales channels, the company was able to set up a sales and distribution system in a short period of time. This has become the operating foundation for the company today. It later developed directly operated outlets and franchise outlets, both of which have greatly contributed to increased revenues and earnings.

One should take note of the following independent efforts of Company D. First, in addition to reducing the effects of seasons on sales by having a broad range of products, it adopted its own sales promotion activities at certain times, such as Christmas and New Year. Secondly, it placed emphasis on harmony and close relations with employees, and introduced financial incentives to stimulate excellent results. Thirdly, it strongly encouraged the reformation of the attitudes of employees transferred from its state-owned partner. This led to cost reductions and consistent product quality. Fourthly, it targeted the middle and upper class Vietnamese market. This allowed it to define itself among consumers in the following way: "Even if Company D's cakes are slightly expensive, I will buy them because the children love them."

Perhaps the most important reason for the company's success was its president's close attachment to the Vietnamese people. Its management strategies matched the feelings of its Vietnamese employees and customers, and it would not be an exaggeration to say that this is dependent on the company president's philosophy and personality.

"Strategic Alliance" between Companies E and F: Low-risk Direct Investment

Company E, a financial firm and member of Corporate Alliance P, set up a joint venture with Company F, also a financial firm and member of Corporate Alliance Q, a state-owned financial firm. The joint venture was set up in November 1997 with identical investments from two Japanese firms, as well as managerial input from the vice presidents of both firms. This is an example of two competitors teaming up to establish an equal-footed joint venture overseas. I will call this a "strategic alliance." By investing jointly instead of independently, companies can reduce associated risks. To this end, such "strategic alliances" illustrate the need, even among large companies, to undertake comprehensive risk management. Those failing to do so will not survive the approaching era of global competition.

Without minimal managerial resources compared with large corporations, small and medium-sized companies should actively consider such "strategic alliances." Success, however, will depend on the individual characteristics of the president and the nature of the business. In the case of Companies E and F, a joint venture became possible because they were selling standardized products (financial policies). Small and medium-sized companies can learn something from this, namely, that in order to become successful with low-risk direct investment, they should actively consider using the resources of "same-industry exchange associations" and "industry bodies." Perhaps companies that decide to undertake overseas investments and the large risks associated with these economically depressed times should give due consideration to risk management.

3 A Message from Vietnam to Myanmar

I have introduced several examples of Japanese companies active in Vietnam, and pointed out the principal managerial issues that apply to Japanese companies. Several of these examples have parallel implications for direct investment in Myanmar. Governments as well as companies, however, determine the frameworks and stages for economic activities. Based on this standpoint, there are urgent problems that the governments of Japan, Myanmar, and Vietnam have in common and should address. The problems may differ in nature, but they exist.

There are two fundamental perspectives for solving these problems. First, political stability is essential for economic growth. Secondly, widespread support of the population is essential for political stability. At the very least, it is my impression that Vietnam is giving its utmost attention to realizing this notion.

Notes

[1] "ASEAN in Figures," JETRO, 1998, pp. 8, 66, 70.

[2] *Ibid.*, p. 100.

[3] *Vietnam News*, 10 September 1998.

[4] United Nations Development Program, "East Asia: From Miracle to Crisis, Lessons for Vietnam," Staff Paper, June 1998, p. 29.

7

Food Sector Development in Myanmar A View from Thailand's Experience

Kitti Limskul
Chulalongkorn University, Bangkok

Introduction

Since Myanmar's adoption of a market economy in 1988, the private sector contribution to the national economy has increased significantly. Although many private companies have been established, they are mainly for import/export and trade. In addition, trade in services, such as in the hotel sector and tourism has been implemented, but not until 1992 did the government begin to promote private industrial development significantly, as can be seen in its land allocation for industrial use. Many new private industries have been established mainly in the Yangon and Mandalay Divisions. Up to the end of December 1995, the number of private companies registered with the Myanmar Investment and Companies Registration Department was as follows:

Import/export companies	5,059
Commission agents	1,733
Limited companies	5,840
Partnership companies	1,085
Foreign companies and branch offices	567
Joint venture companies	81

Although it would appear that entrepreneurs in Myanmar are turning their attention to the industrial field, no clear definition of strategic industries has yet been established. This paper will attempt to identify such strategic sectors, if and where they exist in the country.

Current Developments: Privatization and the Legal Structure

During the period 1992-93 to 1995-96, the annual GDP growth rate was approximately 8%, while the growth rate of the manufacturing sector remained almost constant at about 9%. A look at GDP by sector indicates that after structural changes the agricultural sector's share remains the highest at about 38%, while the manufacturing sector contributed only approximately 9% of total GDP. This is a normal growth phenomenon in developing countries. As a matter of fact, the contribution of the agricultural sector in Indonesia came down from 51% in 1960 to about 24% in 1989, while the manufacturing sector's contribution increased from 9% to 19% during the same period. Similarly in Thailand, the agricultural sector contributed 40% to GDP in 1960 and only 17% in 1989, while the ratio of the manufacturing sector increased from 13% in 1960 to 24% in 1989. Even in India, the agricultural sector's share of GDP decreased from 50% in 1960 to 31% in 1989, whereas the manufacturing sector accounted for 14% and 20%, respectively, in 1960 and 1989. With the increasing importance of the private industrial sector in Myanmar, the contribution of the manufacturing sector is expected to increase during the current five-year plan.

In Myanmar, the number of state-owned enterprises was 1,767 in 1992-93, which was reduced to 1,609 in 1996-97 owing mainly to the country's privatization scheme. The total number of private enterprises, including cooperatives, was 37,225 in 1992-93. This number increased significantly to 47,592 in 1996-97. Counting cottage industries and service enterprises, the total number of cooperatives in 1996-97 would be 1,351. The number of private enterprises registered under the Private Industrial Enterprise Law was, however, found to be 35,191 as of December 31, 1996, which indicates that the number 47,592 quoted above also includes some unregistered entities.

Of Myanmar's total GDP, the share of manufacturing industries was 9.2% in 1996-97. A review of the contributions of the three industrial sectors to the GDP shows that private enterprises play a significant role in national industrial production. The contributions of state-owned enterprises, cooperatives, and private enterprises remained more or less constant at about 28%, 1%, and 71%, respectively. The role of private industry will increase in coming years.

The state-owned enterprises are much larger and more capital intensive than the private enterprises. They come under the control of various ministries: for example, the agro-based industries, such as sugar mills, cotton gins, and rubber processing plants are under the jurisdiction of the Ministry of Agriculture and Irrigation. Similarly, light industries, such as food industries, pharmaceuticals and cosmetics, cement mills, paper mills and spinning/weaving mills and personal goods, are controlled by the Ministry of Industry No. 1; other agricultural machinery/equipment industries and electrical/electronic industries fall under the control of the Ministry of Industry No. 2. The Ministries of Defense, Mines, Energy, Commerce, and Transport each have their own industrial activities. This pre-privatization era of industrial development is similar to development in Thailand over the past thirty years.

Cooperatives come under the Ministry of Cooperatives and are governed by the Cooperative Law. They are private limited companies and are permitted to operate independently like any other private company. The Cottage Industries Department of this Ministry provides for the transfer of technology and technical services to cooperatives. The Cottage Industries Promotion Law has been enacted to provide assistance to cottage industries, whether cooperative or private, which voluntarily register under this law.

Out of the 33,375 registered private enterprises, only 1,194 belong to the large-scale category, defined as enterprises that employ over 100 workers and utilize over 50 hp. of electric power. These large-scale industries account for only 4% of the total. Medium-scale enterprises, using 25-50 hp. and employing 50-100 workers, comprise only 10% of the total. Small enterprises predominate at 86% of the total. Any private enterprise registered under the Private Industrial Enterprise Law or Cottage Industries Promotion Law is eligible to apply for assistance from the government. It can be said that Myanmar's industrial scale is still small relative to those of Thailand and other ASEAN countries.

Under the Privatization Scheme introduced in January 1995, some state-owned enterprises have been converted to private ownership. Private companies or individuals, whether local or foreign, are allowed to enter into an agreement with state enterprises in one of the following ways: (1) on a joint venture basis; (2) on a consignment basis; (3) on a build, operate, and transfer (BOT) basis; and (4) on a rental basis.

The government has instituted an industrial promotion scheme that comprises the following industrial laws:

- The Union of Myanmar Foreign Investment Law of November 1988
- The State Enterprises Law dated 31 March 1989
- Notification No. 1/89 issued on 30 May 1989: Types of Economic Activities Allowed for Foreign Investment
- The Private Industrial Enterprise Law of 1990
- The Promotion of Cottage Industries Law of 1991
- The Myanmar Citizens Investment Law of 1994

In addition to this legal structure, the Myanmar Industrial Development Committee has been established and entrusted with industrial development policy planning and implementation and with the acceleration of the industrialization process. In particular, it functions to: (1) enhance the quantity and quality of industrial products; (2) increase production of new types of machinery and equipment; (3) produce machinery and equipment for industrial use; and (4) create suitable conditions for changing over to an industrialized state.

The Myanmar Industrial Development Bank (MIDB) was established on 15 February 1996 to assist in providing loans to private industries. Recently, new private industries have sprung up in Yangon, and other new industries both local- and foreign-owned will be built during the current five-year plan.

The industrial field is wide open in terms of exploitation both for local consumption and export. With abundant natural and human resources and with government encouragement, the pace of industrialization is quickening and would be even faster if some major constraints were to be removed soon. The government's desire to accelerate industrialization is evident in its strengthening of the Ministry of Science and Technology, which will play a vital role in technology transfer and industrial manpower resources development.

The Development of the Food Processing Industry in Thailand

This paper will provide references relevant to the industrial development and development of the manufacturing sector in Myanmar. The manufacturing sector is important because it can earn the foreign currency needed to finance economic development in the early stages of modernization. Among the many industries in the manufacturing sector, food processing industry, one of the most promising natural resource endowed industries in Myanmar, is an example. The history of the development of the food processing industry in Thailand will be discussed first as it has implications for its neighboring country.

The food industry in Thailand can be traced back more than thirty years. It was originally a small-scale household industry that later developed into medium- and large-scale production. Canned pineapple and seafood were significant products. During 1987-89 the industry for these goods expanded spectacularly, made possible by country's comparative advantages in labor costs and natural resources. During 1987-89 its export value increased from 1.78 billion baht (US$591 million) in 1987 to 6.15 million baht (US$2,77 million) in 1989. It went on to increase to 10.64 billion baht ($US4.26 million) and 14.40 million baht (US$5.76 million) in 1991 and 1994, respectively. In the latter two years the canning industry occupied a 14.66% and 12.66% share of total Thai export value.

In 1992, there were 2,850 processed food factories, which amounted to 2.75% of the total number of Thai factories. In value added terms, the food and other food processing industries accounted for a 26.79% share of total manufacturing GDP in 1988. This decreased to 14.4% in 1993. There were several reasons for this decline including inadequate raw materials, high labor costs, new suppliers emerging from developing countries, and overvalued exchange rates.

It should be noted that Thailand's system of national accounting redefines the status of processed food manufacturing, placing it in a separate category from simple agricultural production, which also includes simple food processing such as cottage industries. In our view, formal food industries are mostly those of export-oriented processed foods, while simple agricultural processed foods mostly go to the domestic consumption market. Thus, the food processing industry in Thailand is recognized to be a very significant indigenous industry, one with very high labor intensity (employment), using mostly domestic raw materials, and with a low import content, except for predominately international products such as canned tuna and some seafood.

The structure the Thai food processing industry can be described as follows in terms of its production capacity, production cost, technology, markets, and distribution channels, as well as the emergence of competitors. Vegetable and fruit exports had a value of 21.11 billion baht (US$844 million) in 1994 as compared with canned seafood, mostly canned tuna, and processed seafood of 37.08 billion baht (US$1.48 million). Processed and non-processed seafood such as prawns were valued at 49.85 billion baht (US$1.2 billion); fish at 9.30 billion baht (US$372 million); and poultry exports at 10.02 billion baht (US$409 million) in the same year.

The largest processed food exports were canned pineapple and other canned fruits, pineapple and other fruit juices, frozen and chilled vegetables and fruits, prawns, canned tuna and canned seafood, and so forth. In the vegetable and fruit industry, thirty-five companies obtained investment infusions during 1987-91. During the same period, the total capacity of these companies exceeded 1 million tons per year. Most of the companies have a capacity above 1,000 Mt. per year; and two, Universe Food and Kaset Thai Samparn Canning, have respective capacities of 439,000 and 145,000 Mt. per year. These companies export almost 100% of their products. The raw materials they use are almost all from domestic sources, and together they absorb 13,582 employees, who are almost all local residents. Their technology is quite modern, as they have intentionally introduced the latest technology from abroad to keep pace with dynamic foreign markets. Their production cost comprises: 40-70% for raw materials; 20-30% for labels and packaging; and the remainder for wages, fuel, depreciation, and interest costs.

Case Study 1: Canned Tuna

Thailand has twenty main packers of canned tuna, with a combined capacity of 360,000 metric tons per year. The actual capacity utilization rate is 75%, which amounts to 40% of national capacity for canned seafood. The combined production output of the industry in 1993 was 200,000 Mt. as compared with 243,958 Mt. and 273,200 Mt. in 1992 and 1991, respectively. Canned tuna products are actually international commodities, as Thailand must import frozen tuna, which amounts to 80% of the total production cost. Labor cost is only 5.5%, packaging cost 6.1%, interest cost 3.6%, fuels and energy 1.7%, and others 2.7% of total production cost. Therefore, the export price of canned tuna to the world market is very volatile, depending on the price of frozen tuna fish.

The largest packer is Unicord Co., Ltd, with a capacity of 126,000 Mt./year. The second and third largest packers are Thai Ruam Sin Industry, with a capacity of 500 Mt./day, and T. K. Industry, with a capacity of 300-400 Mt./day. These three companies consume almost 70% of total imported raw materials, while other local packers use the remaining 30%. Here, 75% of output is destined for export markets.

An expansionary trend in the canned tuna industry has been observed over recent years. The industry produced 39.9 thousand Mt. of canned tuna in 1984 with its output expanding very significantly thereafter. In 1985, Thailand produced 87.1 thousand Mt.; this output jumped markedly to 141.9 thousand Mt. in 1986, increased again to 207.7 thousand Mt. in 1988, and peaked at 272.8 thousand Mt. in 1991. In 1992 and 1993, the output dropped to 243.4 and 200.0 thousand Mt. respectively. The annual output growth rate during 1984-91 was 47.46% on average. Growth has been negative since 1992. Output decreased 10.75% and 17.86% in 1992 and 1993, respectively.

Tuna and its products can be in solid, chunked, flaked, and grated forms. Skipjack tuna, yellow fin tuna, and albacore tuna are the species most used as raw materials in Thailand. The major fishing fleets supplying these fish are from France, Spain, and the US, and Japan, South Korea, and Taiwan in the South Pacific (30% of total catch) and East Pacific, West Indian, and Atlantic Oceans. Their total catch capacity is approximately 2 million tons. In 1994, Thailand acquired 480,000 Mt. of tuna fish as raw material for canning, 80% of which was imported from these major fishing fleets. Twenty percent was from Taiwan, 15% from Japan, 10% each from France and the US, and 25% from Indonesia, New Zealand, Spain, Panama, Singapore, and Seychelles, Maldives, and Micronesia in the Pacific.

Asian countries are the main packers and exporters of the world's canned tuna market. Asian exports account for 70% of world exports, of which 50% are from Thailand. Export growth of canned tuna from Thailand was remarkable during 1984-91, but owing to various factors declined thereafter. The main destinations for these exports can be divided into three groups: (1) the United States, Canada, and Australia, where the American market is the main market; (2) France and the United Kingdom as the main importers, with the rest of the group being Germany, Italy, Belgium, Luxembourg, the Netherlands, Denmark, Greece, and Ireland; (3) Switzerland, as the main importer, and Finland, Austria, Sweden, and Norway. The US market is the major destination of Thailand's canned tuna exports, absorbing 40%, while European countries absorb 27.6%. The UK is the destination of 16.5% of its canned tuna exports, and NAFTA countries 5%.

It should be noted that the US is both a packer and user of canned tuna products. It consumes 40% of the world's canned tuna production and is a net canned tuna importer. More than forty suppliers, mainly from Asia, service the US market. Thailand holds a 50% share of this total market. The import volume of the US market increased from 59,249 Mt. in 1984 to 100,728 Mt. in 1988, for an average annual growth rate of 20%. The market for Thai exports, however, has been declining since 1989 owing to tariff and non-tariff barriers. Thailand's main competitors in the US market are Indonesia, Taiwan, the Philippines, Ecuador, and Malaysia, which hold shares of 8.9%, 7.2%, 4.2%, 1.6%, and 1.6%, respectively.

The thrust of the Thai canned tuna industry has taken a reverse as its competitive edge has eroded. The newest emerging packers are Indonesia and the Philippines; both have lower labor costs and their own fish reserves. Vietnam has also recently emerged as a new packer, spurred by foreign direct investment from Taiwan. Moreover, Mexico has resumed exports to the American market. At the same time non-tariff barriers imposed by the US, such as a quota system, environmental sanctions, and organoleptic and histamine testing by the Food and Drug Administration (FDA), have created impediments to Thai exports. Further obstructions to the sustainability of Thai exports are: the possible lifting of the GSP given to Thailand by the EU; NAFTA's blocking of packers outside member countries; price-cutting among Asian packers; freight charge increases; and, before July 1997, the appreciation of the baht. The devaluation after July 1997 reduced the baht's value more than 80% vis-a-vis the US dollar. This has had an adverse effect on the canned tuna industry, which relies heavily on imported tuna fish. The overall increase in exports may not be as large as expected as other main packers such as Indonesia and the Philippines have also seen their currencies significantly devalued.

In conclusion, Thailand's canned tuna industry has already lost much of its past competitiveness. Its production base will need to be relocated away from Thailand if raw materials cannot be cheaply procured. Its labor costs and exchange rate after the currency crisis in 1997 may be a partial blessing. However, without restructuring the import content ratio of 80%, the industry may not be able to sustain its major share of the world market. Added to the challenges it faces are the fierce non-tariff barriers imposed by the US, NAFTA, and the European Union on Asian packers, especially Thailand.

Case Study 2: Canned Pineapple

The canned pineapple industry is an agro-industry that began twenty years ago. Its main output is destined for export. Thai canned pineapple holds a 40-50% share of the world market with destinations of over sixty countries. Its main importers are the US and the EU.

Currently, the canned pineapple industry produces a mix of pineapple chunks, juices, and other processed fruits. In most cases, the packers contract the farming of pineapple roots. In 1984, Thailand had 302,400 Mt. of production capacity, which increased to 338,080 Mt. in 1986 and to 508,800 Mt. in 1989, for an average growth rate of 50.5% over the latter three-year period. In 1996, Thailand had a 563,200 Mt. production capacity, with utilization normally at 70-80%. In 1996, utilization was at 88.74%. There are altogether approximately twenty-four packers, eight of which are promoted by the Board of Investment. Average registered capital is approximately 15.5 million baht for small packers and 871.5 million baht for larger packers respectively, with an aggregate labor absorption of 20,000 persons. Canned pineapple is one of Thailand's most labor-intensive industries, 90%

of its workers being female. The large packers employ up to 2,195 workers per factory, while the smaller ones on average employ 427 persons.

The raw material used by the industry is pineapple fruit, which exceeds 2 million Mt. (gross weight) a year. Fresh pineapple fruit constitute 40-50% of total production costs, with packaging costs (for example, cans, labels, and paper boxes) at 35%, wage costs at 7%, fuel and electricity costs at 3%, and depreciation and interest charges at 8%. The unit cost for a 20-ounce box of canned pineapple is 210.55 baht per box.

The cost of fresh pineapple is the main determinate of the cost of canned pineapple. When the price of fresh pineapple increases, farmers tended to expand their plantation area. In 1989, an increase in planted area caused a rise in the fresh pineapple supply to 2.01 Mt. as compared with 1.71 Mt. in 1988. This excess supply pushed down the price of canned pineapple to 1.65 baht per kg, whereas the price of fresh pineapple normally ranges between 2-3 baht per kg. In Thailand, 85-90% of total fresh pineapple is earmarked as raw materials for the canned pineapple industry.

Production technology comes from Taiwan. As the canned pineapple industry is subject to a seasonal supply of fresh pineapple, the factories produce these products for only seven to eight months of the year. The rest of time they produce other kinds of canned fruits such as rambutan, lychees, and longan.

Products come in the forms of slices, chunks, spears and fingers, tidbits, diced, cubed and crushed pineapple, fruit cocktails, concentrated juices, and pineapple by-products. Some 90-95% of total production is supplied to foreign markets. However, an increasing trend of domestic use by hotels and the tourism industry as well as the changing taste of Thai consumers from fresh to canned pineapple has been observed. In 1992, Thailand exported 491,367 Mt. or 48.28% of world production. In 1994, exports grew to 511,600 Mt., with an export value of 7,570 million baht (US$303 million) as compared with 341,414 Mt. or 4,675 million baht (US$187 million) in 1988.

The destinations of Thai exports comprise five markets. The first is the North American market, which comprises the US and Canada, and absorbs 40% of Thai exports. The US is the world's largest importer. Main suppliers for this market are Thailand and the Philippines, with shares of 51% and 38%, respectively. The second group is the EU, which imported 37% of Thai exports in 1992. Its main market is Germany, for which Thailand had the largest share at 50.6%, followed by Indonesia and the Philippines. The third group, the Asian market, comprising Hong Kong, Japan, Singapore, South Korea, and Taiwan, absorbs 10% of Thai exports. In Japan, Thai canned pineapple has penetrated up to 50% of the market followed by Malaysia. The fourth group is the Middle East, which absorbs 3% of Thai exports, and the fifth is Australia, Africa, and Scandinavia, which absorbs 8% of total exports.

Among the destination markets, the US imports 175,724 Mt. with a value of 2,451 million baht; Germany imports 59,431 Mt. worth 731 million baht; and the Netherlands imports 45,393 Mt. worth 612 million baht. The canned pineapple industry is now facing severe competition from Indonesia and the Philippines, which have a cost structure 20-30% lower than Thailand's. However, with the de facto devaluation of the baht in July 1997 by at least 80% (as of December 1997), the cost of imported raw materials and other tradable material inputs have increased while export earnings in baht have also increased. The social opportunity cost of exporting canned pineapple and tuna may increase as well. If the opportunity cost of producing canned pineapple and/or tuna is less than the shadow exchange rate, then canned pineapple and tuna will remain competitive in the world market.

Canned pineapple is considered to be preferable to tuna as far as Thailand's resource endowment is concerned: it uses more domestic resources and a higher content of primary input, especially labor inputs. It also uses domestic raw materials in the form of fresh pineapple fruit, while frozen tuna, which must be imported, incurs foreign currency costs. Employment generated both directly and indirectly by the pineapple industry may be larger than that of the canned tuna industry.

Conclusion and Recommendations

Elements of Thailand's agro-industry development, particularly as derived from its historical setting, the current economic crisis, and structural adjustments, can be applied to Myanmar's agro-industry development. My conclusion and recommendations follow.

Canned pineapple and canned tuna are 100% tradable products/commodities that can become important sources of foreign currency for Myanmar. Other fruit and vegetables products and other seafood products are tradable commodities that can be used to seek foreign exchange. However, canned tuna and pineapple are currently subject to very fierce competition in the world market. Thus, the stage of starting development should be determined based on an evaluation of which way to go, either the highly competitive canned pineapple/tuna or the less competitive general fruits/ vegetables/ seafood.

Myanmar's eastern coastal and central areas have the sandy soil and moderate temperatures suitable for growing pineapple. The labor-intensive pineapple plantation is also well suited to the country's cheap wage structure. Most of all, the employment potential generated both directly and indirectly through this kind of development is immense. However, the production of tradable material inputs, such as cans and paper boxes, require certain technology and investment, if they are not imported from the international market. Accessibility to the world market needs to be developed, and research is needed to develop a hybrid pineapple bulb that is suited to Myanmar's soil and climactic conditions and satisfying requirements of market tastes and industry scale.

Alternatives to pineapple may be canned fruits in syrup such as lychees, peach, longan, or canned vegetables in brine and salty liquid such as baby corn, asparagus, ginger, or apricot. Hybrids suited to Myanmar's soil and climate as well as to tastes and production would also need to be researched and developed for these products.

Since pineapple, other fruits, and vegetables destined for international markets are subject to market volatility, certain government measures are designed as a buffer. It should, however, be noted that top-down agricultural planning by the state is not by itself an effective buffer as can be seen in the case of Thailand. This is because the market is very dynamic and volatile. Farmers need to be allowed to cope with new trends and to learn how to adapt by introducing new hybrids, contracting middlemen, and obtaining profit when making right decisions while incurring losses when making wrong ones. The government can promote certain reference prices and contract farming systems to reduce the risk of market volatility. The cost of research and development of appropriate hybrid fruits should be borne by the government, which should also provide long-term land concessions to manufacturers at low rental rates. Contract farming should be carried out based on government-designated systems.

On the production side, technical assistance comes to Myanmar from neighboring countries like Indonesia, the Philippines, and Thailand as fellow members of ASEAN. However, since Thailand is geographically the nearest to it, Myanmar would be well advised to seek technical assistance from the Royal Thai Government. Contact should also be cultivated with some Thai private sector companies such as successful packers in this business in order to gain experience-based expertise, capital participation, and market access to third countries. Myanmar may use Singapore as its port of distribution to international markets to its west, such as Australia, Africa, the Middle East, and some European markets. At the same time, cooperation should be established with Thailand in exporting Myanmar-produced pineapple and other fruit products to markets to the east, such as China, Hong Kong, Japan, South Korea, Taiwan, and even on to North America in the future.

For the time being it is not recommended that Myanmar develop a tuna industry because the cost of the required import content is still too high. For Myanmar to develop its own tuna-fishing fleet would require large capital investment, not to mention the acquisition of related technology and skill. Furthermore, product quality standards are very strict, and market access is highly competitive. The frozen seafood industry may grow along with advances in cold-storage technology. Until the frozen seafood industry reaches maturity, there is still room for development in the canned tuna and seafood field.

To begin with, Myanmar may develop intermediate products such as soybean cake for the feed meal industry or raw soy-crunched oil for the cooking oil industry both for its domestic market and for Thailand. This would have a very high linkage to soybean farmer employment in the rural areas of upper Myanmar, especially in Shan State. Secondly, Myanmar may develop palm oil plantations in the south where crunching factories can be built along with palm oil refineries. This would create an import substitution industry for palm oil, and an export promotion industry for soybean cake and raw soybean oil. Palm oil is a substitution for sesame, groundnut, and soybean oils for cooking in Myanmar. Soybean oil is also regarded as a good cooking oil in Thailand.

Development of the palm oil industry in the south of Myanmar could be on an international joint venture basis with businessmen from the south of Thailand who possess considerable expertise in this field. By making use of vast plantations in Shan State, a soybean oil project could exploit links between the cooking oil industry in Bangkok and industrialists in Mandalay. The development of frozen marine products could be linked with the marine industries of Japan and Thailand, and that of vegetables in salty water or brine with industrialists in Thailand who have access to domestic and international markets. Finally, a packaging industry will need to be introduced in Myanmar to allow the export of last-stage finished products that meet international standards, rather than only intermediate products.

In establishing a bilateral relation between Thailand and Myanmar, consideration should be given to agricultural and food-processing development in Eastern Shan State. This is one of the regions where the government, under the jurisdiction of the Ministry of Agriculture and Irrigation, has implemented special development measures through a program entitled "Progress of Border Areas and National Races and Development Affairs." Several measures have been taken to develop the border areas in terms of physical infrastructure, human resources, and agricultural development. In fact, the Ministry of Agriculture and Irrigation has declared three special objectives in agricultural production: (1) to produce a surplus in paddy production; (2) to achieve self-sufficiency in edible oils; and (3) to increase exportable surpluses and industrial crops.

Agricultural development in Shan State is being carried out consistent with these national objectives. First, the state is a suitable area for cultivating upland paddies, which puts it in line with the objective of creating a surplus in paddy production. Secondly, maize and soybeans are major crops in the state and can increase self-sufficiency in edible oil production. Thirdly, Eastern Shan State is situated close to such marketplaces as southwest China and upper northern Thailand, giving most of its exportable crops and produce access to these markets. For example garlic, soybean and soybean cake, maize, sugar cane and sugar, ginger, coffee beans, fruits, bamboo shoots, cabbage and other vegetables, and wood products made possible by reforestation could be sold to southwest China and Thailand to earn foreign currency. In Eastern Shan State, not only agricultural products, but also processed food industries using local agricultural inputs, have a high potential for development.

Appendix 1

Table 7.1. Food Product Exports of Thailand, 1994-98

Export Products	*1994*	*1995*	*1996*	*1997*	*1998 (January – June)*
Rice	39,187.3	48,626.8	50,734.8	65,093.4	45,641.6
Maize	544.3	468.6	279.1	297.4	214.9
Beans	725.0	479.4	422.4	384.7	290.2
Tapioca	18,773.4	18,253.3	20,651.2	22,458.3	12,327.0
Frozen fruit	377.1	355.8	452.6	548.2	363.7
Chilled vegetables	1,019.3	952.5	812.4	880.2	860.9
Frozen vegetables	931.2	1,221.4	1,430.8	1,498.2	979.3
Herbs and spices	512.4	509.2	630.9	843.0	729.0
Coffee beans	2,147.1	4,610.0	2,445.2	2,075.0	3,433.5
Other grains	168.6	2,159.0	489.3	634.3	287.6
Dried longan	248.2	195.5	1,053.7	2,142.9	32.8
Dry vegetables	145.5	156.0	184.8	327.7	160.2
Frozen and chilled shrimp	49,155.6	50,302.0	43,404.5	47,183.9	29,492.0
Dried shrimp	288.9	350.3	323.5	300.7	187.6
Boiled shrimp	402.2	617.9	250.5	99.4	42.3
Frozen squid	7,056.3	7,175.9	6,958.1	9,321.7	6,519.1
Dried squid	505.0	410.4	338.8	180.5	81.0
Processed squid	365.0	482.6	373.9	953.0	541.6
Frozen and chilled fish meat	5,441.0	6,409.4	5,563.0	7,543.8	3,762.3
Frozen and chilled fish	3,019.1	3,449.3	4,011.0	4,647.5	3,595.3
Dried fish	527.7	640.4	652.0	699.0	378.4
Boiled crab	196.7	323.3	205.6	315.1	191.2
Shell (except canned products)	128.5	110.6	133.6	207.6	124.0
Other crustaceans (except canned products)	586.2	638.9	643.5	626.3	500.3
Dried jellyfish	181.7	161.5	328.4	206.1	24.2
Other marine products (except canned products)	179.0	392.2	299.4	348.8	178.3

Frozen and chilled chicken	9,854.4	9,661.8	9,085.0	10,949.3	8,357.8
Processed chicken	1,849.7	3,088.0	3,371.6	4,950.9	4,173.3
Frozen and chilled duck	362.2	381.4	301.7	306.6	151.3
Fresh eggs	36.0	30.7	98.3	88.4	144.1
Dried eggs	68.2	76.5	132.5	189.6	64.6
Meat and edible livestock parts	83.7	223.4	95.2	309.0	221.2
Canned tuna	15,619.7	13,629.4	12,384.8	17,338.6	13,110.4
Canned sardines	1,032.8	1,295.4	1,215.4	1,299.4	919.0
Other canned fish	690.3	709.9	586.3	705.0	462.2
Canned crab	992.1	1,328.2	1,023.4	1,429.0	1,188.1
Canned shrimp	13,301.8	16,032.3	18,707.0	28,115.4	16,355.9
Other canned seafood	359.1	299.5	327.2	421.8	307.9
Processed seafood	5,087.0	5,857.7	6,217.1	8,083.2	4,930.0
Sugar	17,202.6	28,768.6	32,081.4	31,493.2	20,810.7
Molasses	1,108.0	1,713.1	1,976.6	1,429.0	1,006.6
Canned pineapple	6,608.1	5,763.1	6,510.1	5,901.9	4,210.9
Other canned fruit	2,524.1	3,045.6	2,469.9	3,481.2	1,749.2
Canned pineapple juice	1,681.2	2,348.6	2,988.0	2,215.3	1,505.8
Other fruit juices	974.9	830.8	862.2	1,038.5	603.1
Dried and sweetened fruit	1,051.8	1,140.4	1,229.1	1,351.0	892.1
Canned baby corn	963.7	1,071.9	1,085.3	1,598.4	972.0
Canned bamboo shoots	110.9	1,285.2	1,097.7	1,024.4	444.2
Other canned vegetables	1,142.7	1,489.8	1,764.7	1,990.7	1,229.2
Pickled vegetables	660.5	817.5	1,177.7	1,187.1	412.7
Rice products	3,154.2	2,786.3	3,304.0	3,719.8	1,888.9
Wheat and other food products	3,686.5	4,360.3	5,259.1	5,754.9	3,166.2
Pet food	5,047.7	5,716.3	6,455.8	8,040.7	5,201.3
Source	284.5	337.1	410.0	556.7	381.1
Fish source	383.9	473.0	466.4	606.3	341.7
Curry paste	162.6	180.9	211.7	293.4	151.7
Vinegar	4.9	4.6	7.3	6.5	3.8
Other flavors	426.8	539.9	586.2	943.2	714.6

Diary products	845.8	842.0	889.0	1,104.6	718.6
Chewing gum and snacks	827.2	1,002.1	1,081.0	1,095.9	465.5
Soft drinks	2,300.7	2,647.8	3,541.0	4,382.6	2,136.2
Soup and artificial flavorings	781.4	779.0	1,287.6	940.2	230.1
Fats and oils	643.8	605.0	445.7	2,256.3	1,638.5
Cocoa and flavoring	194.2	341.7	447.9	598.2	339.8
Total	**237,001.7**	**273,762.5**	**277,824.4**	**331,778.8**	**214,965.7**

Source: Government of Thailand, Ministry of Commerce

Appendix 2
Possible Scenario of Industrial Development in Mandalay

In our field survey, I identified the development potential of the Mandalay region as judged from its location, history, culture, and capital accumulation. The city of Mandalay is situated in the central part of the Union of Myanmar and is, therefore, a center of transport and communication for all trade and commerce activities in the upper and northern areas of the country. The Mandalay Hills are to the north and the Shan Plateau to the east, with the Ayeyarwaddy River to its west, and the Yangon-Mandalay highway and the international airport to the south. The city covers an area of about 65 sq. km., and its population is over 700,000. Mandalay is a center for border trade with neighboring countries, especially China and Thailand.

The region has two distinct seasons: the rainy season from May to October, and the dry season from November to January. The temperature is highest, at about 31°C, in April and May, and lowest at about 20°C in January. The average annual rainfall is about 34.3 inches. Mandalay and its surrounding area are ideally suited for agricultural development and for becoming a marketing center for crops and livestock.

As the former capital of the last Burmese king, Mandalay is the gateway to Bagan, a pre-modern civilization. The city was built in square blocks outside the palace wall, with each block having traditional crafts and merchandise trade. The workmanship of handicrafts is excellent, especially in lacquerware. Mandalay is unique for its artists' talents and home industries in such products as gold foils, tapestries, hand-woven silk sarongs, and woodcarvings. The city is the country's second largest and also its second commercial capital as the business center of upper Myanmar.

Mandalay is ready for an economic take-off in both agricultural development, such as food crops, and in industrial development as related particularly to its traditional handicraft skills, such as weaving and garment-making. Also in the area of commerce and trade, future development will be aided by the city's attributes as the center of a transportation network with land and air links, not to mention its traditional position as a site for marketing, storage, and distribution in the upper areas of the country.

The Mandalay City Development Committee (MCDC), the authority responsible for city planning and development, is mainly focused on the construction of roads, bridges, city parks, and recreation centers. Projects for building a stadium and a new housing estate are also emphasized in MCDC's development plan. A new international airport is currently under construction in Tada Oo Township, and on its completion, Mandalay will be more open to and have better links with neighboring countries, particularly its main trading partners, China and Thailand. Many related services will arrive, induced by the growth of the tourism industry in Mandalay. There are already 224 hotels and motels capable of accommodating over 3,500 tourists during peak seasons. About 50% of the hotels are equipped with modern comforts and facilities. Some, like the Novotel and Sedona, are international standard hotels. The development of this sector should lead to a greater local demand for agricultural products, ranging from vegetables, meats, fruits, poultry and eggs, and diary products, to cereals like wheat and flour, to milled rice and edible oils.

In 1990, a regional industrial zone was established in Mandalay having 60 heavy, 25 medium, and over 1,000 light industries. In 1994, the MCDC formulated a plan for implementation in June 1995 to install a 10-megawatt electricity distribution plant to service 950 industries in the present industrial zone. This still leaves another 4,000 heavy, medium, and light industries without adequate power in Mandalay.

The following four major development policies are regarded as most strategic for Mandalay: (1) the Gateway Policy; (2) the Regional Center of Upper Myanmar Policy; (3) the Counter Magnet or Burden-Sharing

Policy; and (4) Mandalay as a Historical and Cultural Center. The main features of these policies are outlined below.

1 Gateway Policy

The government has designated Mandalay as a gateway to Myanmar with national priority given to promoting the economy through international trade and tourism. The following activities are planned:

- Development of an international airport and an EPZ (Export Processing Zone) in the airport development area (under construction with funds provided by the Thai government)
- Development of other infrastructure such as banks, insurance firms, hotels, international communities, etc.
- Assignment of a dry port function to the city with a customs area, bonded warehouse, storage, track terminal, and supporting facilities
- Promotion of a market economy with export-oriented industries within the framework of ASEAN and Asian trade market
- Stimulation of regional agricultural productivity both vertically and horizontally, focusing on expectable cash crops
- Promotion of tourism, including programs, networks and routing assets, and other appropriate facilities.

2 Regional Center of Upper Myanmar

The government has designated an enhanced central function for the socio-economic integration of the Upper Myanmar region include the following:

- Enhancement of regional market functions and institutions
- Encouragement of import substitution industries, such as electrical goods, household goods and construction materials by developing industrial parks
- Structuring the urban fabric of Greater Mandalay
- Improvement of regional transportation networks and telecommunications

- Improvement of the goods shipment network and model function, such as track terminals, cold storage, and similar facilities.

3 Counter Magnet or Burden-Sharing Policy

Under the terms of this policy, Mandalay has been designated as a growth center with burden sharing with Yangon, making it another growth pole second only to the nation's capital city.

4 Historical and Cultural Center of Myanmar

Mandalay's position as a historical center should be developed so as to become a symbol of national pride and spiritual unity. Thus, the restoration of cultural and historical sites is to be given first priority.

Despite the desire of the people of Mandalay to see their community become an international gateway right away, a step-by-step approach will be needed to realize this development plan and development priorities will need to be clearly defined. For instance, in order to develop the Regional Business Center, it will be necessary to reinforce Mandalay's indigenous market capability. Although renovation of existing offices and shops is necessary, priority should be given to strengthening mechanisms for community input. People's associations other than the present Chamber of Commerce need to be promoted. What is particularly needed are federations of industry in Mandalay, including such industries as weaving and garment making, steel casting, food processing, plastic works, wood works, mining, jewelry manufacturing, which can facilitate the routing of international corporations to the city.

One of the highest priorities should be upgrading the grain and bean exchange or central market starting with rice and beans, so that the kind of quality assurance and product grading needed for Myanmar's entry into the world market can be systematically conducted. As a pre-condition to accomplishing this, certain financial institutions, such as private banking and insurance and advanced communications facilities, will first need to be established. This is not to overlook the need for human resource development and an open-door policy toward foreign investment, which will require amendments to certain laws and practices so as to bring them into conformity with international standards.

The Greater Mandalay City Plan calls for value-added product exports and other activities to earn foreign currency, such as jewelry making, food processing, and tin provising as well as a logistics center and dry port functions. It appears that the plan follows the successful economic development scheme used in Asian countries prior to the Asian financial crisis. However, given the crash of 1997, this rapid export-led growth policy may need reassessment. The substantial devaluation of Southeast Asian currencies—for instance, the baht and the rupiah by 100%—makes agricultural production and labor-intensive manufacturing highly competitive again in these countries. Thus, the strategy of rapid export-led growth should be amended in favor of balanced growth in which rescue-based industries, such as agriculture, food, and jewelry, are pursued in cooperation with neighboring countries including Bangladesh, China, and Thailand. For example, Myanmar would be able to produce seeds up to the intermediate stage and export them to Thailand, which would in turn use them to produce goods at the next, or value-added, stage, destined for large domestic and export markets.

A case in point would be soybeans, soybean cake, and vegetable oils made from soybean. Myanmar can grow soybean on a par with US quality. The more than 100% appreciation of the US dollar vis-a-vis the baht has made American imports less attractive in Thailand. Nevertheless, soybeans are treated as a secondary domestic crop in the lower region of northern Thailand, and we can thus expect a shortage of soybean cake, which is the leftover from refining. This will cause a rise in the price of animal feed and household cooking oils. Myanmar's Shan State could supplement this production of soybeans and set up oil refineries to supply raw edible oils to Thailand's cooking oil industry and soybean cake to feed its livestock industry. This is simply one example among many where the two countries might cooperate. Such a refinery could be operated to process oils from other agricultural products, such as castor beans, rapeseed, linseed, or sunflower seed, which Myanmar was a high potential to grow given its abundant land, more or less suitable weather conditions, and extensive labor force.

A similar scenario could be employed to promote economic development in the southern part of Myanmar as well. Myanmar's demand for edible oils may have to be filled by imports of palm oils from Malaysia. The price of palm oils is currently very high owing to the depreciation of the kyat. I propose international cooperation between southern Malaysia, Myanmar, and Thailand in the growing of palm oil in southern Myanmar and in the setting up of a palm oil refinery/agro-industrial estate in the south. The feasibility of such a project is linked to the excess demand for palm oils in Thailand's edible oil production, making cooperation possible among the three countries.

The most crucial issue in Greater Mandalay's development is the serious shortage of energy. It is reasonable to propose the establishment of a regional energy center to meet the rapidly increasing demand for power supply and fuel consumption in Greater Mandalay and its surrounding region.

Appendix 3
Effect of the Asian Financial Crisis on the Development of Thailand's Food Sector

Looking at Thailand's current economic crisis from the perspective of its relativity to Myanmar's economy, both pessimistic and optimistic interpretations are possible. On the pessimistic side, the crisis clearly implies that the baht's devaluation makes Thai agricultural products cheaper in the international market. This is the case with rice, maize, tapioca, vegetables and fruits, marine products, poultry, and meat products. Their price in foreign currency is thus becoming competitive again, after the tough competition that resulted from the exchange rate appreciation before the Asian financial crisis. The devaluation of the baht also means an attractive return on imported agricultural products used in production because the price of their local purchase increases but is still cheaper than the price of their importation. This causes farmers to produce more, increasing the use of local agricultural products and raw materials for food processing. This being the case, demand for agricultural imports should lessen, which will have negative repercussions on the export of agricultural products from and food processing in Myanmar. More importantly, the product cycle of canned pineapple and tuna will lengthen, making them more competitive in the world market. This will make it much more difficult for Myanmar to enter this international business.

On the optimistic side, the baht's devaluation should engender increased world demand for food products from Thailand. Devaluation also induces an increase in the cost of imported material inputs such as chemicals and pesticides. In addition, labor costs in Myanmar are much lower than in Thailand. If trade in agricultural products between Myanmar and Thailand is liberalized, Thailand will eventually import cheap raw materials from Myanmar to substitute local production. Furthermore, Thailand may find feasibility in relocating production sites to Myanmar to save on costs of transporting raw materials.

This optimistic scenario will be adopted in our analysis. A relationship of bilateral trade and investment will benefit both countries. In the medium to long run, enhanced agricultural production will require structural change. Thailand must increase the value added of its food processing activities. Hence, a cheap supply of raw material is a necessary condition for food processing development. Moreover, sufficient quality assurance must be applied to the raw materials used. If these conditions are met, Thailand should start moving toward higher value-added production in food processing, while Myanmar will be able to take responsibility for supplying raw materials and semi-processed products to Thailand. This is exactly what Thailand did several years ago vis-a-vis forerunners like Japan and Taiwan.

In my view, the agricultural sectors of both countries will benefit from gradual adjustment and reform. Thailand must increase its land productivity while preserving its natural resources and environment. A cost-effective approach should be the main principle: if the supply of products meeting required standards is cheaper from Myanmar than from Thailand, trade should be liberalized. Under new international regulations, the quality of food production must be monitored from the stage of raw material production through to the finished product. In this context, intensive application of fertilizers and pesticides is considered to have possible adverse effects on the finished product. Furthermore, the conventional wisdom that the production of food products can be separated from concerns about the environment or the food chain may be obsolete. In order to achieve sustainable development, both countries must join hands. Myanmar may have to reform its agricultural sector to increase its production capacity both in terms of quantity and quality, while adding numerous varieties of new crops, livestock, and marine products suitable to market demand in Thailand. Import market demand in Thailand is not derived from world export market demand, and thus, the quality of its products' food chains must satisfy world standards.

Thailand must push forward with agricultural reform as well. Currently, most of its cash crops (for example, maize, soybean, sugarcane, and rubber) and its marine products (for example, shellfish, shrimp, and squid) are becoming less competitive due to rising labor and material input costs. Some crops are overproduced and face sluggish market prices. Thailand may have to discard some non-competitive crops and turn to partial imports of them from abroad, particularly from neighboring countries like Myanmar. Such imports would include beans, herbs, garlic, maize, marine products, onions, and spices. By reforming its agricultural sector, Myanmar would be able to develop and export more sophisticated fruit crops and vegetables to the Thai market.

8

Industrial Policy in Myanmar Lessons from the Past

Toshihiro Kudo
Institute of Developing Economies, Tokyo

Introduction

When one writes about economic development in Myanmar, it seems to have become the custom to start by deploring its phenomenal failure in economic growth after independence in 1948, in particular during the socialist period between 1962 and 1988, and instead to cherish the memory of its relatively high income level and good export performance among neighbor developing countries before the Second World War.[1] The author will continue to follow this practice.

Most Myanmar watchers and economists, including those in international financial organizations, were optimistic about the country's development prospects when it achieved independence soon after the Second World War.[2] Table 8.1 shows the growth experiences of Myanmar and some Asian countries. Myanmar was among the fastest-growing Asian economies in the 1950s. Therefore, despite the fact that the stern realities of prolonged stagnation in the next three decades betrayed economists' prophecies, it is still hindsight to criticize their failure to foretell the country's later dismal economic record.

Table 8.1 Real Annual GDP Growth of Selected Asian Nations, 1950-96[3] (%)

	1950-60	*1960-70*	*1970-80*	*1980-90*	*1990-96*[a]
Myanmar	6.3	2.6	4.7	1.5[b]	6.4
Indonesia	3.8	3.5	7.2	5.5	7.0
Thailand	5.7	8.2	7.1	7.6	8.3
Philippines	6.4	5.1	6.0	0.9	3.0
India	4.2	3.6	3.4	5.3	4.3

Sources: World Bank calculations from *World Tables* and various issues of *World Development Report*

[a] Average of 1991-96 annual GDP growth rates, except for Myanmar which is 1991-95

[b] 1981-90 for Myanmar

The country was rich in natural resources and had a highly literate population, which was obviously a good sign for its development prospects. Before the Second World War its economy was slightly larger than Thailand's.[4] Its exports reached US$195 million, while Thailand's were only US$76 million. Although Myanmar's economy was substantially devastated during the war period, most economic and development indicators show that by 1950 it was not too far behind Thailand.[5] In the 1950s, it was not at all unrealistic to be optimistic about Myanmar's economic prospects.

Instead of blaming the deficiencies of the economic prophets, one might understand what happened through the perspective of John Wong: "It [Myanmar's detour from the mainstream development path] serves to show how bad politics and wrong development strategies could have delayed a country's development for a generation. Myanmar's experience offers a good lesson for students of economic development."[6] Neither the economic preconditions, although the war shattered the country's economic infrastructure and certainly retarded its economic growth,[7] nor the lack of economic potential prevented the country from joining the circle of the "East Asian Economic Miracles."[8] On the contrary, it was the "policy" long clung to by the Ne Win government that economists in the 1950s hardly fancied. Therefore, there are still reasons for economists and others today to be optimistic about Myanmar's development prospects. The only prerequisite, however, is that correct development strategies be followed by present and future governments.

With this perspective in mind, this essay deals with the evolution of the economic system with emphasis on industrial policies. The economic system, or set of public policies, has undergone several fundamental changes since the country became independent. Among them, the on-going transformation from a centrally planned economy to a market-oriented one is drastic and has attracted particular attention from both academic and business sectors. In order to understand the present transformation and government policies, it is useful to know Myanmar's economic history, by which the reader can "historicize" current government policies.

Industrial policy, which will be the emphasis in this essay, does not necessarily mean government interventionist measures. It may be used as industry-related policy in a broader sense, and, accordingly, also includes liberalization measures under the present government. Industrial policy has been changed following the transformation of economic systems. Industrialization has been a major goal of post-independence governments. Nevertheless, government policy regarding industry has long failed to contribute to this goal. It is high time to learn lessons from the past.

Industrial Development

Table 8.2 depicts the present position and past development of the industrial sector in Myanmar and selected Southeast Asian countries.

The present underdeveloped position of the industrial sector in Myanmar is clear, the industrial sector having composed only 12%-15% of total GDP over three decades.

In terms of employment, it is clear that Myanmar is an agricultural economy (Table 8.3). Out of total employment of 18.36 million in 1997-98, 11.51 million, or 62.7%, were engaged in the agricultural sector, while the processing and manufacturing sector accounted for only 9.1%.

Table 8.2 Shares of Major Sectors in GDP (%)

	Agriculture			*Industry*			*Services*		
	1970	*1980*	*1995*	*1970*	*1980*	*1995*	*1970*	*1980*	*1995*
Myanmar	49.5	47.9	46.1	12.0	12.3	15.3	38.5	39.8	38.6
Thailand	30.2	20.2	10.9	25.7	30.1	42.2	44.1	49.7	46.9
Indonesia	35.0	24.4	15.9	28.0	41.3	42.2	37.0	34.3	41.9
Philippines	28.2	23.5	21.5	33.7	40.5	35.5	38.1	36.0	43.0
Malaysia	–	22.9	13.9	–	35.8	47.1	–	41.3	39.0

Source: Asian Development Bank, *Asian Development Outlook: 1996 and 1997*

Table 8.3 Estimated Employment in Various Sectors, 1997-98

Sector	*Number*[a]	*Ratio (%)*
Agriculture	11,507	62.7
Livestock and fishery	397	2.2
Forestry	189	1.0
Energy	26	0.1
Mining	121	0.7
Processing and manufacturing	1,666	9.1
Electric power	22	0.1
Construction	400	2.2
Transport and communications	495	2.7
Social services	597	3.3
Administration and other services	888	4.8
Trade	1,781	9.7
Workers n.e.s.	270	1.5
Total	**18,359**[b]	**100**

Source: Ministry of National Planning and Economic Development, *Review of Financial, Economic, and Social Conditions for 1997-98*

[a] In thousands

[b] Total employment based on the working age group of 15-59 years

Compared with the rapid industrialization in other Southeast Asian countries, it is striking to see that Myanmar barely underwent industrial development and accompanying structural change. As mentioned above, this was mainly due to the ineffectiveness of the industrial policies pursued by successive governments since independence, in particular the socialist administrations.

Economic System and Industrial Policy

Myanmar has undergone several drastic changes in political and economic systems since independence, and its strategy with respect to industrialization has altered accordingly. Before discussing these changes in detail, a brief chronology of the political economy of the country may be useful (Table 8.4).

When Myanmar achieved independence in 1948, the state was expected to take a leading role in industrializing the economy. This was mainly due to the lack of local private capital and entrepreneurs and partly due to the newly born nation's ideological inclination to socialism. However, economic nationalism in this period was moderate and neutralized with liberal democratic ideas. In March 1962, General Ne Win took power in a coup d'etat and launched "The Burmese Way to Socialism". Under this line, such policies were implemented as radical nationalization, abrupt Burmanization of the economy, state monopolization of external trade, and a stern isolationist foreign policy. Myanmar's economy experienced a continuous series of trials and errors during the first decade of socialism and plunged into stagnation. In 1974, soon after the ostensible power transfer to civilian government under the guidance of the Burma Socialist Programme Party (BSPP), the only ruling party, the government began to relax its grip on the economy to some extent. Nevertheless, the reforms introduced in this period were at most lukewarm and were eventually found to be unsustainable. By the mid-1980s Myanmar's economy fell into depression again. In 1988, the State Law and Order Restoration Council (SLORC) assumed power in conditions of political and economic turmoil.

Table 8.4 Brief Chronology of Political Economy of Industrialization in Myanmar

Period	*Political System*	*Economic System*	*Industrial Strategy*	*Result*
1886-1948	Colonialism	Laissez-faire policy	Export-propelled "agriculturization"	Alien-dominated industrial sector Poor spread-effect for nationwide industrial development
1948-62	Parliamentary democracy	Moderate economic nationalism in the framework of market mechanism	Raw material-oriented Import-substitution industrialization	Moderate industrial performance Alien-dominated industrial sector
1962-74	Military rule ("The Burmese Way to Socialism")	Command economy Radical nationalism Burmanization and stern isolationism	Import-substitution industrialization Self-reliance line	Burmanization of economy and industry Poor economic and industrial performance
1974-88	BSPP rule ("The Burmese Way to Socialism")	Centralized planning Inward-looking policy with exception of ODA acceptance	Import-substitution industrialization Agro-based industries Inflows of ODA (mostly from Japan)	Poor economic and industrial performance Import-dependent industries
1988 to Present	Military rule (SLORC/SPDC)	Transition to market economy	Agriculture-based and export-oriented industrialization Inflows of foreign direct investment	Economic recovery Gradual increase in foreign and local private enterprises

Sources: Based on Mya Than and Joseph L. H. Tan, "Introduction: Optimism for Myanmar's Economic Transition in the 1990s?" in Mya Than and Joseph L. H. Tan, eds., *Myanmar Dilemmas and Options: The Challenge of Economic Transition in the 1990s* (Singapore: ASEAN Economic Research Unit, Institute of Southeast Asian Studies, 1990), Appendix I, pp.14-15, and Maung Maung Lwin, "Industrialization of Myanmar and Economic Dynamism of Pacific Asia," *Kaigai-Jijo Kenkyu* [Studies on Foreign Affairs], 24.1 (Kumamoto: Kaigai-Jijo Kenkyu-jo, Kumamoto Gakuen University, September 1996). Changes by the author. (For example, the original divides post-independence history into four periods, but the author demarcated the period between 1962 and 1988 into two eras. Some descriptions were also subject to change by the author.)

The new regime officially abandoned the socialist economic system and declared itself determined to proceed to a market economy, the transition to which is a focal point of this book.

The Colonial Period

As J. S. Furnivall has described it, the economic development of Myanmar during the British colonial period took place under a laissez-faire regime with free trade.[9] Stimulated by the enhanced opportunities of international trade with the opening of the Suez Canal in 1869, the Ayeyarwaddy delta had been colonized with massive inflows of migrated peasants and was transformed from swamp and jungle into the rice bowl of Asia. While the country was integrated into the world economy as a primary exporter, the domestic manufacturing industry of micro-enterprises was virtually wiped out with the influx of cheap imports.[10] "Agriculturization" rather than industrialization, therefore, characterizes economic development during this period.

Moreover, the process of agriculturization took place in a "plural society" in Furnivall's term. Whereas the participation of the native population in the national economy was largely confined to agriculture, industry and commerce were dominated both by foreign capital and foreign labor. Native Burmans could not compete with Indian workers even for unskilled jobs in dockyards, for example. There was also foreign capital, mainly that of Chettiars, a money lender caste from South India, in the agricultural sector, the only occupation for native people.[11] Such a situation is a key to understanding the interventionist or socialist policy of the independent government, which aimed for industrialization, that is, a more diversified economic structure with the participation of the native population in the industrial and commercial sectors being encouraged.

The Parliamentary Democracy Period: 1948-62

The Era of Ideology

In 1948, the newly independent government was not only influenced by the legacy of colonial rule but also inspired by socialist ideas, which at the time were popular with academics. Reading through the 1947 Constitution will give a sense of its inclination toward socialism. It declares that "the State is the ultimate owner of all lands."[12] Based on this concept, "the State shall have the right to regulate, alter or abolish land tenures or resume possession of any land and distribute the same for collective or co-operative farming or to agricultural tenants."[13] This implied prospective land reforms and even the possible collectivization of agriculture. According to Clause 31, which stipulated that there could be no large land holdings on any basis whatsoever,[14] the maximum size of private land holdings was determined to be up to ten acres.

Although "the State guarantees the right of private property and of private initiative in the economic sphere,"[15] "[P]rivate property may be limited or expropriated if the public interest so requires."[16] Therefore, "individual branches of national economy or single enterprises may be nationalized or acquired by the State."[17] Large investors, foreign ones in particular, must have feared possible nationalization. Moreover, "all sources of potential energy and other natural resources shall be exploited and developed by the Union."[18] The private sector was not necessarily discouraged, but as far as governmental assistance was concerned, "[P]reference shall be given to co-operative and similar economic organizations."[19] All these clauses indicate the socialist inclination of the new state, which meant the end of colonial laissez-faire. With the enhanced government role and policies, the new state intended to overcome the negative legacy incurred from having been a plural society and to promote economic development with elevated economic and social status for the indigenous population.

The economic aspirations of the newly born state were first incorporated in a two-year plan.[20] This plan, written with the help of two eminent economic advisors, J. S. Furnivall and Hla Myint, was publicized just after independence. Even though the plan's implementation was seriously obstructed by the communist and ethnic insurgencies launched immediately after independence, the nationalistic and socialist aspirations formally embodied in it long remained economic principles even in later plans. With respect to industrial development, the plan advocated that all basic industries were to be established and developed by state enterprises and, that first consideration be given to developing consumer goods industries on a state-owned basis.[21]

The second economic plan was the eight-year plan called the Pyidawtha Plan (welfare state plan). This plan was designed with the help of a group of American engineers and economists, and the first report was submitted to the government in January 1952. Due to a lack of information, it took more than a year and a half to produce the final report in August 1953. The plan was formally endorsed and announced by the government the following year. The Pyidawtha Plan adopted a national income target roughly doubling the GDP in real terms from 1950-51 to 1959-60.[22]

Industrial development was naturally one of its priorities. The Plan says that "[T]here is no doubt that a substantial programme of industrial development is needed urgently in Burma to create employment for our growing population, to reduce our dependency on other countries for goods that can be produced economically in our own country, to make larger quantities of more varied products available to our people at reasonable prices, and to strengthen our national defence. Steady industrialization is essential to the realization of our vision of the New Burma."[23] Three major manufacturing centers were planned in the Rangoon, Myingyan, and Akyab areas; sixty-five industrial projects were approved; and the Industrial Development Corporation (IDC) was established to administer them. All these government-led projects may be said to have been ambitious.[24]

The plan was unfortunately interrupted by the sharp decline in the price of rice after the end of the Korean War[25] and replaced by two more modest four-year plans.[26] Due to budgetary and foreign exchange constraints, the plan was scaled down and confined itself to the public sector. Agriculture and irrigation doubled their share in total public investment, while industry and power retained their share, being largely a continuation of committed projects. On the contrary, the share of infrastructure development in transport and communication was considerably reduced.[27]

Conflict between Ideology and Reality

Against such a backdrop, the government began to rely more on private enterprises than on public ones. It is ironic that the military caretaker government led by General Ne Win for the period from September 1958 to April 1960 made a detour from the thoroughfare of socialist and nationalist doctrines.[28] Even though Steinberg writes that "[A]fter downplaying the private sector in the early days of independence, U Nu then acknowledged the need for an enhanced private sector in 1955,"[29] it was Ne Win who actually limited the number of state enterprises and encouraged the private sector. The military caretaker government announced the following four policies:[30] (1) the non-expansion of state enterprises; (2) the promotion of increased efficiency and capacity of existing state enterprises; (3) the closure of commercially non-viable state enterprises; and (4) encouragement to establish of new private enterprises with both domestic and foreign capital.

More importantly, the military caretaker government introduced the first investment act. This not only allowed but also encouraged the inflow of foreign capital.[31] Preceding civil governments had also permitted foreign direct investment, but its promotion was generally regarded as against socialism and nationalism (the Burmanization of the economy) . However, the dire need for foreign exchange after 1955 seems to have urged Ne Win to take a further step forward in increasing foreign direct investment. This policy dramatically contrasts with his xenophobic attitude during "The Burmese Way to Socialism" after 1962.[32]

However, the Ne Win caretaker government also placed severe controls on prices, trade, and other economic activities. The newly introduced countrywide sale of rice at the same retail price without taking into consideration differing transportation costs may be a good example that showed Ne Win's preference for uniform control over the whole economy, as well as his understanding of what socialism meant. Regarding the new investment law as well, there was one clause reserved for nationalist causes. Section 6 (1) says "[N]o enterprise shall be nationalized for a period of 10 years from the date on which commercial operation commences." This must have given the same fears to potential investors as in the early days of independence.

The military also became intimately involved in economic activities through the Defense Services Institute (DSI) in a monopolistic manner.[33] The general success of the DSI may have given the military confidence that it could assume direct control over the economy, which may have misled Ne Win to a belief in "command economy." Therefore, we may need more detailed study of individual policies taken by the caretaker government before judging this period as a deviation from socialist doctrine.

In any case, a cessation of nationalization efforts and slowdown of state-led industrialization programs were supposed to continue during the Second Four-Year Plan (1961-62 to 1964-65). This plan indicates that "the pattern of ownership of means of production and instruments of economic activity has considerably changed in the direction of socialization, accompanied by efforts, not too successful, to transfer foreign-owned enterprises into the hands of nationals."[34] In line with such an understanding, it followed that "since the slicing of the cake has been made as equitable as possible so far, it remains now to enlarge the size of the cake in order for each to get a larger share."[35] The plan admitted that some government policies had hitherto discouraged private initiatives due to their socialist tendency in economic affairs and that the private sector had not achieved its potential rate of investment in the past years. The plan then goes on to state:

> In order therefore to make full utilization of private initiative and energy in the development of the economy, particularly in the field of industry, it is necessary to take measures to strengthen the private

> sector of the economy....The *strengthening of the private sector* will therefore rank as one of the most important objectives of the Second Four-Year Plan [original italics].[36]

However, this accommodation with reality and the emphasis on the private sector in the latter half of the 1950s were regarded as a deviation from nationalist and socialist doctrines, which were cherished during the struggle for independence, and were abruptly and totally arrested by the full-fledged Ne Win regime subsequent to the coup of 1962. The first bout between ideology and reality was, therefore, won by ideology.

"The Burmese Way to Socialism:" 1962-88

"The Burmese Way to Socialism" (hereafter called "Burmese Socialism") was ushered in with the military coup in the early morning of 2 March 1962. [37] The era of Burmese Socialism may be divided into three periods in terms of economic policies and performance: periods of establishment, modification, and crisis.[38] The first period covers the initial ten years, demarcated in terms of politics by the Revolutionary Council's official passing of power to the new legislative body, the People's Assembly, formed under a newly adopted constitution in 1974, and in terms of economic management by the introduction of partial policy reforms. The second period covers the ten years of relatively brisk economic growth, ending in the mid-1980s when the collapse of the economy occurred. The third period, characterized by economic crisis, lasted until 1988, when the military assumed power by force.

The Period of Establishment: 1962-73

Four pillars of economic policy supported Burmese Socialism: (1) nationalization, with which the military pursued the "Burmanization" of the economy; (2) import-substitute industrialization; (3) exploitative policy on agriculture, with which the government tried to finance industrial projects; and (4) a self-reliance line, which turned the country into a hermit state, and yet Ne Win thought it could not only eke out its livelihood but also achieve a certain degree of development.

Nationalization

Even though the civilian government started emphasizing the enlargement of the pie, the military was still unsatisfied with how to share the pie, recognizing that Burmans had not received their fair share. "Burmanization" of the economy must have been a major goal of the nationalist military leadership when it came to power in 1962, and "nationalization" was thought to be a major policy instrument for attaining this goal.

Following the ouster of Aung Gyi, a relatively liberal soft-liner once heir apparent to Ne Win, the abrupt and thorough nationalization policy became clear and was accelerated.[39] By February 1963, Ne Win announced the new policy that declared the nationalization of the means of production and distribution and the import and export of all major commodities, as well as prohibition of the formation of new private enterprises. The government propelled a series of nationalization programs until 1967. Moreover, fifty and one hundred kyat notes, then the largest currency denominations, were demonetized with the purpose of rooting out private businesses, many of which were believed to be in foreign hands.

The abrupt nationalization resulted in the Burmanization of the economy both in terms of ownership and management, as the Ne Win government intended. The ratio of output by state management increased from 30% in 1961-62 to more than 50% in 1965-66. The manufacturing sector in particular underwent a rapid transformation of ownership; the above ratio increased from about 30% in 1961-62 to more than 60% in 1965-66. By the early 1970s, all major economic enterprises except agriculture, small-scale trading, and minor services had been nationalized.

Expanded state-managed economic activities had to be administered mainly by military personnel, who had practically no experience in civilian management. They were appointed to the heads of the state economic enterprises, simply because they had Ne Win's confidence.[40] It took some time before they could learn their jobs, and frequently, after they had been trained, they were moved to new posts or relieved of their duties, either for political or incentive reasons.[41] It is no surprise that the general management efficiency deteriorated. The situation was aggravated by the exodus of skilled foreigners. In the first several years of military rule, about 200,000 Indians and Pakistanis, who had played an important role in the economy, left the country after being affected by the stringent nationalization policy. In the same period, military personnel replaced 2,000 career civil servants. Bureaucratic capacity was also, naturally, reduced.

Import-Substitution Industries

During the first decade of military rule, the government gave priority to industry over agriculture. The ratio of public industrial investment to total capital expenditure increased remarkably from 3.6% in 1960-61 to 37% in 1970-71.[42] However, too great a reliance on import-substitution industries and practically no attention to export-promotion industries led to resource misallocation.[43]

Even though capital-intensive factories and their employees mushroomed, industrial output in the public sector did not increase proportionately. In addition to managerial inefficiency, the shortages of imports of raw materials and spare parts, which occurred whenever the foreign exchange situation became tight, aggravated the capacity usage ratio of expensive machines. Nevertheless, the government, at this stage, adhered both to its self-reliance line and to industrialization based on the import-substitution strategy. The results were disastrous.

Agricultural Policy

Although the Ne Win government followed the socialist line, it did not collectivize agriculture. Instead, it controlled agriculture and the economic life of the peasantry through nationalization of the internal and external trade in rice and other major products.[44] While heavy, implicit though, taxation on farmers was institutionalized with the introduction of the low-priced delivery system, the government attempted, in compensation for low producer prices, to guarantee the security of tenure for the cultivator.[45]

Nevertheless, the government had never implemented complete land reform that included land allocation not only to tenant farmers but also to agricultural laborers.[46] The agricultural policy was inconsistent with the cause of Burmese Socialism, which emphasized the equal distribution of national welfare. The Ne Win government seemed to have been more concerned with extracting resources from the agricultural sector than with the equal redistribution of land. Under the self-reliance line, as explained below, agriculture was the only resource that could finance industrial development.

The Self-Reliance Line

The Ne Win government continued the foreign policy of predecessor governments: a neutralist, non-aligned line. The only difference between them was that the military government went further than its predecessors.[47] While successive governments during the democratic era pursued a positive neutralist line whereby Burma attempted to contribute to alleviating political tension between East and West, the Ne Win government took a negative non-aligned line whereby the military government attempted to be involved in international disputes as little as possible. Placing emphasis on its internal political priorities, the government cut the country off from the outside. Information from outside was strictly restricted, and people were discouraged from making contact with foreigners. The foreign policy the Ne Win government pursued in this period could be called isolationism.

As a corollary of the isolationist foreign policy, the country had been reluctant to accept foreign aid, let alone foreign direct investment, for fear of its accompanying political and economic influence. The annual average amount of assistance received by the Ne Win government during the ten years ending in 1972 was a mere US$26 million. This contrasts starkly with the situation of the ASEAN countries. For example, during the same period, Indonesia received US$272 million in official development assistance, the Philippines US$87 million, and Thailand US$57 million.[48] In addition, these countries were open to private foreign investment.

The Period of Modification: 1974 to the Mid-1980s

The first ten years of the Ne Win regime saw political and social chaos and ensuing economic stagnation. Such factors are responsible for the worsened situation of economic disorder caused by abrupt nationalization and persistent insurgencies, a poor harvest, and inappropriate economic policies. The average economic growth rate was as low as 2% during the period. The government suffered from the significant decline of exports and a resultant current deficit. The Ne Win regime, taking a stark self-reliance line or xenophobic attitude, did not accept either foreign private capital or public assistance and instead forcibly cut imports. Accordingly, the economy faced a chronic lack of capital and intermediate goods. It plunged into a vicious circle of contracted production.

Against such a deteriorating situation, the government launched the Twenty-Year Plan in 1972,[49] calling for some economic reforms, though within the framework of Burmese Socialism, including a priority shift from heavy industry to agriculture and the commercialization of state enterprises. In terms of politics, the military government transferred power to an apparent civilian government according to the new constitution of 1974.

Economic reforms were nonetheless limited and at best lukewarm,[50] and political and social unrest continued. Consequently, the condition of economic severity did not improve, but rather degenerated during this period. The crisis culminated in an attempted coup by young officers in 1976. Ne Win eventually declared a realistic revision of Burmese Socialism in the same year. In retrospect, however, this declaration did not lead to fundamental political and economic reforms but to the frustration of the self-reliance line. Along with the partial liberalization of the economy, the government opened its doors to significantly increased amounts of ODA from foreign donors. The Ne Win government chose ODA, in particular that from Japan, as relatively cost-free funds compared with those of international financial organizations and foreign direct investment, from a political viewpoint, although such aid would after all have to be repaid.[51]

During the Third Four-Year Plan (1978-79 to 1981-82), economic growth recorded a relatively high rate of 6.5%. Without increased foreign aid, this recovery could not even have been imagined.[52] Foreign aid enabled an increase in public investment, which constituted the greater part of total investment. The investment ratio to GDP jumped to 20% from a prolonged low level of 10%-13%. Budget deficits, without adequate measures to increase revenue, were augmented. As a result, public deficits were mostly financed by foreign aid. For example, it is said that 65% of total deficits were financed by foreign aid in 1979.

Economic Crisis: Mid-1980s to 1988

However, the recovery did not last long. The economy stagnated again after the Third Four-Year plan. A sharp fall in international commodity prices in 1982 triggered a deep economic slump. By 1983, the debt problem also had come into the open. In 1983-84 the debt service ratio was already 34.4 % on a commitment basis. An export slump after 1982 aggravated ratios to 52.5% in 1985-86, and 88.2% in 1987-88.[53] This clearly showed that the increased receipt of foreign aid after the mid-1970s could not contribute either to enlarging production capacity or promoting exports. During the period from 1985 to 1988, the economic growth rate plunged into negative figures.

In September 1987, one year before a vehement mass movement for democracy, the government suddenly abolished the delivery system of rice, a pillar policy instrument of the socialist economic system. This was an overture to the precipitous end of Burmese Socialism, which eventually came with the revival of the military government in September 1988.

The Second Bout between Ideology and Reality

Nationalization undermined the business class in general and foreigners in particular. Autarchic controls over the entire economy deprived the private sector of economic freedom by making its day-to-day operations illegal in most cases, such as obtaining inputs from the so-called parallel market. The socialist policy environment successfully withered away private capital and critically damaged the continuity of the residual entrepreneurial class that had developed during the closing years of parliamentary rule.[54]

Under prolonged economic stagnation, partial reforms were introduced in the mid-1970s, and the author regards this as a second trial for the authorities to retreat from socialist doctrine. It may also be called the second bout between ideology and reality. The government wanted to redefine the role of the private sector and to accommodate it into the national economy.

Nevertheless, all reforms and changes introduced at that time were, in retrospect, minor and unsuccessful. Although Steinberg wrote in 1981 that "[T]he industrialization strategy of the nation, the doctrinaire approach to a socialist state, was abandoned,"[55] it remained, the author thought, intact de facto. For example, even though the reintroduction of foreign direct investment into the national economy was considered, and Mutual Beneficial Economic Cooperation (MBEC) was invented in 1977, no actual foreign investments, except one, which had unusually close ties with Ne Win, were realized.

There seem to have been several reasons why the series of reforms in the mid-1970s did not lead to a fundamental restructuring of the economy. First, the Ne Win regime had not yet abandoned socialist doctrine or dogma. The government only admitted practical modifications within the framework of Burmese Socialism. This is clearly contrasted by the anti-socialist attitude of the State Law and Order Restoration Council (SLORC).[56] The latter announced the official abrogation of the socialist economic system immediately after assuming power. Secondly, the substantial inflow of ODA, from Japan in particular, bailed the Ne Win regime out of its economic and political quagmire, without any significant reforms. Without the decision to open the state to official assistance and Japan's positive response to this, the Ne Win government could never have survived the period without making fundamental reforms both in politics and the economy.[57] ODA was politically low-cost funding to the Ne Win government, which, on the contrary, turned out to be nothing but debt in the long run, and bringing about a financial crisis by the late 1980s. Thirdly, the Ne Win regime successfully controlled and prevented the majority of the population from resorting to violence or taking collective action against the authorities with various measures, including intelligence networks across the nation.[58] Whatever the reasons, ideology also won the second bout.

Lessons from the Past: End of a Vicious Circle or Beginning of Another?

SLORC/SPDC officially abandoned establishing a socialist economic system and began to promote a market-oriented economy. Two pillar laws were promulgated: the Foreign Investment Law (November 1988) and the State-owned Economic Enterprises Law (March 1989). The former resumed the intake of private foreign capital after a twenty-five year interval; the latter authorized private enterprises to be engaged in all but twelve stipulated industries.

This essay does not want to elaborate on the on-going reforms to transform the economy from a centrally planned to a market-oriented one. Numerous books and articles explain the detailed policy and reforms of trade, investment, privatization, and so forth.[59] Moreover, other writers in this volume take up such a task. The author would instead like to consider some features of the present policy changes from a historical viewpoint in relation to the country's industrial policy, just studied.

Every government since independence, whether civilian or military, democratic or socialist, has approached the problem of the private sector with great concern and trepidation. Whenever the government wanted to accommodate and integrate the energy of private enterprises into the national economy, socialist philosophy, anti-capitalist attitudes, and a xenophobic disposition based on bitter colonial experience provided obstacles, with the redefinition of the role of the private sector being left vague and halfway.

Table 8.5 Number of Enterprises Registered with the Directorate of Investment and Company Administration

	Myanmar Co., Ltd.	*Foreign Companies and Branches*	*Partner-ships*	*Chamber of Commerce and Industry*	*Joint Ventures*	*Total*
1988-89	21	2	31	-	-	54
1989-90	154	37	345	-	14	550
1990-91	640	43	189	6	18	896
1991-92	494	51	162	12	9	728
1992-93	961	51	123	11	8	1,153
1993-94	1,133	113	99	2	13	1,360
1994-95	1,383	146	106	-	9	1,644
1995-96	1,888	216	53	1	16	2,174
1996-97	2,140	336	58	1	20	2,555
1997-98	2,029	201	48	2	17	2,297
1998-99[a]	739	55	9	1	8	812
Total	**11,582**	**1,251**	**1,223**	**36**	**132**	**14,223**
	81.4%	**8.8%**	**8.6%**	**0.3%**	**0.9%**	**100%**

Source: Ministry of National Planning and Economic Development, Directorate of Investment and Company Administration

[a] Six months from April to September 1998

The present transformation of the economy is the third, and surely the largest, wave of liberalization in Myanmar's industrial history. Compared with the previous two waves, the present government has committed itself much more clearly to market economy principles and the enhanced role of the private sector. Private enterprises registered with the authorities concerned have mushroomed (see Table 8.5); 311 foreign direct investments, amounting to more than US$7 billion, were approved as of September 1998 under the Foreign Investment Law. The share of private investment in total capital formation reached 50% in 1990 and peaked at 65% in 1993, although the share of the private sector afterwards declined due to increased infrastructure projects undertaken by the government (see Figure 8.1). All these figures may prove the government's commitment to the enhanced role of the private sector.

Figure 8.1 Share of Private Investment

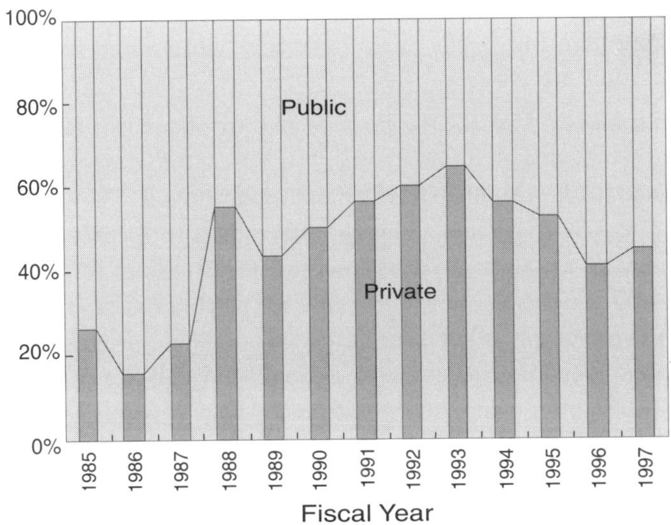

Source: Ministry of National Planning and Economic Development, *Review of Financial, Economic, and Social Conditions for 1996-97*

Its history still nonetheless exhibits a reserve to be fully confident in government policies toward a market economy. To be sure, there is much room for improvement in public policies. For example, state-owned economic enterprises are still much more favorably treated than most private enterprises, in terms of access to inputs (raw materials, electricity, petroleum, etc.), finance, foreign exchange,[60] and in the process of bureaucracy. Many private enterprises are far from satisfied with the surrounding policy environment.[61] Large-scale privatization programs have long been planned, but no single significant case has actually been implemented.[62] Moreover, since the onset of the Asian financial crisis in 1997, the government has extended administrative, and sometimes oppressive, measures to control foreign exchange transactions for fear of its spreading influence on the economy. Some foreign exchange dealers have been detained under an accusation of speculative transactions; the remittance of foreign currency to the outside has been restricted; and a new set of regulations on imports and exports has been introduced. Such interventionist responses will not only add uncertainty into the economic environment but also, more harmfully, may again raise suspicions about public policy in entrepreneurs' minds.

Unless the government addresses the deep-seated problems mentioned above, the private sector may continue to recall its past bitter experiences and lack confidence in the country's investment environment. The same is true of foreign firms, both present and prospective. This is the only way that the government is to steadily promote concrete economic reforms toward a free and fair market economy to make the private sector firmly convinced that the vicious circle between dirigiste (or control-prone) ideology and economic freedom has come to an end, and that the private sector is properly accommodated with the regime's ruling principles. This should be one of the most important lessons from the past.

In order to enhance the transformation toward a market-oriented economy, allow the author to present some guiding principles learned from past failures.[63]

- Myanmar's industrial development should be carried out in the framework of free markets and an open economy. Ending the vicious circle in a victory of the market over dirigiste and narrow-minded nationalist ideology is critically important for the country's industrial development.
- Myanmar should utilize foreign capital, technology, and markets. In order to do so, the government should end the stark self-reliance line and abandon its xenophobic attitudes.
- At the same time, the participation of local industrial entrepreneurs should be encouraged. They should play a significant role in the country's industrial development in order to prevent the re-emergence of the plural society of the colonial era. One important lesson from history is that a foreign-dominated economy will never render social and political stability. In order to encourage local entrepreneurs to play a more active role in the national economy, the government should recognize the importance of human resource development.
- The government should also pay attention to the possible inflows of drug money into legal economic activities. Most private enterprises in Myanmar are in their rudimentary stage, and are just beginning to make their first steps in the business world. Given their vulnerability as latecomers, once Myanmar's legal economy is contaminated with large inflows of drug money, they may easily be swept out of the economic sphere, and dirty money may easily come to dominate the private sector, distorting economic incentives. Clean and sound local private capital can only play a sustainable role toward economic development.
- The government should develop appropriate administrative and social infrastructure as well as physical infrastructure. The role of the government is still significant in a market-oriented economy. Market-friendly government activities, not protectionist measures, should be taken in order to enhance industrial development.

- Last but not least, the government should be responsible for macroeconomic stability. The present government has failed to display discipline in this regard. The inflation rate is grossly high; public deficits are persistently large; the money supply is out of control; and the local currency is plunging toward a record low. Without achieving a certain degree of macroeconomic stability, the private sector will never be confident and as a result long-term and large-scale investment will never be forthcoming.

Notes

[1] This essay is the revised version of "Industrial Policy in Myanmar: From a Historical Viewpoint" in Minoru Kiryu, ed., *ASEAN and Japanese Perspectives on Industrial Development and Reforms in Myanmar: A Survey of Selected Firms* (Bangkok: Chulalongkorn University Printing House, 1998), pp. 7:1-45.

[2] Mya Than and Joseph L. H. Tan, "Introduction: Optimism for Myanmar's Economic Transition in the 1990s?" in Mya Than and Joseph L. H. Tan, eds., *Myanmar—Dilemmas and Options: The Challenge of Economic Transition in the 1990s* (Singapore: ASEAN Economic Research Unit, Institute of Southeast Asian Studies, 1990), p. 1.

[3] This table is cited from David Dapice "Development Prospects for Burma: Cycles and Trends" in Robert I. Rotberg, ed., *Burma: Prospects for a Democratic Future* (Cambridge, Mass.: World Peace Foundation and Harvard Institute for International Development, Brookings Institute Press, Washington, DC), pp. 153-64.

[4] Tun Wai, "Part Two: Myanmar" in Pradumna B. Rana and Naved Hamid, eds., *From Centrally Planned to Market Economies: The Asian Approach—Vol. 3: Lao PDR, Myanmar, and Viet Nam* (Hong Kong: Oxford University Press for the Asian Development Bank, 1996), p. 151.

[5] Research Group for the Economic Development of Burma, *Economic Development of Burma: A Vision and A Strategy* (May 1997), pp. 1-2. GNP

estimates for Myanmar and its neighbor countries in those early days were not accurate. For example, John Wong stated that Burma's per capita income was higher than that of Hong Kong, Korea, Malaysia, and Thailand in 1950 ("Why has Myanmar not Developed like East Asia?", *ASEAN Economic Bulletin*, 13.3 [Singapore: Institute of Southeast Asian Studies, March 1997], p. 344), while the former Research Group provided quite a different picture. The divergence in the development stages between Burma (now Myanmar) and Thailand, however, seems to have been small at that time.

[6] Wong, p. 345.

[7] It took almost fifteen years to recover the peak of GDP in the pre-war period, and still the per capita income of 1959-60 was lower than that of 1938-39 by 13%. The volume of rice export in 1959-60 was only two thirds of that in 1938-39 (Ministry of National Planning, *Second Four-Year Plan for The Union of Burma: 1961-62 to 1964-65* [Rangoon: Superintendent, Government Printing and Stationary, Union of Burma, 1961, Chapter I, pp. 1-20, 21]).

[8] See the International Bank for Reconstruction and Development/The World Bank, *The East Asian Miracle: Economic Growth and Public Policy* (Oxford: Oxford University Press, 1993).

[9] See J. S. Furnivall, *An Introduction to the Political Economy of Burma*, 3rd edn (Rangoon: Peoples' Literature Committee and House, 1957).

[10] Furnivall describes the situation as follows: "They [Burman industries] have gone backwards under the British government. Spinning and weaving used to be carried on in almost every village but imported cloth has killed the product of the village loom. The blacksmith cannot easily make tools as cheap and efficient as those which are imported and sold in all the Bazaars. Ship-building was at one time an important business in Rangoon and Moulmein. But ships are no longer built of timber" (p. 161).

[11] About half of total land under cultivation in Lower Burma as of the end of 1947 was held by non-agriculturalist landlords, most of whom were non-residents; Thakin Tin, "The Speech of the Hon. Thakin Tin, Minister for

Agriculture and Forests, on the introduction of the Land Nationalization Bill, 1948, at the Sixth Session of the Parliament on the 11th October 1948" in Ministry of Agriculture and Forests, *The Land Nationalization Act, 1948* (Rangoon: Superintendent, Government Printing and Stationary, Union of Burma, 1948), pp. 1-11.

[12] *The Constitution of The Union of Burma (1947)*, Sect. 30 (1), Chap. III.

[13] *Ibid.*, Sect. 30 (2), Chap. III.

[14] *Ibid.*, Sect. 31, Chap. III.

[15] *Ibid.*, Sect. 23 (1), Chap. II.

[16] *Ibid.*, Sect. 23 (4), Chap. II.

[17] *Ibid.*, Sect. 23 (5), Chap. II.

[18] *Ibid.*, Sect. 219, Chap. XIII. See also Sect. 44 (1), Chap. IV.

[19] *Ibid.*, Sect. 42, Chap. IV.

[20] Wai, p. 157.

[21] Ministry of National Planning, *op. cit.*, Chap. I.

[22] The Economic and Social Board of the Union of Burma, *Pyidawtha: The New Burma* (Rangoon, 1954).

[23] *Ibid.*, pp. 84-85.

[24] However, the plan also admitted that some developing countries rushed headfirst into "ambitious schemes for rapid and extensive industrialization without adequate study or preparation" and that Burma should not make such mistakes (Economic and Social Board of the Union of Burma, p. 85.) The Pyidawtha Plan appears to have been more practical, compared to the former plan, even though it contained much nationalistic sentiment and socialistic ideals.

[25] The average price of rice per ton was almost halved from 1952-53 to 1958-59, while the Pyidawtha Plan assumed a very gradual decline by less than 14% (Ministry of National Planning, p. 10.)

[26] The first four-year plan was, however, a series of annual budgetary schedules, which may not deserve to be called a mid-term plan, and it was

interrupted by the military caretaker government. The second was abandoned by the military coup in 1962.

[27] Ministry of National Planning, Chap. I.

[28] However, as mentioned before, Ne Win introduced a stern socialist system after 1962. See the next section.

[29] David I. Steinberg, *Burma's Road Toward Development: Growth and Ideology under Military Rule* (Boulder: Westview Press, Westview Special Studies on Southeast Asia, 1981), p. 48.

[30] Noboru Yamamoto, et al., *Economic Development in Burma* [in Japanese] (Tokyo: Institute of Developing Economies, Research Report Series No. 14, 1961), p. 210. These four are my translation.

[31] *The Union of Burma Investment Act, 1959.*

[32] The FDI inflows received official encouragement following issuance of the Investment Policy Statement of 1955, which was later enacted as the Union of Burma Investment Act of 1959 with more incentives for investors (Mya Than, "The Union of Burma Foreign Investment Law: Prospects of Mobilizing Foreign Capital for Development?" in Than and Tan, eds., p. 187). The author has no evidence that may give plausible reasons why Ne Win allowed the first investment act to be promulgated. It is not sure whether he himself promoted the act in order to improve the foreign exchange situation despite his antipathy to foreign capital, or whether he simply respected the decision of the preceding civilian government to do so. This topic may be important for understanding his true motives regarding Burmese Socialism, to which he had long clung but abruptly abandoned in 1988. Most scholars and Myanmar watchers attributed the birth of Burmese Socialism to the military's or Ne Win's belief in socialism that was equated with nationalism.

[33] Steinberg, pp. 17-18.

[34] Ministry of National Planning, p. 21.

[35] *Ibid.*

[36] *Ibid.*, p. 23.

[37] Regarding this section, see also Chap. 3 in Toshihiro Kudo, "Political Basis of Economic Policies under Burmese Socialism," *Southeast Asian Studies*,

No. 4 (Tokyo: Tokyo University of Foreign Studies, 1998).

[38] As mentioned, however, the period of Burmese Socialism may be divided into two eras according to the political system in effect, that is, direct military rule by the Revolutionary Council (1962-74) and Socialist Republic rule (1974-88).

[39] Steinberg, p. 77.

[40] Wai, "The Myanmar Economy at the Crossroads: Options and Constraints," p. 22.

[41] Wai, "Part Two: Myanmar," p. 159.

[42] Steinberg, p. 37.

[43] Wai, "The Myanmar Economy at the Crossroads, p. 25.

[44] Robert H. Taylor, *The State in Burma* (London: Hurst, 1987), p. 351.

[45] *Ibid.*, p. 349, and Akio Takahashi, *Biruma-Deruta no Beisakuson: "Shakaishugi"-Taisei-ka no Noson-keizai* [A Rice Village in the Burma Delta: Village Economy under the Rule of "Socialism"](Tokyo: Kenkyu Sosho [IDE Research Series], No. 423, 1992), pp. 83-84.

[46] Takahashi defined tenant farmers as those who had the right to work on the land, holding a degree of agricultural capital consisting mainly of working animals and harrows, and agricultural laborers as those who did not have the right on the land and were without such agricultural capital. The former employed the latter (Chap. III).

[47] Steinberg, p. 39.

[48] Institute of Developing Economies, *Basic Survey for Promotion of Official Loans to Burma* [in Japanese] (Tokyo: IDE, 1983), pp. 181-82.

[49] The Twenty-Year Plan consisted of five four-year plans. It was formally adopted by the Central Committee of the BSPP in 1972. However, due to the economic crisis in 1973 and 1974, as well as a change in the fiscal year, the first four-year plan was frustrated halfway and the second started from April 1974.

[50] For example, despite so-called autonomy given to state economic enterprises, they were still centrally controlled and decision-making was slow (Wai, "The Myanmar Economy at the Crossroads", p. 32).

[51] For details, see Toshihiro Kudo, "Japan's Aid to Burma: History and Problems" [in Japanese], *Tsushin*, 11 November 1993 (Tokyo: Institute for Study of Languages and Cultures of Asia and Africa, Tokyo University of Foreign Studies), pp. 1-18. Regarding the current ODA situation in Myanmar, see Toshihiro Kudo, "ODA to Myanmar: Actual Situation and Problems" [in Japanese], *World Trends*, No. 37 (Tokyo: Institute of Developing Economies, August 1998).

[52] Agricultural reforms also contributed, though. The introduction and spread of high-yielding varieties were strongly propelled during this period.

[53] Institute of Developing Economies, *Report on Economic Assistance—Myanmar and Bangladesh* [in Japanese] (Tokyo: IDE, 1991), p. 65.

[54] Tin Maung Maung Than, "Myanmar Democratization: Punctuated Equilibrium or Retrograde Motion?" in Anek Laothamatas, ed., *Democratization in Southeast and East Asia* (Singapore: Institute of Southeast Asian Studies, 1997), p. 180.

[55] Steinberg, p. 47.

[56] SLORC was dissolved in November 1997, and the State Peace and Development Council (SPDC) was formed simultaneously.

[57] For details, see Kudo, "Japan's Aid to Burma."

[58] The author once attributed the main factor that prevented the farmers from resorting to desperate actions including violence to the village class structure and rice production features. See Kudo, "Political Basis," pp.157-61.

[59] These include Than and Tan, eds.; Wai, "Part Two: Myanmar"; and Myat Thein and Mya Than, "Transitional Economy of Myanmar: Performance, Issues, and Problems" in Seiji Finch Naya and Joseph L. H. Tan, eds., *Asian Transitional Economies: Challenges and Prospects for Reform and Transformation* (Singapore: International Center for Economic Growth, Institute of Southeast Asian Studies, 1996), pp. 210-61.

[60] The grossly overvalued official exchange rate is instrumental in providing the SEEs with implicit subsidies. One of the main reasons why the incumbent government is reluctant to unify the multi-stratified exchange rates into the single market one may stem from the rent-seeking motives of the public sector, both organizations and individuals, that have access to the overvalued official exchange rate. As many economists have pointed out, the unification of exchange rates should center the structural adjustment program.

[61] Such problems are identified in Nu Nu Yin's essay in this volume.

[62] Except for small cases, such as cinema halls and sawmills.

[63] See also the Research Group for the Economic Development of Burma, Chap. 3.

9

Recent Banking Sector Developments and Current Monetary Status in Myanmar

Takanori Wajima
CRC Research Institute, Tokyo

Introduction

After the Ne Win government nationalized private banks, financial resource allocation was carried out exclusively through state-owned banks in Myanmar. Less than two years after the State Law and Order Restoration Council (SLORC) assumed power, the Financial Institutions of Myanmar Law was promulgated in line with the new government's private-sector orientation. By this provision, the banking sector, prescribed by the previous law, the State-Owned Economic Enterprises Law of 1989, as exclusively state-owned, was explicitly opened to private-sector participation. As of November 1997, nineteen private banks and forty-one representative offices of foreign banks had been established as the result of this relaxation. The law also prescribed the establishment of three state-owned banks: the Myanmar Economic Bank (MEB), the Myanmar Foreign Trade Bank (MFTB), and the Myanmar Investment and Commercial Bank (MICB).

Laws relating to financial system reforms were enacted the same year. The Central Bank of Myanmar (CBM) Law of 1990 was designed to strengthen monetary control over the financial market in the new era. Unlike the former system, the CBM is vested with relative independence from the government in the decision-making process concerning the government budget. The Myanmar Agriculture and Rural Development Bank (MARDB) was established under the MARDB Law of 1990, not only taking over the business of the Myanmar Agricultural Bank (MAB) but also with newly assigned purposes. The law stipulates the main aim of this bank as the support of the development of rural enterprises and the agriculture and livestock sectors through banking services.

The market-oriented economy, which Myanmar lacked for over twenty-seven years until the socialist economic system was revoked, is being introduced gradually but is being promoted consistently by the participation of private entrepreneurs in various kinds of economic activities. Needless to say, for the further development and activation of the economic system that was revived at the beginning of the 1990s efficient and stable financial resource allocation is a precondition. After a brief review of the historical background of the financial sector in Myanmar, this paper will attempt an analysis of the characteristic aspects of the current situation.

Figure 9.1 Credit by Sector per GDP, 1949-88

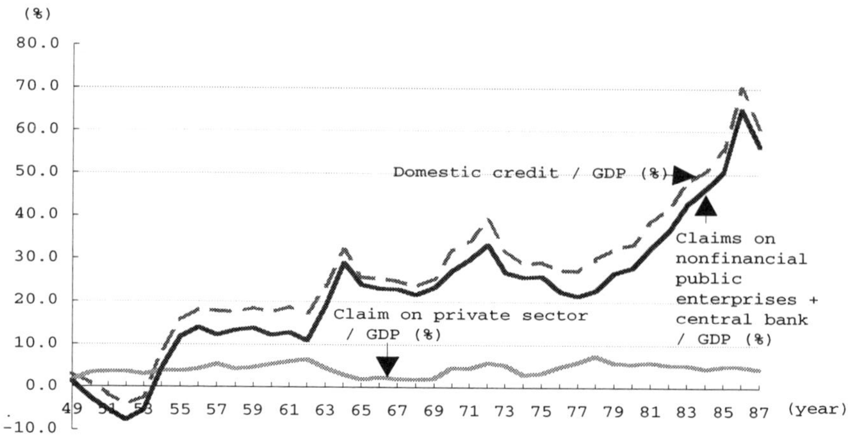

Source: International Monetary Fund, *International Financial Statistics Yearbook*

Historical Background of the Myanmar Financial Sector, 1963-89

1.1 Nationalization of Private Banks in 1963 and Decentralization of State-Owned Banks in 1976

In 1963, one year after the Ne Win government replaced the previous government, twenty-four private banks, of which fourteen were foreign-owned, were nationalized in line with the nationalization of the entire economy. The new government banks at that time were integrated into a monolithic bank with specialized functions under the People's Bank of the Union of Burma Law of 1967. Eight years after integration, this centralized bank was divided into four banks by the Bank Law of 1975 accompanied by the reform of state economic enterprises (SEEs). In 1976, state banks consisted of four specialized banks, namely: the Bank of Union Burma (UBB), the Myanmar Economic Bank (MEB), the Myanmar Foreign Trade Bank (MFTB), and the Myanmar Agriculture Bank (MAB).

1.2 Cumulative Loans to State Economic Enterprises

The reform of the SEEs, which aimed at the rationalization of inefficient enterprises, also restricted their funding measures only to borrowing from banks at the same time. In the late 1980s, the period of stagnant economic growth, lending to SEEs accumulated at a rapid pace due to expanding losses caused by inefficient management. The outstanding bank credit to the public sector amounted to 38.5 billion kyat, which equaled 65.2% of GDP in 1986 (Fig. 9.1).[1] This disproportionate resource allocation resulted in a heavy burden on the sluggish, anemic Myanmar economy. The undisciplined and almost unlimited lending disbursed to the SEEs was eventually followed by a cumulative money supply. Due to the lack of an efficient monetary instrument for absorbing money circulating in the market, the government was compelled to demonetize large bank notes, for dread of a monopoly of farm products in 1987.[2]

1.3 Conversion of Outstanding Loans to Government Securities in 1989

The year after the replacement of the government, budgetary control over the SEEs was placed under a centralized system called the State Fund Account (SFA), as executed in the previous era. Under this system, all government receipts and payments as well as those of SEEs are channeled through one account, with any overall deficit being financed by the issue of treasury bills (which pay 4% per annum) to the central bank. The deficits of individual SEEs, whether due to operating loss or capital expenditure, are met from the SFA at no interest cost to the enterprise.[3] There, bank financing is generally not available, partly because of the difficulties encountered by the central government before 1989, when SEEs enjoyed unlimited borrowing from the government banking system.[4] Accompanied with this alteration, the outstanding loans disbursed to SEEs by state-owned-banks (SOBs) were converted to government equities.[5]

Recent Financial Sector Reform and Current Status, 1990-97

2.1 Promulgation of the Financial Institutions Law

The reorganization of the budgetary system and abolishment of the socialist economic system were soon followed by the promulgation of the Financial Institutions of Myanmar (FIM) Law. As Clause 3, Sub-section (a) defines, financial institutions shall be established as limited liability companies. The law thus explicitly declared the relaxation of the financial sector.

2.2 Establishment of Private Banks and Representative Offices of Foreign Banks

Under the FIM law, the following private banks and representative offices of foreign banks have been opened (Tables 9.1 and 9.2) as of July 1998:

Table 9.1 List of Local Private Banks (as of July 1998)

Name of Bank	*Date License Issued*	*Date of Commencement*
Myanmar Citizens Bank	25/5/92	2/6/92
Cooperative Bank	3/8/92	21/8/92
Yadanabon Bank (Mandalay)	27/8/92	11/9/92
First Private Bank	25/5/92	6/10/92
Myawaddy Bank	1/1/93	4/1/93
Yangon City Bank	19/3/93	1/4/93
Yoma Bank	26/7/93	14/8/93
Myanmar Oriental Bank	26/7/93	18/11/93
Myanmar Mayflower Bank	17/3/94	9/6/94
Tun Foundation Bank	8/6/94	14/6/94
Kanbawza Bank	8/6/94	1/7/94
Asia Yangon International Bank	17/3/94	18/10/94
Myanmar Universal Bank	21/11/94	24/1/95
Asia Wealth Bank	21/11/94	30/4/95
Myanmar Industrial Development Bank	12/1/96	15/2/96
Myanmar Livestock and Fisheries Development Bank	9/2/96	15/2/96
Cooperative Promoters Bank	2/3/96	6/7/96
Cooperative Farmers Bank	22/3/96	6/7/96
Sibin Thayar Yay Bank	26/6/96	4/7/96
Inwa Bank	15/5/97	28/11/97

Source: Aung Aung and Associates

Table 9.2 List of Representative Offices of Foreign Banks (as of July 1998)

No.	*Name of Foreign Bank*	*Date License Issued*	*Date of Commencement*
1	Development Bank of Singapore	10/11/93	29/3/94
2	United Overseas Bank	10/11/93	2/8/94
3	Siam City Bank	8/2/94	5/8/94
4	Keppel Bank of Singapore	8/2/94	20/12/94
5	Overseas Chinese Banking Corporation	8/2/94	15/11/94
6	Thai Farmers Bank	8/6/94	9/12/94
7	Panin Bank International, Nauru	8/7/94	1/3/96
8	Overseas Union Bank, Singapore	18/7/94	10/7/95
9	Malayan Banking Berhad (MAYBANK)	12/8/94	11/4/95
10	Public Bank Berhad, Malaysia	12/8/94	1/11/94
11	Bank of Commerce (M) Berhad, Kuala Lumpur, Malaysia	18/10/94	12/6/95
12	Global Commercial Bank, Phnom Penh	24/10/94	20/6/95
13	Hong Kong and Shanghai Banking Corporation	24/10/94	9/2/95
14	Bangkok Bank Public Company	24/10/94	18/8/95
15	Arab, Bangladesh Bank	22/11/94	1/8/95
16	Krung Thai Bank	22/11/94	4/8/95
17	Banque Nationale de Paris	29/12/94	18/12/95
18	Banque Française du Commerce Extérieur	23/1/95	17/11/95
19	Standard Chartered Bank	23/2/95	27/4/95
20	ABN AMRO Bank NV	23/2/95	14/3/96
21	Société Générale	9/5/95	29/11/95
22	Bank Dagang Nasional Indonesia	14/6/95	10/6/96
23	National Bank	6/7/95	16/7/96
24	Brunei Investment Bank	18/9/95	1/7/96
25	Fuji Bank	10/10/95	22/12/95

26	ING Bank	24/11/95	1/3/96
27	Korea Exchange Bank	20/12/95	18/11/96
28	Deutsche Bank	5/4/94	28/5/96
29	First Overseas Bank	30/4/96	15/5/96
30	Sumitomo Bank	30/4/96	19/6/96
31	Tokai Bank	14/5/96	5/6/96
32	Sanwa Bank	17/5/96	4/7/96
33	Dai-Ichi Kangyo Bank	12/6/96	4/10/96
34	Asahi Bank	12/6/96	1/11/96
35	Sakura Bank	12/6/96	7/10/96
36	MBF Bank	16/8/96	9/4/97
37	Credit Lyonnais	4/7/96	15/1/97
38	Hana Bank	28/3/97	16/9/97
39	Korea Long Term Credit Bank	28/3/97	7/8/97
40	Daewoo Bank (Hungary)	10/6/97	1/10/97
41	BII Bank	27/8/97	-
42	Bank of Tokyo-Mitsubishi	17/9/97	19/9/95
43	First Commercial Bank, Singapore Branch	20/11/97	5/5/98
44	RHB Bank Berhad	28/11/97*	-
45	Crédit Agricole Indosuez	1/1/98**	19/1/95

* New license for merger issued
** New license for transfer issued

2.2.1 Increase in Loans by Private Banks

Loans by private banks increased drastically in 1995 and 1996 (Fig. 9.2). Outstanding loans (consolidated loans and advances) amounted to 3,529 million kyat, more than fifty times the 179.6 million kyat in 1992, when four private banks were initially opened.

Figure 9.2 Consolidated Balance Sheet of Domestic Private Banks (Assets)

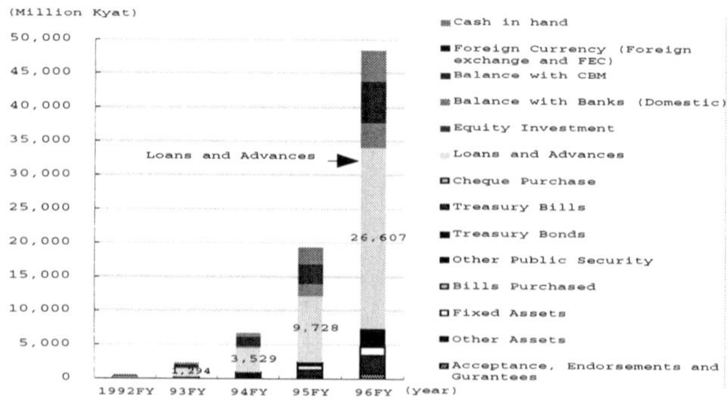

Source: Central Statistical Organization, *Statistical Yearbook, 1997*
Note: Data for each year include the following numbers of private banks, respectively:

Year	1992	1993	1994	1995	1996
Number of private banks	4	8	13	15	21

This remarkable increase also continued in 1996. That year, outstanding loans expanded to 26,607 million kyat, approximately three times the figure for the previous year. Through these expansions, the ratio of outstanding loans to GDP showed surges in the last two years. Bank claims on private sector per GDP (including SOBs) are shown in Figure 9.3. In financial year 1996, this index slightly surpassed 10%, demonstrating a growth of private finance demand. The private banking sector, of which loans and advances accounted for 36% as of the end of 1996,[6] is thus expected to meet it by expanding finance capability.

Figure 9.3 Claims on Private Sector per GDP (%) by Country

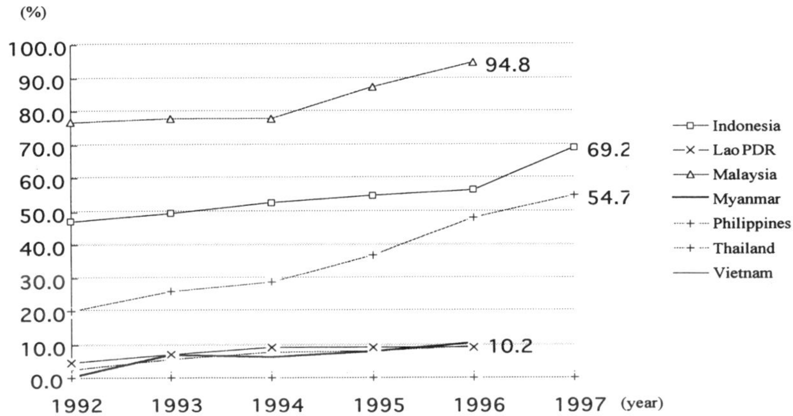

Source: Asian Development Bank, *Key Indicators of Developing Countries in Asia and Pacific*
Note: Data on the Lao PDR, Myanmar, and Vietnam for 1997 not available

2.2.2 Increase in Deposits with Private Banks

Since the beginning of private participation, deposits for certain terms (savings deposits and time deposits) with private banks have strikingly increased, compared with those for SOBs (Fig. 9.4). As a result of the accelerated growth, the ratio of the savings deposits with SOBs surpassed 65% in fiscal year 1996. However, this steady increase of saving deposits took a downturn in late 1997. Outstanding deposits with private banks recorded a 2.5% decline to the previous year in August 1997 until which it had continuously increased since March 1995 (Fig. 9.5). Its momentum was accelerated in May to 9.5% and soared to 17.4% in the month prior to the drop. Outstanding SOBs deposits plunged following it, and lagged for one month. As no obvious recovery is currently found for both, outstanding since September 1997, this is unlikely due to the seasonal trend observed for other kinds of deposits (Fig. 9.5), but a reactive adjustment occurs with some certainty. As for time deposits, the order between both shares reversed in fiscal year 1993, and the level of the private banks is currently overwhelming that of SOBs.

Figure 9.4 Savings and Time Deposits with Private Banks and State-Owned Banks

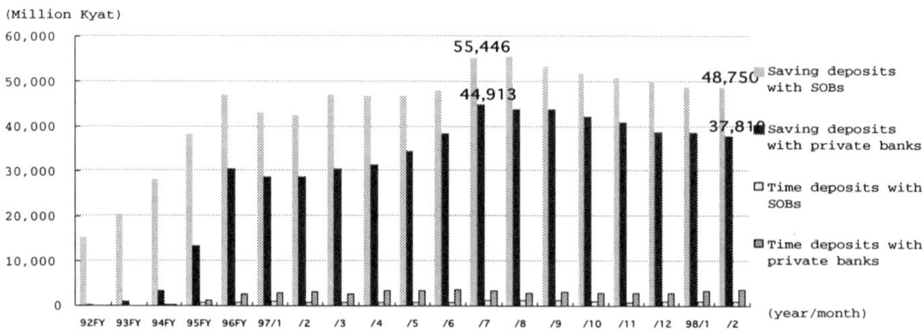

Source: Central Bank of Myanmar, *Selected Monthly Economic Indicators*

2.2.3 Composition of the Money Supply

The composition of the money supply for 1989-96 is shown in Figure 9.6. Since 1992, the initial year of private participation in this sector, the share of demand deposits with private banks has been on the rise, while that with SOBs has been shrinking. However, as the share of currency in circulation, always accounting for around 90% of the total, remains as dominant as before the relaxation, the share of the private banks has not so much expanded as merely eroded that of the SOBs. Certain kinds of rationalization, as some private banks have actually implemented with

Figure 9.5 Annual Change of Deposits Outstanding, 1996-98

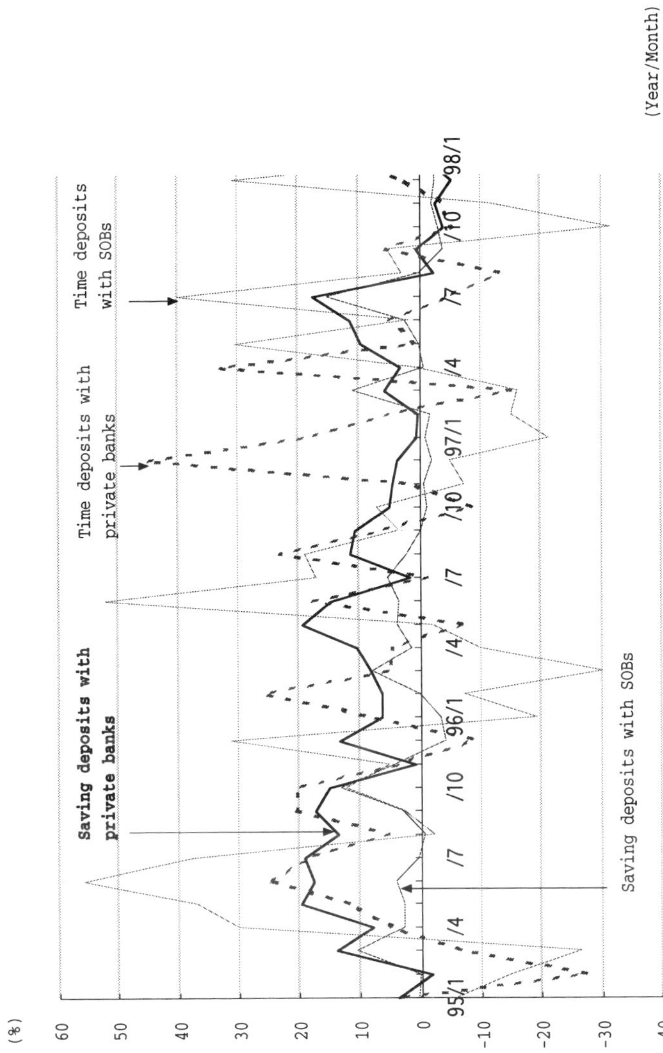

Source: Central Bank of Myanmar, *Selected Monthly Economic Indicators*

computerized business procedures, such as automatic teller machines, may lead to a rapid and wide penetration of banking services into the economy.

Figure 9.6 Composition of the Money Supply, 1989-97

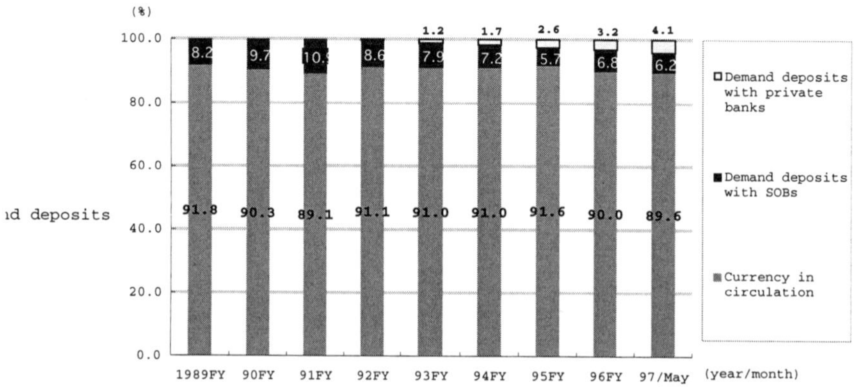

Source: Central Bank of Myanmar, *Selected Monthly Economic Indicators*

This illustrates that private participation in the banking sector is to some extent proceeding successfully. However, if limited within the availability of clearance via banks, one can say that banking services in the economy as a whole have not yet come into wide use. M2/GDP of Myanmar, which is supposed to represent "financial depth," is shown in Figure 9.7 with selected neighboring countries. Since fiscal year 1994, Myanmar's M/GDP has curved upwards, although gradually, approximating the lowest level of ASEAN 4. The status of further development in this sector after fiscal year 1996 is to be expected with a rise in this index, in terms of rational financial resource allocation.

Figure 9.7 M2/GDP (%) by Selected Southeast Asian Country

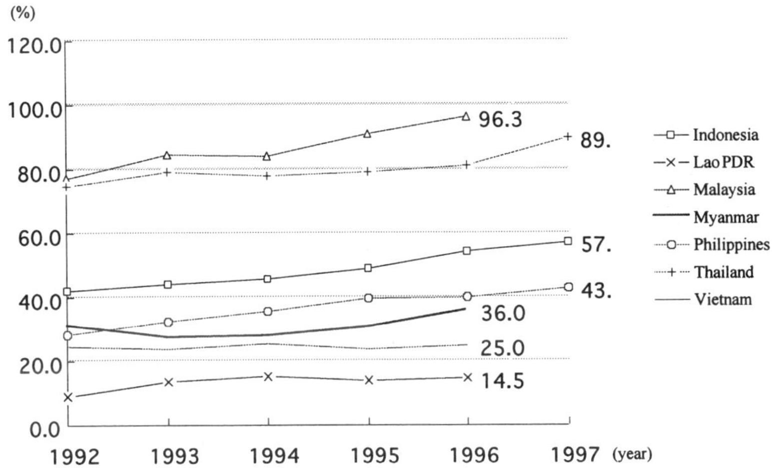

Source: Asian Development Bank, *Key Indicators of Developing Countries in Asia and Pacific*
Note: Data on the Lao PDR, Malaysia, Myanmar, and Vietnam for 1997 not available

2.3 Separation of Myanmar Investment and Commercial Bank from Myanmar Economic Bank

The Myanmar Investment and Commercial Bank (MICB), which had formerly belonged to the Myanmar Economic Bank (MEB), the largest bank in Myanmar, was separated from the latter in 1989 and established as an independent entity under the FIM law in 1990. Simultaneously with undertaking the government's market-oriented policy, the bank specializes in investment and commercial banking. It is deemed that, by doing so, the government intended to supplement financial demand resulting from private-sector development until the establishment of private banks after the relaxation.

2.4 Establishment of Myanmar Agricultural and Rural Development Bank

The Myanmar Agricultural and Rural Development Bank (MARDB) was established under a specific law, differently from the other three SOBs, except the Central Bank of Myanmar. Clause 5 of the MARDB Law defines the main aim of the bank as to support the development of agricultural, livestock, and rural socio-economic enterprises in the country by providing banking services.[7] In addition to taking over the business of the Myanmar Agricultural Bank, the bank's predecessor, new objectives were assigned to the bank. These are defined in Article 6, Subsections (a) to (f), including Subsection (b), which mandates promotion of rural banking, and Subsection (d), which mandates support of socio-economic development in rural areas.

2.5 Promulgation of Central Bank of Myanmar Law of 1990

Accompanying the new laws relating to financial sector reforms, the Central Bank of Myanmar (CBM) Law was promulgated in 1990. The bank's main aim is stipulated in the law as preserving the internal and external value of the nation's currency.

2.5.1 Objectives of the Central Bank of Myanmar

The objectives of the CBM are also stipulated in the CBM law as follows (Clause 6 of the CBM law): (1) to promote efficient payment mechanisms and the liquidity, solvency, and proper functioning of a soundly based financial system; and (2) to foster monetary, credit, and financial conditions conducive to orderly, balanced, and sustained economic development. As stipulated in Clause 8 of the law, these objectives are to be implemented by ten functions vested in the bank, including those of acting as: (1) the sole issuer of domestic currency, both notes and coins; (2) the banker to the government by maintaining its accounts; and (3) advisor to the government in respect to such economic matters as the government may require, including economic development policies and plans and the state budget.

2.5.2 Organization and Management of the Central Bank of Myanmar

The members of the Board of Directors, their terms of office, and their appointment are subject to Clause 25, Subsections (a) to (e) of the law as follows:

(a) The government shall appoint the members of the Board of Directors of the central bank. Such board shall be constituted with seven members.

(b) The board shall consist of the following persons:

- (i) The Governor, the Deputy Governor, and four members appointed by the government.
- (ii) A director appointed ex-officio by the Ministry.

(c) The term of office of the Governor and Deputy Governor of the Board of Directors shall be five years. The term of office of the other members shall be four years. Such persons shall be eligible for reappointment for more than one term.

(d) The Governor and Deputy Governor shall devote their whole time to the functions and duties of the central bank and shall not engage in any other remunerated employment.

(e) The board shall assign an officer of the central bank as secretary of the board.

Furthermore, Clause 29, Subsections (a) to (f), stipulates that the following persons be excepted from appointment: (1) salaried personnel of the government and any organization subordinate to the government (Subsection b); (2) a person who is not a citizen (Subsection c); (3) personnel or the principal shareholders of a bank or financial institution (Subsection f) .

According to Subsection (b), the bank is constitutionally walled off in its decision-making process from influences by other ministries except the Ministry of Finance and Revenue. Compared to the statement that "financial controls over the state enterprises were never exercised" in the previous era, the bank has actually obtained independence thus far.[8]

2.5.3 Relationship between Assignments to the Central Bank of Myanmar and the Government Budget

In relation to the government budget, Clause 55 of the law provides that the Ministry of Finance and Revenue may assign to the bank the issuance of different types of securities under the Government Securities Act and the management of public debt under the State Budget Law enacted annually. In addition, this clause requires that the assignment be in accordance with the terms and conditions agreed to between the Ministry and the CBM. Moreover, Clause 56 requires the bank to advise the government on the placement of its debt instruments with financial institutions and the public.

Current Monetary Status Pertaining to Government Finance

3.1 Expansion of the Public Deficit

The public deficit, composed chiefly of deficits of the state administrative organizations and SEEs has been sharply increasing since fiscal year 1994 (Fig. 9.6).[8] Its level jumped from 15.5 billion to 29.7 billion kyat in fiscal year 1994. A structural change is also to be found in its composition for fiscal year 1996. Since fiscal year 1994, the former has boosted this steady increase, while the latter decreased slightly in fiscal year 1995 to the previous year. By dissolving the expenditure of the SEE into two elements, current and capital expenditures, changes of both compositions are traceable (Fig. 9.8). After the bottom of fiscal year 1993, the share of capital expenditure has risen, reaching 10.8% in fiscal year 1996 when the SEEs' deficit showed about a twofold increase in the same year. The following year, the balance of SEEs considerably worsened due to an expansion of current expenditure, which was incurred mostly by the trade sector (Fig. 9.9).[9]

Figure 9.8 Deficits of State Administrative Organizations and State Economic Enterprises, 1990-97

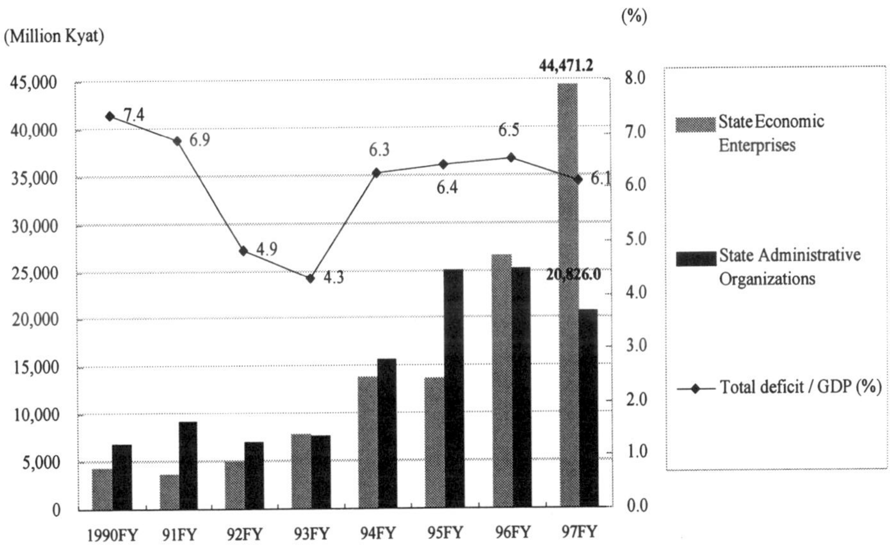

Source: Ministry of National Planning and Economic Development, *Review of Financial, Economic, and Social Conditions*, Various years

Figure 9.9 State Expenditure by Sector, 1994-97

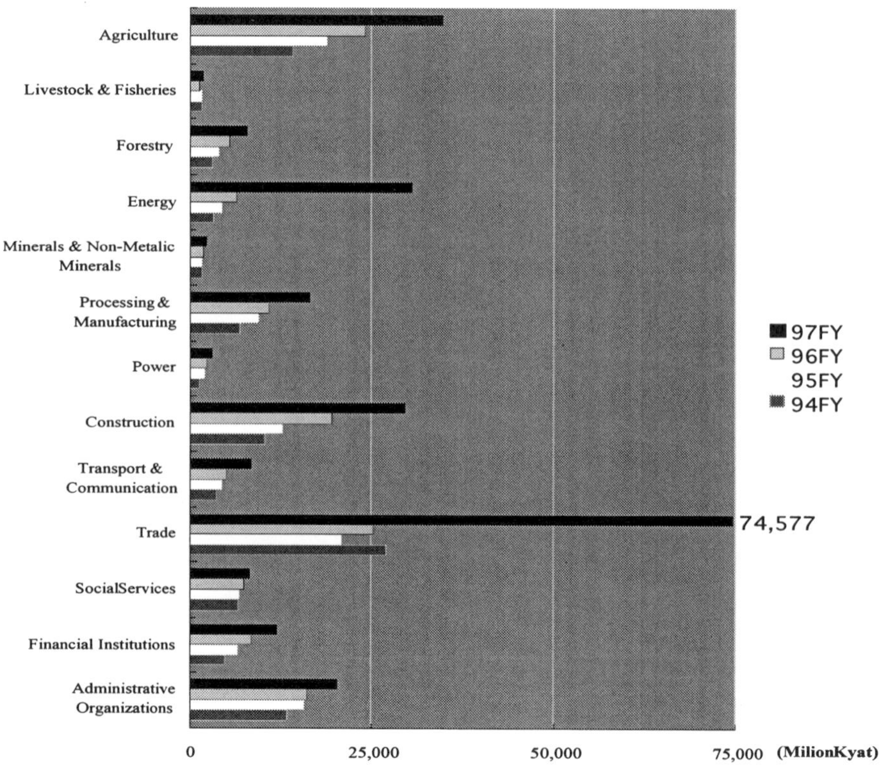

Source: Central Statistical Organization, *Statistical Yearbook, 1997*

Figure 9.10 Overall Expenditure of State Economic Enterprises, 1990-97

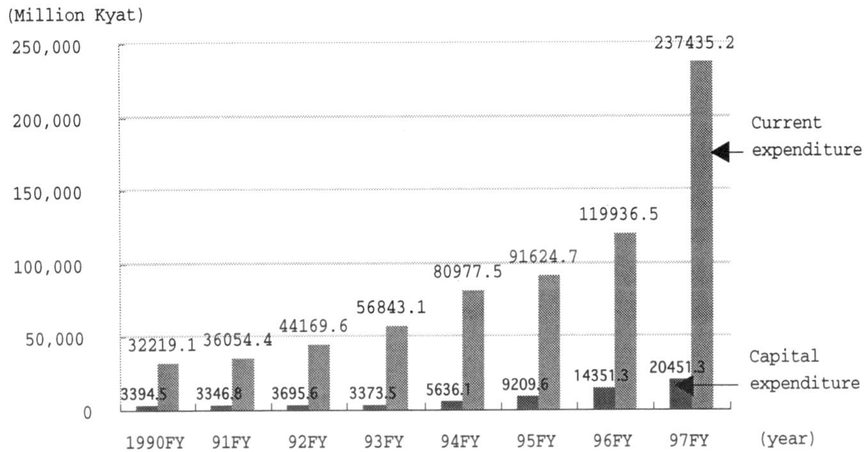

Source: Central Statistical Organization, *Statistical Yearbook, 1997*

3.1.1 Expansion of State-Owned Banks' Investment Account

In the assets of the consolidated balance sheets of SOBs, some apparent changes are observed that seem to be attributable to institutional reform. As shown in Figure 9.8, the amount of "investment," which had remained at the same level until 1988, started to increase abruptly in 1989.[10] This increase has accelerated year by year, and its current level accounts for 31.1% of total assets, second to that of "others" (60.9%). At present, the sorts of valuable instruments that can be held in "investment" accounts are so restricted in Myanmar that it is presumed that its content is government securities or similar items. Assuming this, the securities should have been issued in order to compensate for public revenue and to cover the consequent public deficit.

Figure 9.11 Composition of Assets of State-Owned Banks

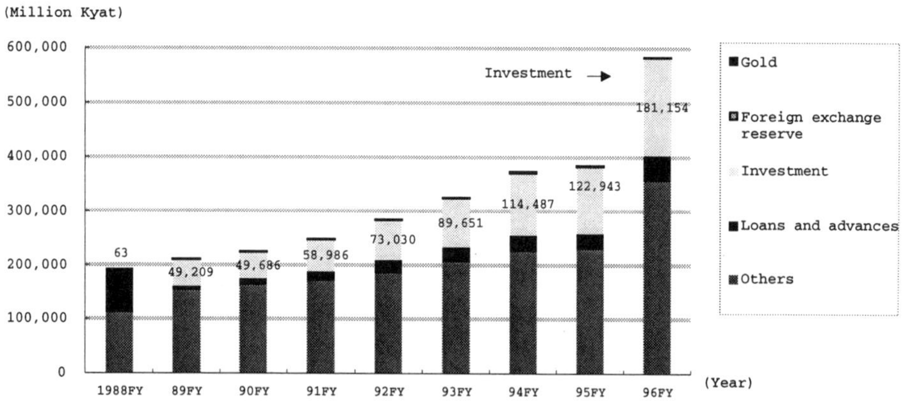

Source: Central Statistical Organization, *Statistical Yearbook, 1997*

3.1.2 Short-term Lending through the Central Bank to the Government

The CBM Law stipulates that the bank may provide various types of loans and advances (hereafter referred to as "short-term lending") to the government that shall be guaranteed by interest-bearing government securities with a maximum term of 184 days (Clause 49, Subsection b).[11] The total of the loans and advances extended within any given year shall not exceed 20% of government receipts of the previous year (Subsection c). In addition to these provisions, the law also provides that the Ministry of Finance and Revenue may assign to the CBM the issuance of various types of securities under the Government Securities Act and the management of public debt under the State Budget Law enacted annually. The increment of "investment" and short-term lending to the government at the maximum facility are shown in Figure 9.12 with the aforesaid public deficit.

3.1.3 Financing Measures for the Public Deficit

Government securities of two types, with a maturity of three years and five years, respectively, were initially sold in 1993.[12] Compared to the level of the public deficit, the aggregate amount of both securities is apparently inadequate for compensating it, even if short-term lending is added to the amount.[13] These can be covered only by including the increment, except that for fiscal year 1995, one year before it augmented to about seven-fold that year. Under a consistent budgetary system, any public deficit that is to be financed must have certain financing measures. Although there is no firm evidence to hand, based, however, on the exemplifying facts above, the approximate amount of the "investment" increment to the public deficit is suggested to be the main measure itself. Thus, due to the expanding public deficit, SOBs seem to be accumulating low-performing assets in the form of government securities, which are so difficult to negotiate that SOBs must inevitably hold them inside themselves. Moreover, unless the public deficit is largely retrenched, the cumulative money supply will follow in consequence. Referring to Clauses 5 and 55 of the law,[14] as for the substantiality of the provisions, how these have actually been applied to prevent deterioration of the currency should be examined.

3.2 Status of Interest Rates: Rise in the Central Bank Rate

Since 1989, when the CBM raised the official discount rate, which had remained unchanged at 4% for nineteen years, to 11.0%, the bank has attempted to bridge the disparity between interest and inflation rates. The bank then raised the interest rate to 12.5% in January 1995 and to 15% in April 1996, respectively, keeping pace with growing inflation rates. However, the level of real interest rates still remained strongly negative (Fig. 9.10) despite repeated hikes in the nominal interest rate. Moreover, the upsurge of the inflation rate (Consumer Price Index at Yangon) since late 1997, which is to be noted as historical with its level of 67.0% in June 1998, is sinking, respective to real interest rates, to less than -46% (Fig.

9.13). Both the maximum lending rate and minimum deposit rate are stipulated, respectively, within +6 points the central bank rate for the former, and -3 points for the latter.

Figure 9.12 Increment of Investment Amount, Deficit Total, Short-Term Lending Facility, and Outstanding Government Treasury Bonds

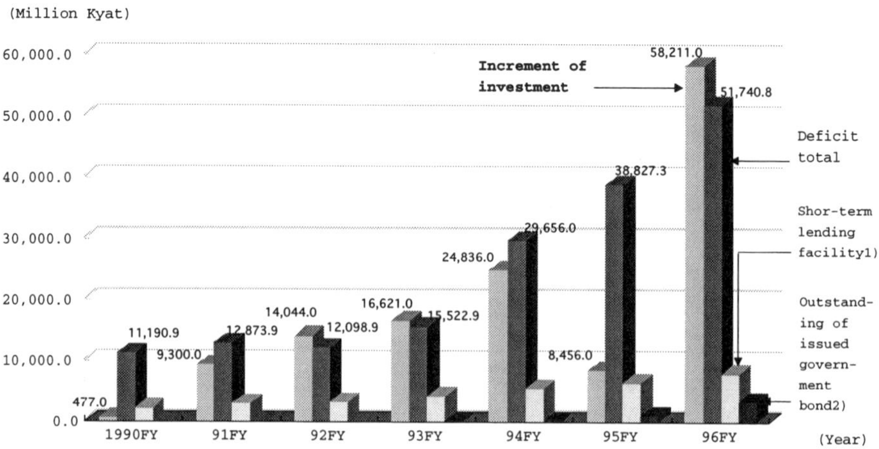

Sources: *Review of Financial, Economic, and Social Conditions for 1996-97*; *Statistical Yearbook, 1997*; *Selected Monthly Economic Indicators*

The previous high was likely caused by the money supply, which quickly expanded and continuously increased then to constantly augmenting public finance demand. As shown in Figure 9.14, the growth rate has a correlation with the lagging inflation rate. The current surge, which has never been recorded, began in 1997, when flooding caused paddy production to fall from government expectations by 8.4% (basket). At the same time a steep devaluation of the kyat resulted in a rise in the imported petrol price that caused a sharp increase in transportation costs, following the aforesaid pile-up of the money supply. In term of saving mobilization as well as the preservation of the kyat's value, it must be said that this level of the real interest rate is nothing more than abnormal. In order to pluck away an already foreseeable seed of hyperinflation and to halt a deterioration of reliance on the kyat, the nominal interest rate should be promptly raised to an adequate level.

Figure 9.13 Real Interest Rates in Myanmar, 1990-98

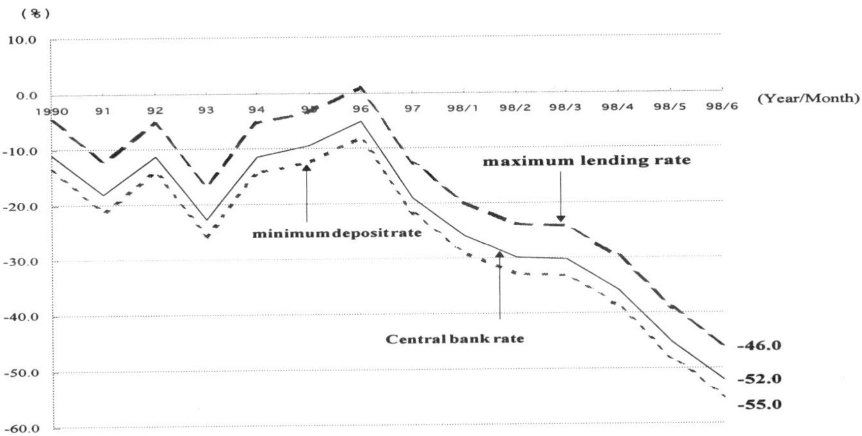

Source: Central Bank of Myanmar, *Selected Monthly Economic Indicators*

3.2.1 Informal Sector Finance

Contrasting with the repressed bank rates, interest rates, which prevail in the informal sector, jut out from the inflation level. According to results of a survey conducted by the Overseas Economic Cooperation Fund of Japan (OECF) in the form of a questionnaire in 1995, more than 40% of money lenders in Yangon Division (51 money lenders) offered 60% of lending rate for working capital to individual borrowers, and a quarter, the same rate for investments by individuals.[15] Converted to real terms, its

its level reached 38.2% that year, when an inflation rate of 21.8% was recorded, while the real interest rate in the formal sector remained at -3.3%. This considerable disparity suggests that any borrower from the formal sector is allowed to enjoy unrealistically discounted interest rates, while the banks renounce their task of strengthening deposit augmentation. However, a scale of this privileged group should be extremely limited, since, as mentioned in 2.2.1 above, the share of bank loans to GDP still remains very limited. Most money lenders, who chiefly rely on their own funds or on close relationships for fund raising, are to a large extent merely inducing the accumulated money into circulation within the same kind of the group (see Figs. 9.21 and 9.22).

Figure 9.14 Year-on-Year Change of General Consumer Price Index at Yangon and Relevant Indices, 1990-98

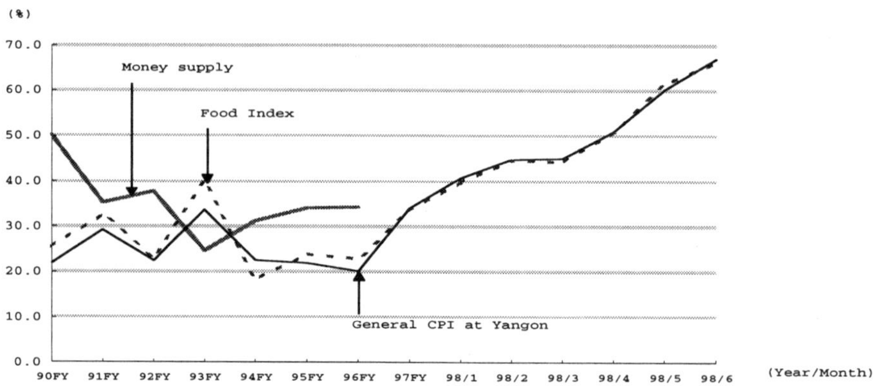

Source: Central Bank of Myanmar, *Selected Monthly Economic Indicators*

Conclusion

It is highly anticipated that Myanmar's economy will for a certain time largely be rooted in and promoted by the small and medium-sized enterprises (SME) that presently dominate whole business entities (Fig. 9.23). In order to foster their sound and stable development, appropriate financial intermediation is apparently indispensable. Conditional upon the effective reduction of the money supply for soothing current rising inflation,

Figure 9.15 Lenders by Lending Interest Rate and Type of Loan for Individuals, 1995

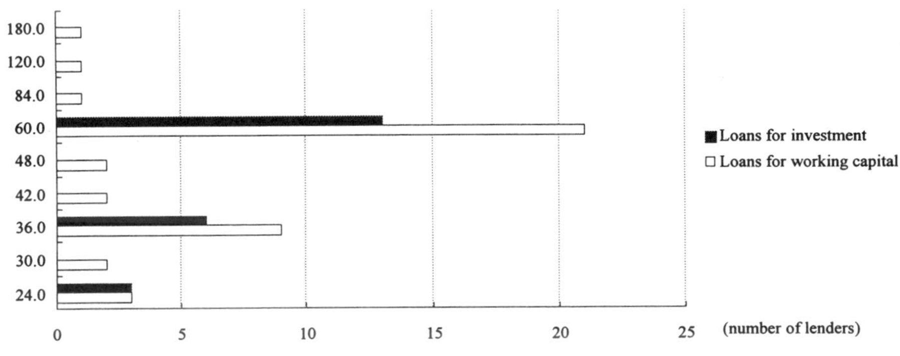

Source: Overseas Economic Cooperation Fund of Japan, data aggregated by author

Figure 9.16 Lenders by Lending Interest Rate and Type of Loan for Private Companies, 1995

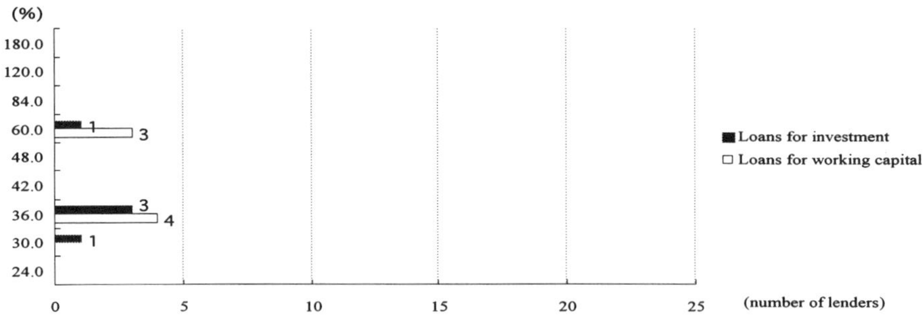

Source: Overseas Economic Cooperation Fund of Japan, data aggregated by author

Figure 9.17 Lenders by Industry of Borrower for Individuals, 1995

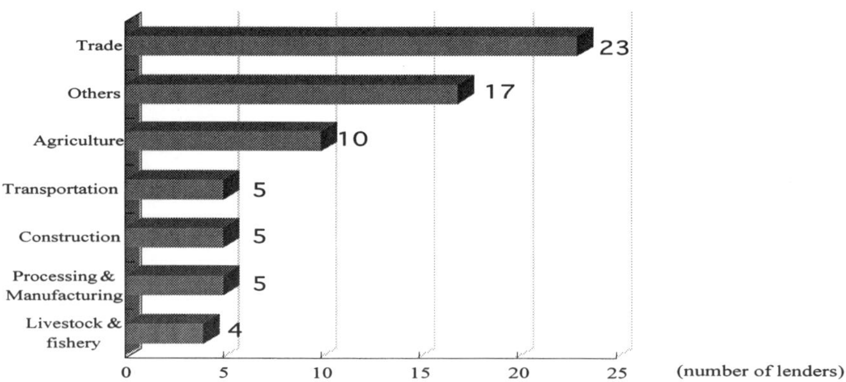

Source: Overseas Economic Cooperation Fund of Japan, data aggregated by author

an adjustment of interest rate levels upward will surely contribute much to this aim. The reduction may be gradual or not, but it should be firm and consistent. This might be as follows: seen from the supply side, so as to implement substantial savings mobilization, the deposit interest rate offered by banks can be raised to a certain extent, at the inflation level, or, alternatively, at least near it. The lending rate must also then be simultaneously raised. However, taking into account the necessity of providing lending in adequate volume to as many entrepreneurs as possible for the long- and medium-term at a rational rate, it needs to be much lower than the rates for the informal sector.

Figure 9.18 Lenders by Industry of Borrower for Private Companies, 1995

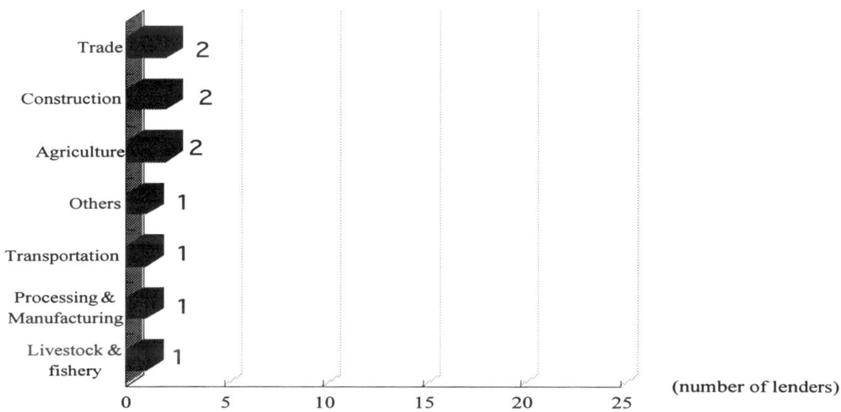

Source: Overseas Economic Cooperation Fund of Japan, data aggregated by author

Figure 9.19 Lenders by Term of Lending for Working Capital, 1995

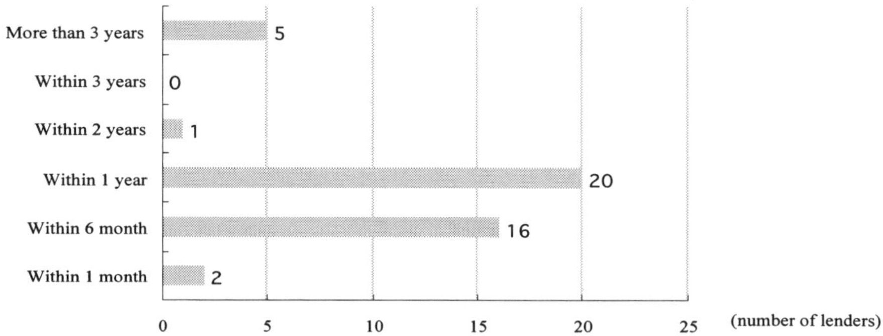

Source: Overseas Economic Cooperation Fund of Japan, data aggregated by author

Figure 9.20 Lenders by Term of Lending for Investment, 1995

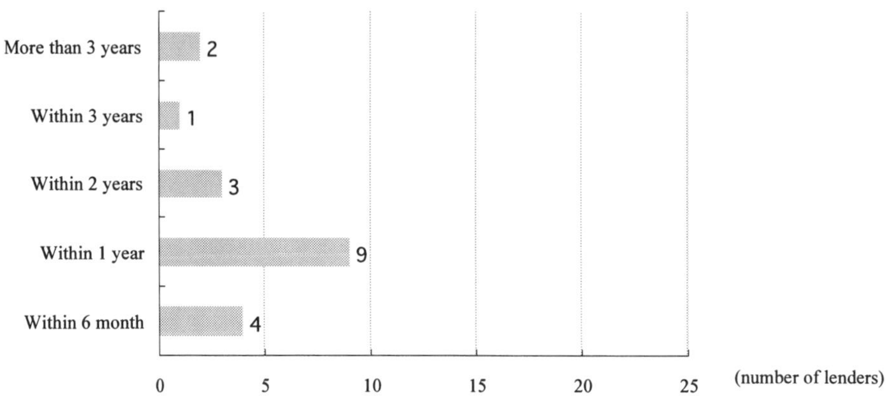

Source: Overseas Economic Cooperation Fund of Japan, data aggregated by author

Figure 9.21 Lenders by Type of Fund-Raising Source

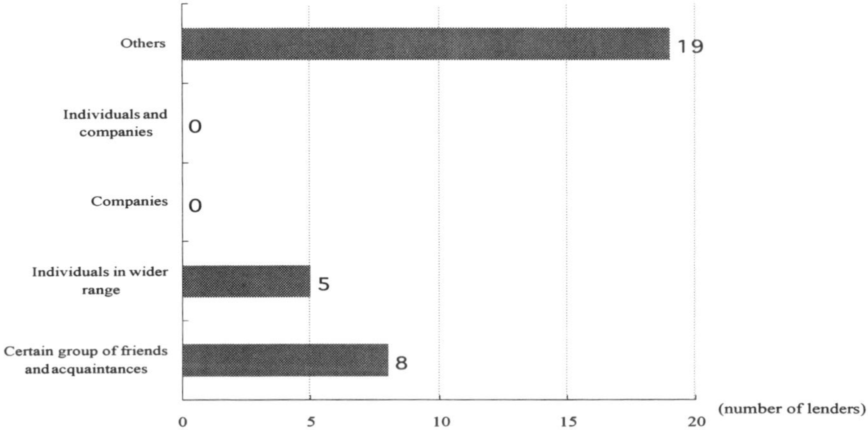

Source: Overseas Economic Cooperation Fund of Japan, data aggregated by author

Figure 9.22 Lenders by Type of Borrower

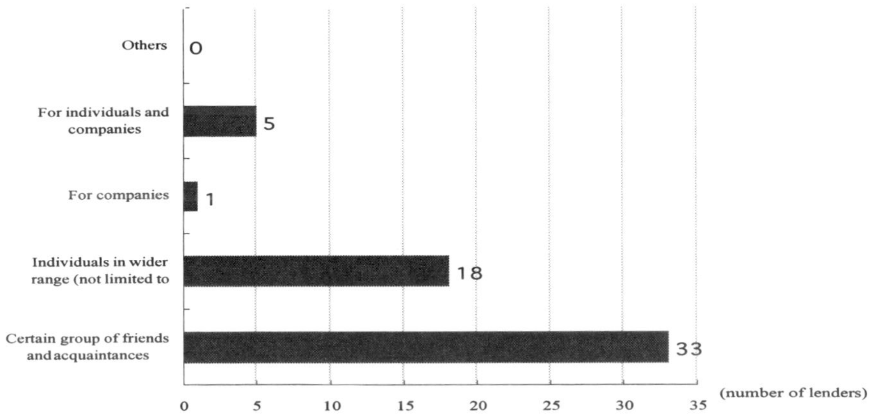

Source: Overseas Economic Cooperation Fund of Japan, data aggregated by author

Figure 9.23 Factories and Establishments by Number of Workers (FY1997, provisional)

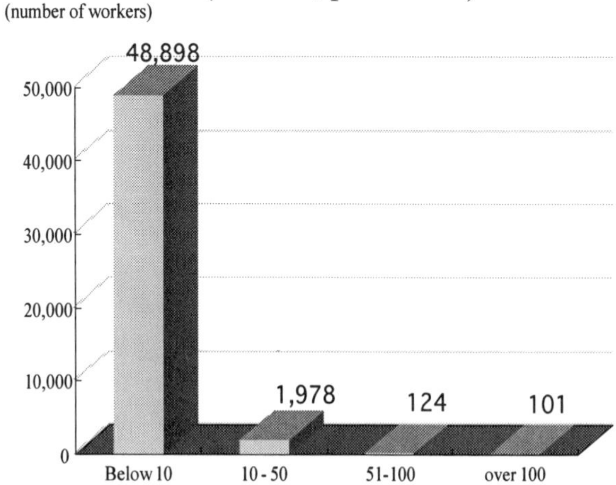

Source: *Review of Financial, Economic, and Social Conditions for 1996-97*

Notes

[1] Credit to the public sector comprises claims on non-financial public enterprises and the central government.

[2] The government exchanged old bank notes with newly issued notes at prior demonetizations in 1964 and 1985 but not in 1987.

[3] Myanmar: Sustaining Economic Growth and Development, *Asian Development Bank, August 1995. Par. 92. The SEEs are expressed here as SOEs (state-owned enterprises).*

[4] *Ibid.*, Par. 112.

[5] *Ibid.*, Par. 92.

[6] Calculation based on "Loans and Advances" in "Consolidated Balance Sheet" of *Statistical Yearbook, 1997.*

[7] Rural socio-economic enterprises are defined in Clause 2, Subsection (i) as "agro- and livestock-based industries and rural development activities."

[8] Pradumna B. Rana and Naved Hamid, eds., *The Centrally Planned to Market Economies: The Asian Approach* (New York: Oxford University Press for the Asian Development Bank, 1995-96), Vol. 3: 201.

[9] In the *Statistical Yearbook* as well as the *Review of Financial, Economic, and Social Conditions*, public finance comprises three kinds of budgets, including the two aforementioned, and "Development Committees Receipt" in which surplus (+) and deficit (-) items are stated. Those of the Development Committees for the term of fiscal years 1990-96 are, in millions of kyat, -13.1, +562.5, -4.0, +5.5, +8.8, +7.8, +7.8, respectively.

[10] Refer to 1.4. "Conversion of Outstanding Loans to Government Securities in 1989."

[11] Moreover, Clause 49, Subsection (e) of the law stipulates that notwithstanding anything contained in Subsection (b), the CBM may agree to purchase, hold, or sell government securities with a maturity of not more than 365 days.

[12] Since the interest rates for both kinds of government securities (10.0% per annum for three-year bonds, 10.5% for five-year bonds) existed even before 1993, it is probable that they had been issued before then.

[13] Refer to Section 1.4. "Conversion of Outstanding Loans to Government Securities in 1989" and, above all, to the restriction to financing measures for SEEs under the SFA system, Section 2.5.3.1."Expansion of the Public Deficit."

[14] For Clause 5, refer to Section 2.5. "Promulgation of the CBM Law in 1990," and for Clause 55, refer to Section 2.5.3. "Relationship between Assignments to the CBM and the Government Budget."

[15] The interest rates on a monthly basis filled in in the questionnaire are converted to an annual basis (simple interest rate).

10

Industrial Development and Inter-Firm Division of Labor in Myanmar

Tetsuo Minato
Aoyama Gakuin University, Tokyo

The Asian Miracle and Technological Progress

According to Paul Krugman, economic growth in East Asian countries—which have been highly commended as a successful example of economic development—has mainly been driven by the quantitative expansion of the factors of production, such as labor and capital.[1] His work has stirred widespread controversy because of its shocking claim that a reduction of manpower reserves would bring an end to high growth. Indeed, the severity of the Asian financial crisis since July 1997 would appear to prove Krugman's assumptions. However, the severity of the crisis varies within East Asian countries, and some countries in the region even retain a potential capacity for high economic growth.

The most important implication of Krugman's work is that in order to maintain growth the economic growth must be greater than the portion of quantitative expansion of production factors. In other words, one must raise the productivity of the production factors and accumulate innovations in the broad sense, such as shifting the production function itself to a high level. Econometricians usually adopt the production function of the national economy and deduct the contribution portion of quantitative increases in capital and labor in economic growth to arrive at the residual portion, which is estimated as the contribution of technological progress. In the case of the Japanese economy, it is estimated that the contribution degree of this residual portion from the beginning of the twentieth century to the mid-1960s reached approximately 50%.[2] This means that the contribution of quantitative expansion of production factors introduced and the contribution of technological progress were practically even.

What can be achieved by such technological progress in developing economies? There are two types of innovation: product innovation (the manufacture of new products) and process innovation (the modernization of production processes). In many cases, product innovation has been accomplished in the advanced economies, while for developing economies the major issue is how effectively such product innovations can be introduced and applied. Therefore, the source of technological progress for developing economies is not product innovation but process innovation. What type of industrial system is needed to achieve efficient process innovation? In modern industry, production processes are well divided into specific and specialized areas. This division in turn spawns the division of labor and improved productivity—the essence of none other than Adam Smith's "wealth of nations." Economic development in modern times has certainly brought about the division of labor. As a result of industrial development, production processes became complex and specialization lines longer. In today's industrial society, it is impossible to organize such long lines within single company units; production activity is the result of a division of labor among many companies. The level of process innovation dictates the ideal system of the division of labor.

There are two types of corporate sector—large companies, and small and medium-sized companies—each with different management characteristics. If the inter-firm division of labor is organized along the lines of these two sectors, significant economic progress becomes possible. Large companies and small and medium-sized companies are equally important elements in the industrial structure of various countries. Small and medium-sized companies are not concentrated in urban areas but scattered throughout a country, using technologies and resources at the grass-roots level. They serve as the "vital majority" by together accounting for the major share of a country's employment.

Large companies possess abundant managerial resources and excel in terms of capital, technological, and marketing power. By contrast, they are unable to undertake focused technological development, their decision-making processes are complicated and time-consuming, and providing motivation for a large number of employees is not simple. On the other hand, small and medium-sized companies lack managerial resources. Such companies, however, enable fast decision-making, flexible adjustment, and close communication between management and staff. Accordingly, managers in small and medium-sized companies can get to know the personalities, strengths, and weaknesses of individual employees and can assign the most appropriate tasks to each. Moreover, they can accurately assess the contribution level of each employee and provide more precise work incentives. In addition, although each small and medium-sized company is responsible for production processes in an extremely narrowly defined scope, all their attention is focused on their specific field. As a result, incremental progress in production technologies can be expected. The actual experience of Japan has been that subcontractors initially received production technology-related assistance from their parent companies. Over the years, such contractors mastered the technologies and eventually reached more advanced levels of process technologies than their parent companies. In these ways, the specialization of production processes automatically led to a division of technological territory, and the level of the division of labor rose so high as to cause fractionalization among companies.

For small and medium-sized companies, raising funds externally is not easy, and the cost of interest in raising such funds is higher than for large companies. As a result, they have a strong incentive to refine production technologies that save capital. Compared with large companies, they have lower labor productivity but a higher capital productivity. By smoothly integrating large companies and small and medium-sized companies—

with their differing managerial characteristics—and separating production processes to maximize the advantages possessed by each, the potential for technological progress driven by process innovation increases. This is a decisively important factor for maintaining the technological progress rate necessary for sustained economic growth and also for securing a competitive position in markets open to international competition.

Global Mega-Competition and Inter-Firm Productivity

In the twenty-first century, Asian economies will look toward abolishing industrial protection import restrictions and integrating into the world economy. ASEAN, of which Myanmar is a member, is seeking to shift toward implementing the ASEAN Free Trade Agreement (AFTA) early in the twenty-first century. In the increasingly border-free world economy, mega-competition will become normal, and any nation lacking an effective industrial "competitive edge"—namely, a strategic system of a division of labor across companies—will probably not survive.

Various developing nations have adopted import substitute policies under trade protection. These policies have led to the increasing production of "import substituted goods," but many of these goods will not be able to withstand global competition. Creating "merchandized products" that can compete in internationally open markets is fundamentally different from producing "import substituted goods under protection." It is vitally important that this difference be recognized. Survival against global competition calls for certain product characteristics, namely, continuous cost reductions, ceaseless quality improvements, incorporation of the latest technologies, and abundant and readily accessible product variations. Acquiring all these product characteristics would be difficult for a single company since doing so requires establishing a production system of efficient inter-firm production sharing, namely, high "inter-firm productivity."

The direct cause of the Asian financial crisis that began in mid-1997 was, as many economists have pointed out, the unstable movement of large volumes of short-term capital, an international financial problem. However, the more substantial problem causing the Asian crisis was that those countries were late in building the industrial infrastructure that serves as the foundation for international competitiveness that, in turn, is essential in the era of mega-competition.

Since the mid-1990s, exports from China to the world markets have expanded at an accelerated pace, and in 1996 the share of Chinese imports to the United States surpassed that of the six major ASEAN economies combined. In Japan, too, imports from China are approaching the ASEAN level. Many Chinese exports are labor-intensive products competing directly with traditional exports from the ASEAN nations. In order to avoid direct competition with China and secure competitiveness in international markets, ASEAN economies turned to developing mass-production-type machinery-based industries, manufacturing such items as automobiles and electronic products. Such industries require a large number of suppliers of numerous components and of supporting industries to handle the growing number of production processes. In other words, suppliers must provide a diverse range of materials and components, and producers must organize a stable and efficient parts supply network with numerous suppliers. Indeed, entire national economies must foster the formation of inter-firm transaction networks based on deep trust. Only by creating such a system of efficient inter-firm division of labor as an industrial infrastructure can an economy begin to supply products that are internationally competitive. However, some Asian countries undertook large-scale investments to establish mass-production systems to make such items as automobiles and electronic products without having an efficient inter-firm division of labor system in place. This is similar to attempting to construct a multistory building without laying a foundation.

By contrast, Taiwan could respond flexibly to rapid changes in technology and the market because of its developed network of inter-firm division of labor driven mainly by its small and medium-sized companies. It now has the top world share for production of personal computer motherboards and enjoys overwhelming international competitiveness in the electronics industry. Accordingly, the Asian financial crisis had a minimal effect on Taiwan.

We can conclude that the level of severity of the Asian financial crisis in various nations is proportional to the insufficiency of development of the social division of labor networks serving as a production foundation, as compared with the level of actual dependence on industry of the mass-production type. In order to extricate themselves from the crisis, therefore, Asian nations must do more than simply tightening controls on international capital flows and other adjustments to financial systems; instead, they must construct efficient inter-firm production sharing systems with a built-in potential for more sustained technological progress.

Division of Labor Determined by Accumulation of Trust Value

As explained above, the process of economic development is synchronous with the inter-firm division of labor. What factors determine the development of such a division? The prophecy of Adam Smith that the "extent of division of labor is limited by the size of the market" remains strongly supported even today as the determining factor for the level of division of labor. Certainly, economies with small market sizes cannot expect to raise productivity through the division of labor. However, the modern era is different from Adam Smith's time. In today's industrial society, with its accomplished market economies, it is generally not difficult to secure the minimum market size necessary for creating an inter-firm division of labor. In today's production processes, where lines are long and complex, a system in which all production processes are integrated into a single company would clearly be inefficient. The problem is the cost involved in integrating specialized inter-firm production processes into the final production process via market mechanisms. In other words, transaction cost size determines the level of the division of labor. If the implementation of the division of labor requires high transaction costs—to the extent that the cost negates the benefits of higher productivity expected to result from division of labor—the progress of the division of labor will be impeded. Therefore, a social system that restricts transaction costs is necessary for developing the inter-firm division of labor.

The inter-firm division of labor is implemented through transactions, but one important factor raises such transaction costs: the cost of suppressing the danger of opportunistic behavior among transacting parties. To put it another way, the size of various transaction costs necessary to suppress opportunistic behavior is determined by the amount of a certain invisible value existing in society, namely, the trust value needed to restrain inter-firm transaction costs.

Kenneth Arrow sums it up excellently: "Societies in their evolution have developed implicit agreements to certain kinds of regards for each others, agreements which are essential to the survival of the society or at least contribute greatly to the efficiency of its working. It has been observed, for example, that among the properties of many societies whose economic development is backward is a lack of mutual trust."[3] Nevertheless, he argues: "The agreement to trust each other can not be bought, as I have said; it is not even necessarily very easy for it to be achieved by a signed contract saying that we will work with each other."[4] Arrow also states: "Now trust has a very important pragmatic value, if nothing else. Trust is an important lubricant of a social system. It is extremely efficient; it saves a lot of trouble to have a fair degree of reliance on other people's word. Unfortunately this is not a commodity which can be brought very easily."[5]

Oliver Williamson takes Arrow's argument further: "One would expect, accordingly, that vertical integration would be more complete in a low-trust that a high-trust culture, *ceteris paribus.*"[6] In other words, he demonstrates an important opinion that could be expressed as: "The level of division of labor is determined by the level of trust." If we follow Williamson's argument, we can say that good development and the spread of a Japanese subcontracting production system stems from the abundant supply of "trust value." Perhaps an underlying factor in the retarded development of specialized inter-firm production systems in many developing nations is the insufficient accumulated trust value that can be utilized for the benefit of the entire economy of each nation.

Creation of Trust Value and Social Norms

To answer the question of how trust value is generated and accumulated in Japan's inter-firm transactions, we must closely examine the socio-cultural context from a historical perspective. The evolution of a stable socio-economy during the long Tokugawa period may have played a major role in promoting widespread awareness of the importance of "trust" or "good will" in conducting transactions. In any case, the foundation for the evolution of trust-based relationships in inter-firm transactions has notable historical backing. There is more to this than the foundation, however. The reason that trust-based relationships have continued to this day without major loss and that smoothness of inter-firm transactions has been maintained is that a socio-economic framework prioritizing maintenance of trust-based relationships has been established.

Inter-firm transactions have been managed smoothly without depending on legal basics, such as written contracts, because social norms concerning transactions have been established. Jeffrey Pfeffer has the following to say in regard to social norms that regulate mutually dependent inter-organizational relationships:

> The presence of a norm may be inferred by two means. When all social actors behave in a similar way in a particular situation there is a possibility that they are being influenced by a norm. This is an imperfect way of knowing that a norm exists, for in fact the actors could be behaving independently, having arrived at the same decision because it represents the best way to behave. When theatergoers arrive for a play at eight, they are not following a norm, but rather responding to the schedule established by the producer. More telling evidence of a norm is discovered when the norm is violated. If sanctions are applied when the actors behave in certain ways, it is likely that a commonly shared norm is operating. Even this method, however, fails to distinguish between norms and the power of another to impose constraints. Norms are commonly or widely shared sets of behavioral expectations.

> Although it is possible to be sanctioned by a single social actor, it is only when most social actors sanction the behavior that we can say a norm exists.[7]

It is a fact that in inter-firm transactions in Japan, social norms, as pointed out by Pfeffer, exist. Such norms help stabilize inter-firm relationships and allow people to depend on tacit agreements without legal contracts.

In many developing nations, it is not unusual to see situations within certain community-based business groups such as the *pang* of the overseas Chinese, whereby group norms are established in order to restrict and control opportunism in the economic activities of group members. However, there are not necessarily numerous cases in which uniformly available trust-based relationships and social norms are established throughout a national economy. As a result, while there is no problem if business activities are limited to certain business group members, there are major restrictions in realizing the advanced industrial structure necessary for numerous inter-firm transactions nationwide.

Myanmar's Industrial Development and Inter-Firm Division of Labor

The impressions obtained from our survey of Myanmar is that there is no shortage of small and medium-sized enterprises that form supporting industries, such as casting and machine processing. However, the formation of organic linkages or close business relationships between large companies and small and medium-sized companies is retarded, and apart from imported parts and components, almost all production processes occur within a company. Even in small and medium-sized companies, the share of components procured from outside is very low, and almost all processes handled within their small factories are done in a manner that is close to hand-made.

There are several reasons why the development of Myanmar's inter-firm division of labor system has lagged. First, as stated in Adam Smith's words: “The extent of division of labor is limited by market size.” Market expansion strong enough to stimulate inter-firm division of labor is not evident in Myanmar, and mass-production-type machinery-based industries, for example, for making durable goods, are underdeveloped. Secondly, the economy has not faced international market competition for a long period, and thus the incentive to create “competitive products” via the inter-firm division of labor has been low. Thirdly, there is an insufficient accumulation of trust among firms, which results from indecision about expanding mutually dependent transaction relationships with outside companies. Nevertheless, there are two important issues for the future. First, there is a crucial need to introduce mass-production-type industries that will foster further industrialization. Secondly, if Myanmar is concerned about pressure to shift to a market economy open to international competition, it will need to develop its inter-firm production system.

Overview of On-Site Survey

We conducted an interview-style survey of fifteen companies in the Yangon and Mandalay regions in August 1998. Despite the limited number of companies surveyed, we were able to gain an understanding of the current situation of the inter-firm division of labor in Myanmar, and began studying the potential of progress in this area.

Let us begin by looking at the status of the supporting industries necessary for developing mass-production-type industries. Small and medium-sized companies involved in metal foundry and machine processing account for at least half of the companies in supporting industries. There are apparently nearly 1,000 metal foundry factories in the Mandalay region alone. In addition, in the industrial zones of the two regions surveyed there are numerous very small machine-processing factories, most having fewer than ten employees. However, many of the machine-processing factories are not processing components at the request of mass-production industries, but are engaged in the production of replenishment components by re-using second-hand parts. Therefore, they do not constitute a supporting industry.

Among metal foundries, several provide a supporting industry role by producing intermediary commodities on order from companies manufacturing pumps and other metal-based products. Many companies produce end-products, such as water pipes. There are a number of plastic-molding companies, producing daily-use items such as washbasins, buckets, and baskets. Also plentiful are metal-molding production factories and very small companies used by the plastic-molding companies. We were able to visit one company that makes precision metal molds for industrial products, but since mass-production-type industries necessary for precision metal molding are almost completely undeveloped in Myanmar, such factories languish because of a lack of customers.

On the other hand, although there are some large state-owned enterprises engaged in metal forging and heat processing, which are essential for production of durable machine components, there are practically no specialist corporations that can be used by private sector small and medium-sized companies. In order to solve the problem of a lack of such supporting industries, large state-owned enterprises must split off these production processes, and a reformed system must be put into place that can respond to demand from private-sector companies.

Although there are some kinds of supporting industries for making basic forms of products in Myanmar, there are practically no supporting industries necessary for making high-quality products. As a result, small and medium-sized businesses, which have made almost no progress in the inter-firm division of labor, conduct most production processes in-house. To cite an example, we visited a medium-sized food- processing machine manufacturer in Mandalay that makes food blenders. All production processes are handled in-house except for electric plating. One component of its products, a receptacle, was not made using a press process but by hand-welding two sheets of stainless steel. In addition, the foundry-made gears had not been heat-treated. To be sure, while the food blenders functioned satisfactorily, they could not be competitive in a market open to international competition. (Picture 1)

Typical Cases of Surveyed Small and Medium-Sized Companies

The T. F. A. Company, Yangon, is involved in plastic mold processing, and manufactures some of the metal molds necessary for such in-house processing. The company employs forty-five people. It has a 450-ton injection-molding machine, and produces daily-use items, including seven types of bucket, seven types of washbasin, and two types of basket. The company was established in 1991, but for twenty years prior to that the current management was involved in molding on a self-employed basis. It contracts out the manufacture of 40% of its metal molds, with orders for precision models going to Taiwan. It has transactions with ten domestic metal mold companies, but there are numerous problems with deliveries and quality. The company's products are sold to various regional wholesalers. Since it limits sales to stores with which it has built up good will over many years, there are few sales-related problems. However, its policy is to terminate transactions with those late in paying. It has transactions with one bank but has almost no borrowing ability since this would require collateral. (Picture 2)

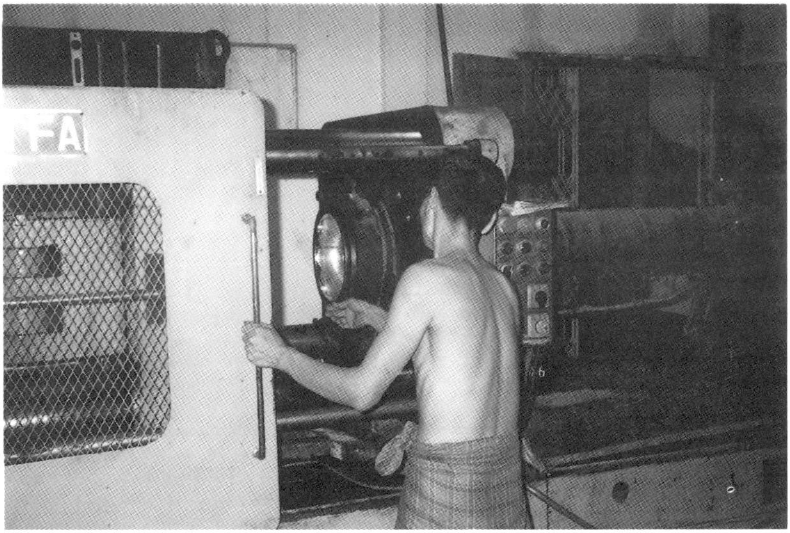

The M. I. Z. Company, Mandalay, established in 1978, produces replacement machinery parts at its single factory in an industrial zone. It has eleven employees. A technician who studied machinery at university is the manager and supervises the actual workings of the factory. The company is particularly strong in the production of gears for replacement use including gears for textile machines, flourmills, and automobiles. It has accounts with two hundred companies, with continuous transactions with around twenty. It orders cast metal ingredients from outside, namely, three companies for pig-iron casting and two each for aluminum and copper. Apart from casting, it rarely makes outside purchases, and there appear to be no transactions with companies in the same industry. Heat treatment is done using a small hand-made charcoal burner set up in a corner. (Picture 3)

The S. L. Company, Yangon, is a precision metal-molding company established in February 1997. It has five employees all of whom are trainees recently graduated from high school. The manager studied applied chemistry at university, then worked in a metal-molding company in Hong Kong for eighteen years, learning various technologies before returning to Myanmar. While in Hong Kong, he was appointed supervisor at his company's Chinese subsidiary and was responsible for managing one hundred employees. Based on this experience, he designs metal molds using computer-aided design (CAD). He has advanced production technologies, including a second-hand CNC machine. Although such precision metal-molding companies are essential for developing mass production industries, there is practically no mass production industry in the country at present, so the company's technologies do not seem to be properly used. Currently, there are a few orders for metal molds for industrial-use components and only small-lot orders for regular-use molds, so the company repairs imported molds. In order to overcome the order slump, the company has purchased a small plastic injection-molding machine, and uses metal molds made in-house to produce high-precision plastic containers. As a result, it manages to maintain a flow of business. The company requires 50% payment up front at the time of contract for metal mold orders. (Picture 4)

The S. E. M. Company, Yangon, manufactures transformers and compact electricity generators. The company's manager graduated from a technical high school in 1970 and immediately started a business repairing electrical goods (motors, transformers, and generators). In the 1990s, the company became a manufacturer of large-scale transformers and compact electricity generators. It is currently the sole maker of large transformers in Myanmar. The company employs more than fifty people, seven of whom are technicians. The reason for its success as a manufacturer of finished industrial-use transformers lies in the management's emphasis on product quality. Employees are subject to technical training to ensure that quality control is firmly implemented at the manufacturing stages. The company has also rebuilt a second-hand television broadcast vehicle imported from Japan for use as its service car. The car travels to various regional areas to install transformers and provide meticulous after-sales service. The company has also employed a retired former technical college principal with a degree in engineering from an American university as its technical manager. This is another factor raising the company's technological level.

Companies like this, where management places high priority on product quality, are not common in Myanmar. The reason can probably be traced to the manager's twenty years of experience in equipment repair from which he gained familiar insight into strong user demands for trouble-free products. (Picture 5)

Although the company makes electrical equipment, namely transformers and generators, it rarely contracts work outside. Its main material, silicon steel, is imported from a major producer in Japan; it imports copper wire from a Japanese-related company in Thailand, insulation wire from Singapore, and ceramic insulation from Italy. Therefore, the company depends on imports for materials that are directly related to product quality and function. Domestic procurements are limited to bolts, nuts, craft paper, and packaging materials. The cost of purchasing these materials and parts accounts for 25% of total production costs, and the value-added component produced by the company is estimated at nearly 70%. The company is currently building a new large-scale factory. Construction funds mainly come from borrowings from the owner's acquaintances. The company is not seeking bank financing due to the complex procedures involved.

The H. H. K. Company, Yangon, manufactures knitted and embroidery products for export. Products are mainly exported to the United States and Western Europe. The company has a 50:50 joint venture with a Malaysian firm and capital is procured domestically. The company's manager is operating a trading company, after having been a Myanmar military officer and working at Myanmar Airlines. The actual general manager supervising operations is the manager's younger sister, who has experience in a state-owned textile company. Today, the company produces 4,000 units of knitted products per month, using twenty-seven Chinese-made knitting machines. Its yarn is imported from Indonesia. A separate firm conducts sales, and the company specializes in manufacturing as a subcontractor for an export trading company, which consequently provides instructions for all designs and other specifications. The company employs around 300 people, but pays female employees according to output (by the number of pieces). Since operations only recently began, there is still not enough workload and some female employees are thus idle. The factory is new and neatly maintained, with lighting at appropriate levels. To help get production under way, the company is receiving guidance from three textile technicians, from China, Hong Kong, and Taiwan. (Picture 6)

The T. S. Company, Yangon, an apparel manufacturer established in 1994, is a private company under the umbrella of the Ministry of Cooperatives. It has ten investors, three of whom are directors. The top manager was a doctor in a national hospital with no experience in running a company. Accordingly, the niece of the company's president, who has fifteen years of experience in a state-owned textile firm, is responsible for operations. The company's principal production equipment consists of fifty used sewing machines purchased from Daewoo. For the first six months of operation, the company served as production subcontractor for Daewoo. This was because, at the time, Daewoo was receiving steady orders that exceeded its production capacity. Although the sub-contractual relationship ended after six months, it helped the company master production technologies as it was getting its factory up and running, which was very beneficial. The company currently employs 180 people. New employees undergo two weeks of basic training as apprentices. After a further six months to one year of work, they are rewarded as technicians. Since Myanmarese women are usually trained in knitting at home, they have great capacity to master technical skills. The wage system is based on efficiency, and skilled workers make an average of 5-6,000 kyat per month.

The company does more than receiving design instructions and raw fabric from its export trading company. It also receives a supply of peripheral materials (knitting yarn, buttons, cloth tape) and manufactures under subcontract. It has continued transaction relationships with two trading companies. Recently, there has been an increase in apparel production in Myanmar, centering on subcontracting. This is due to the abundant supply of low-cost labor as well as to a surplus in the export quota under the multinational textile agreement. In a country where supporting industries are underdeveloped, Myanmar relies almost completely on imports not only for production equipment but also for raw materials. Since the trading companies that place the orders supply production materials, there are few problems, but maintaining production equipment is proving difficult. Apparel subcontractors depend on simple attachments for their sewing machines, but these are also imported; and at US$2-3 per unit, importing traders do not actively handle such items. As a result, manufacturers must purchase large numbers of these items and keep them in stock. (Picture 7)

The S. M. Company, Yangon, established with Norwegian capital, received its business authorization in 1993 and commenced operations in 1994. Using Myanmar-made teak, it manufactures high-quality household furniture and high-quality wooden rowing boats for export to Western European countries. In addition to three hundred production staff, it has fifty non-production employees involved in such areas as security. The average monthly salary for an operator is 4-5,000 kyat per month, which rises to about 7,000 kyat when overtime is included. The salary for managers is about 20,000 kyat.

Myanmar-made wood accounts for a large portion of production materials, and the company uses imported sandpaper and cutting tools. It orders brass foundry parts from domestic foundry manufacturers, of which it has continuous relationships with three companies. When it began operations, the companies sent a prototype model when it ordered its brass foundry parts, but most of the products delivered were defective. It has since made part of its payments in hard currency and endeavored to invest in production equipment (such as transformers, telecommunications equipment, and personal computers) necessary for improving its production technologies. As a result, it has raised product quality and reduced defective product ratios to below 10%. Although 10% is a fairly high level, it is still better than the minimum level necessary for receiving continued subcontracting orders in a developing economy.

Outlook for Developing Linkages between Large and Small Businesses

In order to study the potential for the development of the inter-firm division of labor in Myanmar, two factors must be considered. First, the current status of production and management technologies in various companies involved in supporting industries must be evaluated. To gain insight into the future potential of these technologies, the systematic frameworks for diffusing and absorbing technologies must also be studied. Secondly, since the inter-firm division of labor takes place via inter-firm transactions, the social systems for saving transaction costs—namely, the level of accumulated trust—must also be evaluated. This will involve looking at the effectiveness of market mechanisms or determining the level of transaction costs necessary for utilizing markets.

To look at the technological side first. Quantitatively speaking, the small and medium-sized companies visited had sufficient production equipment. The machine processing factories had numerous machines lined up in a very limited space. Many of the machines are old, Chinese-made, and second-hand, and we even saw an English-made drilling machine made in the 1920s. We saw practically no computerized numerically controlled (NC) machinery.

Even with such old equipment, it is possible to produce satisfactory processing precision if the equipment is properly set up and operated by skilled technicians. Until the early 1960s, much of the machinery in small and medium-sized Japanese machine factories was old, second-hand equipment. Companies actively purchased such equipment, which was operated by skilled workers who maintained well and monitored closely the equipment's characteristics, leading to a high level of processing accuracy. In Myanmar's small and medium-sized machine processing factories, however, there are few skilled workers. It is not unusual to see youths aged 13 or 14 operating machinery. (Picture 8, page 292) It normally takes nearly ten years of on-the-job training to become a skilled operator, but in Myanmar operators are considered skilled if they complete a six-month apprenticeship followed by two to three years of work experience. Because even skilled operators receive a mere 200 kyat per day (5,000 kyat per month), there is little incentive to acquire higher skills. Consequently, many shift to different jobs rather than remain as mechanics for long periods of time.

In Myanmar today, there is little industry that requires high-precision processing and minimal interest among machine processing factory managers in nurturing such skills. Instead, attention is focused on how many costs can be reduced. As a result, people do not develop the craftsmanship required for high-precision processing, so industries related to high-precision processing do not evolve, leading to a vicious cycle. The problem is not so much the age of machinery but the absence of a system conducive to the formation of skills for the effective use of production equipment. What is needed is a social system that generates a positive upward spiral. Such a system would entail the objective evaluation of the skill levels of factory workers, with systematic remuneration that reflects such skill levels. This will help enhance social appraisal and the pride of the workers, emphasizing skill development on the production floor that in turn will further raise technical levels.

The pace at which a country's industry raises its technological level depends on how well the system has evolved in which advanced technologies can be transferred smoothly from one sector to another with a lower technological level. In the case of Japan, the system of subcontracting production had a decisive effect on technology transfers between firms.

In the early stages of machine industrial development, production technologies were transferred from parent companies to subcontractors. After that, the subcontractors became proficient in production technologies in narrowly defined areas of specialization, allowing them to propose a diversity of improvements related to processing technologies, where they now specialized, to the parent companies. At the same time, the parent companies provided information on the latest technological and product trends. Accordingly, a two-way flow of technologies began.

In Myanmar, state-owned enterprises are generally large-scale and possess extensive technical resources. Many of the private sector companies established in recent years employ technicians scouted from state-owned enterprises. In this way, technologies are being transferred from state-owned enterprises to the private sector, but there are various limitations on such transfers. First, market-based competition is practically non-existent, so that state-owned firms are not motivated to refine their products and technologies to withstand market competition. Similar to the difference between home cooked and restaurant meals, they can make "goods" that cannot withstand market competition and cannot produce "merchandized products" that are competitive. Their technologies would not survive in an open market economy. Many privatized former state-owned enterprises in China and Russia, which have moved to more open economic systems, have been defeated by competition and management deterioration. This is because they lack the technologies to make competitive "products." Moreover, technologies acquired by hiring retiree technicians from state-owned enterprises may have been viable until the time of retirement, but they are subsequently unable to make further technological progress. This is different from the situation where technologies are transferred continuously through on-going and long-term business relationships with parent companies. Consequently, Myanmar must also create a system that allows inter-firm technological transfer via close business relationships.

Many company managers who responded to questions during interviews cited insufficient electric power and insufficient demand as major problems. Almost all of them had confidence in the technological levels of their companies and did not feel that there were any technology-related problems. Objectively speaking, aside from one or two exceptional cases, the technological levels of the companies surveyed would never withstand international competition. To cite the example of the foundry company, the top manager took pride in the fact that his company was receiving technical guidance from the Institute of Technology and the Ministry of Cooperatives and had a hundred technical advisors. But a foreign-capital company with which it had transactions pointed out problems with production technologies, such as quality control, and despite receiving inquiries from Japanese corporations, the fact that these have not translated into orders is probably due to quality control problems. As seen above, solving these technological problems requires the formation of specialized skills on the production floor, the creation of a system of continuous technology transfer, and an objective awareness among managers of their companies' technological levels.

The second issue is the effectiveness of the market mechanism function. In the case of Myanmar, before a market economy could evolve the "The Burmese Way to Socialism" was in place. As a result, market formation and development lagged, falling behind other developing nations in Asia. In order for the market to perform effectively, it is necessary that information about transactions be disclosed and transmitted quickly and fairly to market participants. The backwardness of telecommunications and other forms of infrastructure further hinder the development of the market function.

As individuals, the Myanmarese are loyal and well mannered. However, it is hard to say that there is significant accumulated trust value, which is a necessary prerequisite for smooth transactions. Nor is there an ample set of social norms common throughout the national economy. Social sanctions guaranteeing that such norms are protected are also lacking. As a consequence, transactions are conducted only among a limited number of people who can be trusted, and there is a clear trend among managers toward limiting transactions to their own family members. In order to stop the trend of economic activity toward nepotism, it is necessary to raise awareness about the importance of good will in corporate circles, and to establish strong sanctions to suppress trust-betraying actions.

The lack of trust in business activities is one cause for the complexities of bank financing screening procedures. Due to their dislike of complex financing procedures, the number of people using banks is extremely limited. Fund-raising depends largely on private borrowings based on individual credit. Accordingly, corporate growth is restricted for financial reasons.

Although the level of accumulated trust in Myanmar is not sufficient to ensure the smooth functioning of a market economy throughout the nation, there does not appear to be any of the racial conflict experienced by some other Asian nations, and economic activity between races is functioning harmoniously. Naturally, there are some contrary examples, such as the plastics-molding company in which almost in the entire management is Chinese. However, Myanmar must maintain its tradition of racial harmony in order to achieve economic progress.

Another positive factor in our evaluation of Myanmar's economic development was that corruption among government bureaucrats is not as structurally entrenched as in certain other Asian countries. The issuance of permits to conduct economic activity is done in a comparatively fair manner and has won generally high praise from managers of foreign companies. However, recent inflation has caused real reductions in the salary levels of government bureaucrats. There is word that policemen and other low-paid civil servants are accepting bribes, so investor caution is recommended. The level of cleanliness of government institutions is closely linked to the nation's potential capacity for economic development, and it is important that Myanmar maintain this positive tradition.

Establishing a Model Project for the Inter-Firm Division of Labor

Finally, to turn to the level of development of the inter-firm division of labor systems, which are considered to have strategic importance in the context of Myanmar's economic development. In order for a system of inter-firm division of labor to spread, such a system must actually be set up, and individuals must be made aware of its benefits. To this end, evidence provided by a model project could be effective. Indeed, in the early days of Japan's adoption of the subcontracting system, many company managers were suspicious of the technical and managerial capabilities of small and medium-sized companies. In the latter half of the 1930s, however, the subcontracting production system was enforced under a government-led initiative, centering on production to meet military demands. The system received high marks. Based on that experience, the system has since developed under the guidance of the private sector, without government involvement. The productivity and competitive advantages of Japanese industry has grown dramatically as a result.

In Myanmar, the domestic production of diesel engines is a significant example of a model project for setting up a subcontracting production system. Diesel engines are in demand for a wide variety of uses, including fishing boats, irrigation, and household electricity generation, so there is considerable potential for mass production. Moreover, the basic technologies can be feasibly introduced and shared. In addition, diesel engine production requires numerous components and processes that would be suited to the inter-firm division of labor. In fact, two large Japanese companies, Yamaha and Suzuki, began as diesel engine manufacturers supported by subcontractors.

In Myanmar, a plan to produce diesel engines domestically is coming into shape. It should be implemented not via the comprehensive production systems of large corporations but instead by using numerous small and medium-sized companies as subcontractors. We obviously cannot expect top-quality products to be manufactured from the very beginning. However, if technological transfers to small and medium-sized companies are implemented continuously, and if a good balance of competition and cooperation is maintained between subcontracting firms, we can expect that internationally competitive products can be manufactured within several years.

Notes

[1] "The Myth of Asia's Miracle," *Foreign Affairs*, November-December 1994.

[2] Kazushi Okawa, "Production and Distribution in the Japanese Economy, 1905-63: Residual Analysis," *Keizai Kenkyu Hitotsubashi University Bulletin*, 19.2 (1968) [in Japanese].

[3] Kenneth Arrow, *The Limits of Organization* (New York: Norton, 1994), p. 27.

[4] *Ibid.*

[5] *Ibid.*, p. 23.

[6] Oliver Williamson, *Economic Organization: Firms, Markets, and Policy Control* (New York University Press, 1986), p. 98.

[7] Jeffrey Pfeffer and Gerald R. Salancik, *The External Control of Organizations: A Resource Dependence Perspective* (New York: Harper & Row, 1978), p. 147.

11

Formation and Features of Entrepreneurship in Myanmar and Japan

Johzen Takeuchi
Nagoya University

Introduction

Business conditions in Myanmar were at their bottom in 1988 but look to be steadily recovering. A journalist who noticed the dynamic business activity of tourism in 1996 wrote that: "Economic development is far more active than foreign tourists imagine, especially in Yangon, Myanmar's capital. We can no longer feel the atmosphere of a non-democratic state or a least developed country, where until very recently the situation has been severe."[1] These days Yangon can boast modern hotels and skyscrapers, and its main streets suffer traffic jams during morning and evening rush hours. New industrial zones have been established, and more zones are to be provided. Foreign direct investment (FDI) has already proved popular, and a number of companies are experiencing adequate business performance.

The basic macroeconomic indices of Myanmar, however, are not always positive. Some decisive technical changes have been made in the government's statistical estimations, but this topic lies outside the purview of this paper. Official statistics indicate a decided upturn in GDP depending upon data given in the national currency, the kyat (Table 11.1). The trend of official data for the real economic growth rate has also been favorable, but there are still fundamental problems with these statistics.

Table 11.1 Macro-Index of the Economy of Myanmar

	GDP (million kyat)	*Growth rate (%)*	*CPI (%)*	*OFD (US$ million)*
1981	5,862	6.4	5.0	1,754
1982	5,918	5.5	5.3	-
1983	6,117	4.8	5.7	-
1985	6,617	4.3	6.8	-
1986	7,974	3.7	9.2	-
1987	9,975	25.1	24.8	-
1988	11,746	-11.4	16.1	-
1989	16,621	7.4	27.2	-
1990	23,970	2.7	17.6	4,675
1991	28,415	-1.0	32.3	4,800
1992	37,830	10.9	21.9	5,326
1993	40,330	5.8	26.0	5,404
1994	79,189	7.5	22.5	-
1995	108,200	9.8	21.8	-
1996	114,784	6.1	-	-

Sources: Institute of Developing Economies, *Annual Report on Asia and the Middle East*, Annual edition, and Institute of Developing Economies, *Annual Report on Asia*
Notes: CPI = consumer price index
OFD = official foreign debt

There is a serious gap between the kyat's official and black market exchange rate, and its fluctuations have also been serious. While the consumer price index (CPI) does not take black market activity into account, it nonetheless shows a notable rise. Official statistics for 1997 indicate that per capita income for 1996 was nearly equivalent to that for February 1986.[2]

Among macroeconomic indices, the increase in official foreign debt symbolizes one of the most serious problems, even though adequate official data have not been published.[3] This factor has had a strong impact on the balance of payments. There are also problems of political instability, and not only the balance of trade but the current account has been in the red both in dollar and in kyat terms (Tables 11.2 and 11.3). This imbalance has sometimes brought the economic policy of the country into deadlock, and the recent "liberalization policy" is one factor making matters worse.

Taking a bird's-eye view of Myanmar's economy as above, it is possible to say that the prospering urban areas are the exception in this large, stagnant, and traditional country. Generally speaking, Myanmar is still a very traditional country, heavily dependent upon an out-dated primary sector. Most of its people have never had a chance to experience or appreciate a modern standard of living. However, it is one of the major subjects of this paper and our research that the country might have a high potential for raising new entrepreneurs even under severe conditions not only in the newly transferred urban sectors but also in traditional and rural ones. To identify the features of the country's economic prospects, some historical experiences in the economic development of Japan will be introduced in the second part of this paper.

This paper relies upon official statistical data, but these have frequently changed without explanation. The latest available data have been used. The Myanmar government adopts a budgetary year beginning in April and ending in March of the next year, and only the starting year is given here when the year in question is identified. With respect to population statistics, the statistical office adopts data from the middle of the year.

Table 11.2 International Trade Indices, 1981-94 (US$ million)

	Exports	*Imports*	*Balance of Trade*	*Ordinary Balance*	*Gold and foreign currency reserves*	*Official foreign debt*
1981	530	860	-329	-315.3	239.2	1,755
1982	421	882	-460	-468.8	114.0	-
1983	-	-	-	-	98.6	-
1984	-	-	-	-	70.7	-
1985	-	-	-	-	43.6	-
1986	300	306	-6	-	43.9	-
1987	264	377	-113	-	39.7	-
1988	147	241	-94	-	89.2	-
1989	215	191	24	-	275.0	-
1990	425	535	-110	-	325.3	4,675
1991	471	878	-407	-	271.0	4,800
1992	591	1,010	-420	-275.0	292.0	5,326
1993	678	1,182	-508	-284.0	303.0	5,404
1994	740	1,250	-519	-250.0	422.0	-

Source: *Op. cit.*

Table 11.3 Balance of Trade, 1973-95 (million kyat)

	Exports	*Imports*	*Balance*
1973	967	575	392
1974	926	1,015	-90
1975	1,323	1,443	-121
1976	1,716	1,628	88
1977	1,757	2,087	-329
1978	1,853	3,224	-1,371
1979	2,696	4,310	-1,614
1980	3,225	4,635	-1,419
1981	3,453	5,611	-2,159
1982	3,036	6,814	-3,277
1983	3,420	5,197	-1,778
1984	3,195	5,941	-1,847
1985	2,654	4,802	-2,148
1986	2,514	3,936	-1,422
1987	1,679	4,066	-2,386
1988	2,193	3,443	-1,250
1989	2,807	3,596	-790
1990	2,966	6,027	-3,060
1991	2,702	5,285	-2,583
1992	3,590	6,140	-2,550
1993	4,249	7,952	-3,703
1994	5,405	8,766	-3,360
1995	5,945	9,880	-3,936

Source: *Op. cit.*

1 Features of Entrepreneurship in Myanmar

Industrial Sector and Entrepreneurship

Official population statistics (Table 11.4) indicate that the rate of increase is not as high as in many developing countries and shows a decrease over three decades. However, maintaining a rate of about 2% a year, the total population of the country almost doubled during the period 1963-96. Despite this rapid increase, the country's basic industrial structure did not change drastically or, rather, has stagnated. Certainly, there has been no consistent statistical framework, but data from the industrial structure are available (Table 11.5). It is surprising that the GDP share of the primary sectors swelled nearly 50% after going down to the 20-40% range at the beginning of the 1980s. On the contrary, the manufacturing sector's share was constant, or stagnant, at a level of less than 10%. It is noteworthy that the electricity, gas, transportation, telecommunications, and construction sectors took a larger share than the manufacturing sector. In the ordinary industrialization process, the former would take on the role of arranging social infrastructure for the latter's development. However, this country set up a unique but contradictory structure, and it is possible to find various business people in the construction sector in which private enterprises are expanding. State-owned enterprises occupied the major share of electricity, gas, transportation, engineering, and telecommunications, and at present it would be hard to find a new trend of entrepreneurship in these sectors. However, we are able to find numerous human resources in these sectors, and it will be impossible to promote Myanmar's industrialization without the spontaneous collaboration of business people.

It is also possible to examine sectoral features in terms of employment (Table 11.6). Doing so reveals characteristic features of the country's socio-economic conditions. As Table 11.6 shows, the primary sector, excluding mining, shared 66.9% in 1982 and increased to 68.9% in 1991. The manufacturing sector's share decreased, falling from 7.93% to 6.99%. This means that the primary sector's relative labor productivity decreased during the period. The share of the electricity, gas, transportation, and construction sectors contracted in 1991, and this means that their relative labor productivity increased and the gap with the manufacturing sector widened. The wage rate of these sectors is better than the manufacturing sector and decidedly higher than the primary sectors.

This is related to the high labor productivity of these sectors and means that the motivation of employees in the primary and manufacturing sectors has not adequately improved for workers. It also means that the per capita income of state-owned enterprises is traditionally more favorable than income in the private and rural sectors. This is one reason why numerous small businesses are emerging from conservative organizations concentrated in the construction sector.

Table 11.4 Population of Myanmar, 1963-96

	Population (thousands)	*Growth rate (%)*
1963	23,187	2.20
1966	24,218	2.20
1969	26,444	2.23
1972	28,262	2.26
1975	30,170	2.20
1978	32,284	2.03
1979	32,939	2.03
1980	33,608	2.03
1981	34,287	2.02
1982	34,976	2.01
1983	35,680	2.01
1984	36,392	2.00
1985	37,115	1.99
1986	37,850	1.98
1987	38,595	1.97
1988	39,350	1.96
1989	40,030	1.88
1990	40,790	1.88
1991	41,550	1.86
1992	42,330	1.87
1993	43,126	1.88
1994	43,967	1.95
1995	44,740	1.75
1996	45,570	1.85

Source: *Op. cit.*

Table 11.5 Sectoral Share of GDP, 1981-95 (%)

	Primary	*Manufacturing*	*CTEG*	*Others*
1981	37.7	10.2	52.8	
1982	38.3	10.3	51.4	
1983	37.8	10.2	52.0	
1984	37.4	10.4	52.2	
1985	25.7	26.8	47.5	
1986	25.5	27.3	47.2	
1988	47.4	8.9	43.7	
1989	48.3	9.3	11.9	30.5
1990	47.8	9.1	12.3	30.8
1991	47.0	8.8	12.4	31.8
1992	47.4	8.9	12.7	31.0
1993	46.7	9.1	13.3	31.9
1994	46.0	9.3	13.6	31.1
1995	46.3	9.4	14.2	30.1

Source: *Op. cit.*
Notes: Data for 1994 and 1995 show a temporal estimation
CTEG= Construction, telecommunications, electricity, and gas

The primary sector has been the most important sector of the country's economy. However, major agricultural products showed a fatal decline throughout the 1980s and at the beginning of the 1990s (Table 11.7). Among dominant items, only paddy production showed an upward trend after 1992. An official statement indicates that 20.9 million tons of paddy rice was produced in 1996, the highest level in the country. It is difficult to identify whether this growth is related to the government's liberalization policy or to a market situation that succeeded in supplying incentives to farmers. Depending upon official data, it is easy to say that other prod-

Table 11.6 Occupational Structure, 1982-91 (million)

	Primary	*Manufac-turing*	*Con-struction*	*TTEG*	*Public service*	*Commerce*	*Other*	**Total**
1982	9,483	1,150	219	705	852	1,386	609	**14,185**
1983	9,675	1,198	225	496	872	1,413	618	**14,497**
1984	9,787	1,234	240	504	885	1,444	628	**14,792**
1985	10,052	1,285	246	519	919	1,472	637	**15,130**
1986	10,217	1,348	258	533	994	1,507	648	**15,505**
1987	10,380	1,369	265	538	1,047	1,556	658	**15,813**
1989	10,614	1,137	174	402	956	1,405	455	**15,221**
1990	10,867	1,132	188	405	1,205	1,396	465	**15,730**
1991	11,076	1,124	283	411	901	1,255	474	**16,070**

Source: *Op. cit.*
Notes: "Manufacturing" excludes mining
TTEG = Transportation, telecommunications, electricity, and gas

ucts did not show a sufficient upturn or remained stagnant. It is true, however, that the agricultural products available in the local market increased rapidly during the decade. In the course of our survey we encountered individuals who stressed the new development of regional market economies and the increasing desire to have access to the market and commodities. Such vigor in the agricultural sector could be an accelerating factor for future prospects because the potential of the country's primary sectors is enormous. Together with some other Southeast Asian nations, Myanmar is an exception in having sufficient potential for an extensive agro-business among over-populated Asian countries. The country still has vast and various fallow and cultivable land (Table 11.8), precious spaces for future development and requiring intensive care and proper ecological planning.

The importance of the primary sectors can also be seen from exported commodity items (Table 11.9). Agricultural, fishery, and forestry products supply the bulk of exported goods. Even after the agreement on border trade, the export of these commodities increased. In Thailand, the agro-business became the key to the rapid expansion of regional big business groups. It would be difficult to predict whether Myanmar will employ the same strategy as Thailand or establish a new system; however, it is clear that the country should use the large potential of its primary sectors for its development, whether through public organizations or private enterprises.

Taking into account modern international relations and the varied resources for tourism, tourism can play a unique role in the country's economic growth. Historical and cultural monuments and the facilities in the large urban areas of Yangon, Mandalay, and Pagou as well as regional locales like Pagan and Sagain have the potential of attracting international interest and investment. The country's complicated and spectacular coastline offers the prospect of new resort projects with sufficient possibilities for further development. There is also a high potential for eco-tourism in certain highland areas, in the Shan State, and northern forestry districts.

Table 11.7 Major Agricultural Products, 1981-96 (thousand tons)

	Paddy	*Wheat*	*Maize*	*Peanuts*	*Sugar cane*	*Tobacco*
1981	14,146	124	206	573	2,736	41
1982	14,372	130	239	550	3,719	28
1983	14,287	214	309	532	3,662	30
1984	14,226	206	303	667	3,767	36
1985	14,317	190	299	560	3,727	44
1986	14,126	192	285	544	3,318	41
1987	13,636	157	224	519	3,368	68
1988	13,164	130	193	438	2,346	9
1989	13,803	124	194	459	2,008	8
1990	13,969	123	187	472	1,962	10
1991	13,201	143	191	378	2,308	17
1992	14,790	144	205	451	3,285	17
1993	16,760	-	-	-	-	-
1994	18,195	-	-	-	-	-
1995	19,568	-	-	-	-	-
1996	20,865	-	-	-	-	-

Source: *Op. cit.*

Table 11.8 Land Utilization (100 acres)

	1984	*1986*	*1988*	*1990*	*1992*
Cultivated land	20,286	19,939	19,506	20,127	20,859
Fallow land	4,590	4,917	5,289	4,724	4,068
Cultivable land	21,055	20,868	20,898	20,635	20,260
Administered forests	24,747	24,840	24,883	25,062	25,272
Other forests	54,831	55,185	55,223	54,970	54,812
Others	41,677	41,437	41,387	41,678	41,915

Source: *Op. cit.*

Table 11.9 Export Commodities (million kyat)

	1986	*1988*	*1990*	*1992*
Agricultural products	800.5	127.6	942	1,299
Livestock and fishery	124.5	66.5	170	261
Wooden products	1,084.1	701.5	1,131	1,120
Mineral and gems	283.9	127.7	740	155
Others	125.5	1,100.6*	641*	754*
Total	**2,418.5**	**2,168.9**	**2,953**	**3,590**
Re-export	95.4	24.1	9	65
Grand Total	**2,513.9**	**2,193.0**	**2,962**	**3,655**

Source: *Op. cit.*
*Includes border trade

Surprisingly, these resources have remained untouched until recently. International organizations and the government of Myanmar have now noticed the value of these resources, and there will be intensive strategies for developing tourism. According to official statistics, tourism expanded so quickly that 86,695 foreigners visited the country in 1994, and local income from tourism was estimated to be as much as US$175 million. In light of this expansion and success, the government estimated visits by a half a million foreigners in 1997, but because of the Asian financial crisis, re-estimated this as 0.3 million. Despite this downward revision, the international revenue from tourism is estimated at US$600 million, assuming the same level of consumption as 1996 or before. The trade imbalance is equivalent to US$700 million, and the deficit of the current account balance is US$300 million. In addition to these red-letter areas, the government has an official foreign debt of approximately US$5.5 billion and must pay US$300 million annually to service this debt. If the country receives as many foreign tourists as officially estimated, its economic condition will drastically improve. At an early stage of modern economic development, the functions of tourism will be far more important than at a primitive stage of industrialization in advanced countries. It is quite natural and reasonable that both the Myanmar's public and private sectors have a keen interest in the tourism sector. This sector will also be important for encouraging new business people.

Business Scale and Management

In the numerous areas of manufacturing, most manufacturers are small businesses employing fewer than ten persons. These share more than 90% of all workshops in the country (Table 11.10). There are an estimated 40,000 workshops and factories. However, excluding factories employing fewer than fifty workers, the major part of Myanmar's manufacturing sector is sustained by state-owned enterprises. Table 11.11 shows that state-owned enterprises have been organized in various sectors from some large-scale key industries to small-scale houseware manufacturing and food processing. U Aung Myint vividly explains the over-representation of state-owned enterprises in each sector.[4] Among these enterprises are numerous small-scale enterprises and even very small enterprises, but the leading enterprises of each industrial sector are exclusively state owned.

The large-scale state-owned enterprises are usually equipped with modern machinery produced abroad, but as there are inadequate facilities to produce basic materials, similar machines, and crucial parts, they depend heavily on the supply of production goods from abroad. This fatal condition has long been a major cause for the country's serious trade deficit. Table 11.12 shows Myanmar's heavy reliance on imported capital goods and industrial materials. Strategies are needed to improve the present condition of dependency.

First, state-owned enterprises should promote research and development for technology and design to substitute imported goods and materials. Secondly, the government would do well to set up a self-supporting research and development plan at its own cost, as modern technologies cannot be obtained without a sufficient sense of cost management and risk-sharing. It is not difficult, of course, for newly established public organizations to utilize some foreign aid, but they should intend to maintain and expand their systems at their own expense and under their own responsibility, for otherwise, foreign aid will be only a tentative stimulus lacking long-term effects. Thirdly, the public sector should not yield to the temptation of all-round activity to develop self-supporting industrial technologies and systems but should concentrate on certain limited technological areas and/or items that will not have sufficient marketability in international trade. As for the manufacturing of marketable common goods, they can fully depend upon small and medium-sized private enterprises, on the strict condition that managers are willing to keep modern bookkeeping systems and pay taxes in line with profits. Fourthly, it should be emphasized that modern technology does not maintain its efficiency potential without forming adequate human resources. However, it is worthwhile to note that, under present international conditions, it is easier to have an adequate supply of engineers than to employ enough human resources to support the activity of the former. Modern engineers can supply ideas and designs for modern manufacturing but cannot supply the commodity of enough marketability without a basic accumulation of production skills and skilled workers. It is the responsibility of a vocational education system to supply adequate human resources. Fifthly, state-owned enterprises enjoy favorable conditions and have strict responsibilities to ensure that their skilled workers and highly sophisticated engineers spin out to become independent manufacturers, as Japanese naval arsenals once tried to intensify the social division of labor in Japan.

An additional point should be stressed as regards state-owned enterprises. Among them are various tiny factories employing fewer than ten workers. The author could not afford to conduct an intensive survey on this point, but it is open to question whether it is still necessary to sustain as many as 1,000 very small factories. If these state-owned concerns are competing with ordinary private enterprises, the public sector should give way to them, thus intensifying the social division of labor, not competition within the traditional market. If there are to be some public functions like inspection, quality advice, and information service, they should focus their attention on obtaining more sophisticated information from industrialized countries.

Factories under the Ministry of Cooperatives are mostly small or tiny, with the majority concentrating on foods, beverages, textiles, and garments, sectors in which private enterprises are also engaged. More intensive sectoral surveys are needed to identify whether their business relations will set up a new industrial system or whether they are only competing on similar business grounds.

The number of private enterprises has steadily increased during the 1990s. Data on this matter are limited, but it is possible to see a developing trend (Table 11.13). The number of state-owned enterprises is decreasing, that of cooperatives is stagnant, and only private enterprises are rapidly expanding. For their development, there are some institutional backups such as the Industrial Enterprise Law promulgated in 1990 and the Cottage Industries Promotion Law promulgated in 1991. However, these laws order the registration of private enterprises, and, on the contrary, this means that public offices do not follow the actual business activities of unregistered enterprises. Here is another trap of socio-economic surveys, and on this point empirical investigation is needed.

Table 11.10 Manufacturing Enterprises by Scale, 1992

Scale of employment	*State-owned enterprises*	*Cooperatives*	*Private enterprises*	**Total**
Fewer than 10 persons	909	259*	33,649*	**35,817***
10-50 persons	292	266*	1,897*	**2,433***
51-100 persons	141	68	67	**276**
101 or more	425	22	19	**446**
Total	**1,767**	**593**	**36,632**	**38,992**

Source: Institute of Developing Economies, *Asian Annual Report, 1994* (p. 446)
*Number questionable but this table adopts the original

Table 11.11 Manufacturing Enterprises by Sector, 1992

Sector	*State-owned enterprises*	*Cooperatives*	*Private enterprises*	**Total**
Food and beverages	242	299	20,634	**21,175**
Garment and textiles	59	165	2,239	**2,463**
Construction materials	128	75	3,342	**3,545**
Daily necessities	14	16	1,225	**1,255**
Home wares	15	12	156	**183**
Printing and publications	28	8	326	**362**
Industrial material	928	3	1,867	**2,798**
Mineral processing	23	2	1,923	**1,948**
Agricultural materials	3	-	35	**38**
Industrial machinery	7	-	105	**112**
Vehicles	5	-	110	**115**
Shipbuilding and yards	305	-	-	**305**
Others	10	13	4,670	**4,693**
Total	**1,767**	**593**	**36,632**	**38,992**

Source: *Op. cit.*

Sixty percent of private enterprises concentrate on food and beverages, with construction materials, and garments and textiles constituting the remainder (see Table 11.11). Most enterprises are principally involved in traditional material processing. Their business activity is not limited to urban areas but is expanding to include rural areas and remote districts and their business dealings have thus become a social catalyst promoting the market system in such areas. In many places, one can find various improvements of market places and market systems.

The most decisive preconditions for a modern market economy are: (1) improvement in the living standards of ordinary people; (2) the formation of the positive will and intention to improve; and (3) social institutions to assure free access to the market. Small business activities and autonomous transactions in provincial areas will impact on some fundamental conditions for social development. More detailed investigations are required on this topic, and it remains to be seen if Myanmar will follow a strategy similar to Thailand's through business activity or will follow its own path in utilizing its abundant natural resources and take advantage of its particular circumstances. In Thailand, major business groups mainly started as agro-businesses and gradually expanded their lines of business. This is the very reason why Thailand's economic growth has sometimes been called the development of a newly agro-based industrializing country (NAIC)

To turn now to features of Myanmar's industrialization. It is noteworthy that the formation of small- and medium-scale enterprises is slightly different from that in Japan or the United States. One of the critical conditions for the prosperity of the market system is the creation and development of new businesses and enterprises. We can find new and vivid formation of enterprises in Myanmar; however, there are different streams of business formation in the country, and it is difficult to identify which will become the mainstream in the future. Some industrialized countries, especially at the early stage of economic development, experienced high social mobility with respect to skilled workers and engineers. There were

Table 11.12 Import Commodities (million kyat)

	*1986***	*1988*	*1990*	*1992*
Capital goods	2,522.2	1,406.6	1,905	1,750
Construction	538.5	285.8	500	591
Machinery	1,484.0	638.5	924	395
Transportation	336.5	425.6	400	713
Others	118.2	46.7	82	41
Industrial materials	1,158.1	813.5	1,662	1,128
Raw materials	643.3	451.7	1,068	764
Tools and parts	514.8	361.8	594	364
Consumption goods	234.1	184.4	487	913
Durable goods	80.2	85.4	231	231
Food and beverages	2.5	12.0	109	525
Textiles	16.1	22.2	34	56
Pharmaceuticals	104.8	43.3	95	14
Others	30.5	22.7	20	79
Other Goods	21.7	1,038.5*	1,469*	1,574*
Total	**3,996.1**	**3,443.0**	**5,523**	**5,365**

Source: *Op. cit.*
*Includes border trade
** Original data questionable

Table 11.13 Factories by Management Type

	1991	*1992*	*1996*
State-owned enterprises	1,769	1,767	1,609
Cooperatives	617	593	637
Private enterprises	35,518	36,632	47,592

Source: *Op. cit.*

numerous cases of spinning out as people preferred to be independent in their businesses and lives. At the same time, there were a number of cases of large enterprises or political organizations establishing small businesses for the benefit of privileged individuals. The former can be called the "spin-out type" and the latter the "hang-on type." The fate of industrialization in Myanmar cannot be defined at present because of a lack of empirical surveys and detailed case studies.

2 Formation of Japanese Small- and Medium-Scale Entrepreneurs

Downstream and Upstream Industries

The role of the wide variety of minor sectors of industry known as SMIs in supporting the downstream regions of various major industries also deserves positive evaluation from the viewpoint of industrial structure. Even if a large corporation is set up in a specific upstream sector without the stable establishment of its downstream region, it will be extremely difficult to create a large enough market for intermediate products and final consumer goods that matches the dimensions of the upstream sector. Large-scale enterprises were typically established in certain sectors producing basic materials, relying on economies of scale. These, for example, include the cotton-spinning industry at the end of the nineteenth century, the iron and steel industry at the beginning of the twentieth century, and the petrochemical industry after the Korean War, when these sectors had sufficient downstream markets.

In 1858, after Japan formally abolished its self-isolation policy, foreign trade rapidly expanded, leading to a drastic but unfavorable change in the production of domestic commodities. The Japanese cotton industry experienced a serious decline. British cotton goods, cheaper and of better quality, flooded the market, and their impact affected the entire cotton industry: cotton plant cultivation, ginning, spinning, dyeing, and weaving. The efforts of small-scale weavers, however, saved the Japanese cotton industry from a fatal decline. They managed to keep domestic market share by adopting imported cheap threads as a material input. At the time, Japanese handlooms were simple and wooden framed, but they had partly been improved to facilitate the use of newly transferred technological gadgets like the flying-shuttle and the Jacquard. Combining new technologies with labor-intensive production, Japanese manufacturers began to expand their share both in the domestic and overseas market. In 1885, Japanese weavers succeeded in achieving a larger market share than that held by imported goods suppliers. Owing to the development of cotton-weaving productivity and market demand, weavers were required to possess a stable and effective supply of raw thread.

Some Japanese entrepreneurs were able to make use of this opportunity to establish a modern spinning industry based on the market conditions made possible by the numerous efforts of the small-scale weavers. In 1882, the first large-scale modern cotton-spinning factory was established in Osaka. It succeeded in gaining a major share in the domestic market within seven years and surpassed the British share in the Korean market after the Sino-Japanese War (1894-95) and the northeastern Chinese market after the Russo-Japanese War (1904-05).

In Japan, weavers succeeded in developing not only the weaving but also the garment sector. The latter was much more labor intensive so that weavers could export their products easily only if they had enough productivity, capacity, and sufficient skill accumulation to supply the overseas market. Garment exports began to increase from around the turn of the century. In this way, they could arrange the downstream industries and industrial conditions for the upstream textile industries to develop rapidly and with capital intensity. Compared with those in Japan, Chinese weavers could not develop favorably partly because they could not expand into the overseas market and partly because they preferred to use foreign threads. Until the 1920s, they were unable to achieve a modern cotton-spinning industry that needed a high demand to meet its high productivity. In India, even the weaving industry was faced with the misfortune of shrinking, and textile industries could not fully develop until after independence in the late 1940s.

When Japan was still a newly developing country, what was essentially competitive in the international market were, first of all its labor-intensive sectors, without which no foreign exchange could be earned to finance the import of technologies and equipment for advanced industries. These labor-intensive sectors occupied the main items of Japanese exports prior to the First World War. Only four out of thirteen major export goods—cotton thread, coal, cement, and beer—were products of the capital-intensive sectors in that period. All other items were labor-intensive products. What is more important, however, is that developing the labor-intensive sectors formed the downstream of each major industrial sector and eventually paved the way for the rapid expansion of the large enterprises producing basic materials.

Adaptation and Differentiation

One of the characteristic features of the formation of Japanese technologies is that they promoted a historical process of adaptation and differentiation. As a late starter, Japan could not immediately achieve a revolutionary system of technologies that would surpass international standards, and, what is far more important, establish new technological developments. An attempt at achieving these aims through political intervention or regulation was seemingly very easy but in the event proved difficult with most attempts resulting in something like caricature.

In the silk-reeling industry, SMEs promoted adaptation much more positively. In the latter half of the nineteenth century, France had supremely developed the silk industry. The Japanese Meiji Restoration government imported a whole set of silk-reeling equipment from France and established a national pilot plant in 1872. Fixed capital expenditure amounted to 250 yen per worker in the plant; however, in the case of a silk mill established in 1874 in Matsushiro, this was only 57 yen per worker, and in the case of SMEs in the Suwa District only 5-15 yen per worker. The equipment at those mills was hand-made by traditional artisans, who had referred to sketches and explanations by those who had worked and made observations at the pilot plant. The managers of these mills substituted water mills for steam engines, wooden frames for iron ones, wire for glass, bamboo for brass, and dirt floors replaced brick ones. They attempted to simplify the equipment and to make it easier to maintain or to improve within their capacities. The modern pilot plant collapsed, and the Suwa District became the largest silk-reeling district in Japan.

Adaptation, however, was not one of the decisive factors in promoting Japanese industrialization. The need to substitute the intensification of traditional skills for the decrease of productivity per machine played a role. Factory owners and managers attempted to combine modern ideas with their own traditional labor intensity. Further, they began to divide each process into a number of smaller processes so that skills could be easily accumulated, and simple tools and machines, developed at lower costs, were substituted for modern machines. It was more efficient to have workers and craftsmen become independent than to integrate all of them into limited large-scale factories. In this way, small workshops began to emerge rapidly and numerous industrial sub-sectors were organized. Even for a simple item like shell button manufacturing, one could find numerous types of businesses like two types of dealers, seven independent processors or manufactures, and many household industries as supplementary employment. The organizing agent was the key person to integrate modern and traditional technologies and transactions, traditional human relations, traditional skills, and each troublesome quality control activity. A detailed study of this subject cannot be attempted in this short paper, but it can be pointed out that this process of adaptation and differentiation increased the number of SMEs and SMIs in a short period. It is interesting to note that despite the inflow of increasingly modern technologies small-scale businesses and even the number of traditional artisans and craftsmen did not decrease.

Japanese small-scale producers divided up a new technology in a labor-intensive manner or divided up a production process into simpler sub-processes. By doing so, they profoundly affected the subsequent Japanese path of technological innovation. On this point, certain characteristics common to the course of Japanese industrialization can be observed. These include: (1) the sufficient degree of perfection to which final products were completed; (2) the stringency with which finished products were evaluated; (3) the thorough penetration of this stringency not only into a final-process inspection but also into ordinary operations and quick responses to the process control needed; (4) a deep intellectual interest in the processes themselves and the final products resulting from them; (5) a general recognition that workers as well as entrepreneurs need to take an interest in the quality of intermediate and final products.

All these characteristics began to be observed at a relativity early stage of Japanese industrialization because the income of SMEs was reduced whenever defective intermediate products were supplied to succeeding processors. In the case of the shell-button industry, it was cruel but reasonable for Japanese enterprises, while taking advantage of this type of manufacturing system, to build up their own simplified technologies first in the regions of the final finishing process and then in those of the processing of intermediate products. Because adequate funds for initial investment and the maintenance of newly imported machines were lacking it was necessary to substitute a labor-intensive production network for a modern machine system. Even if in many cases owners and managers had to maintain very traditional skills and feudal human relationships, they also had a chance to grow into large manufacturers, controlling various kinds of subcontractors, after working extremely hard to achieve that status. Sometimes, they went so far as to be parasitic landlords when they retreated from the manufacturing sector.

The Japanese subcontracting system developed by a process of adaptation and differentiation, and, at the same time, was a key factor in accelerating social mobility.[5] Nowadays there are many individuals in the business elite who began their career as workers or apprentices and later became independent processors, subcontractors, organizing agents, and finally owner-managers of famous manufacturing companies. Owing to this high level of social mobility, social stratification and class confrontation were not as severe as in Western Europe and North America. Furthermore, the higher the mobility, the more nervously and earnestly did the managerial personnel of large enterprises concentrate on establishing a stable employment system and maintaining a favorable human relationship environment because workers could easily leave their jobs when dissatisfied with their conditions.

Evolution of Human Relations in Small and Medium-Sized Enterprises

It should be explained clearly here that the basic characteristics of industrial human relations apparent in Japanese enterprises after the Second World War mostly evolved in the developing process of SMEs or SMIs. One of the most significant factors was the close relationships among entrepreneurs, engineers, skilled workers, and common laborers, together with their common faith in "on the job" experience. The author believes that this kind of relationship is based on a certain kind of empiricism or actuality.

Many cases of managerial success and failure demonstrate that a vital key to the social success of a small enterprise lay in the human relations environment within it. Workers more or less shared the same attitude toward work and a similar sense of responsibility as did the entrepreneurs. This fact is related to the existence of such social conditions as would give them reasonable prospects to become independent entrepreneurs some day after climbing a number of steps on the social ladder.

When an entrepreneur intended to keep such workers, whether skilled or unskilled, in his employ, he needed to maintain certain specific conditions. He had always to be very careful to maintain favorable informal relations with his employees and to share a similar value system with them because labor intensity depends upon the voluntary creativity of each individual. Employees' tasks had to be constantly improved and sophisticated in order for workers to have better incentives and the motivation to promote their productivity and improve product quality. They required a "sense of development" to remain at the same work place for a long period. The organizational scale of management had to expand consistently so that employees would be given various chances to attain higher positions. Employees staying long in the same work place were expected to have better long-term prospects for receiving responsibility and common rewards.

In this kind of human relationship, a number of cases existed in which employees without any academic background were promoted to managerial or engineering posts if and when they acquired a sufficiently high evaluation from their superiors. Such cases were quite common in companies that had developed from tiny workshops into medium- or large-scale enterprises, where failure to expand management would mean the beginning of collapse. A characteristic feature of Japanese society, which tends to give over-riding priority to quantitative growth, may also explain this tendency.

Prototype of So Called "Japanese Style Management" and Technological Development

This paper will now touch upon the important implications of the development of SMEs and SMIs as they relate to the creation of the unique image of Japanese entrepreneurship and management. Both local and foreign observers have drawn attention to the many peculiarities that constitute the secrets behind the strength of Japanese business administration. Various surveys refer to these as the "Japanese way of business management," or "the Japanese pattern of industrial relations," or the "Japanese form of skill mastery," and so forth. These concepts more typically describe large businesses that have developed from smaller ones than large corporations that have enjoyed generous government protection since the earliest stages of industrialization. It is not within the purview of this paper to portray various cases of such businessmen, but they typify the new breed of Japanese business leaders, especially following the Russo-Japanese War.

The founders of Suzuki and Toyota, for example, shared many their personal characteristics. Both began as carpenters specializing in making wooden handlooms, and this laid the base for the later development of their major automobile manufacturing companies. In the case of Hitachi, today one of the largest manufacturers of electrical machinery and appliances in Japan, the company had at first been a humble subsidiary of a mining company. Sony began as a tiny workshop and Honda emerged from only a repair shop after the Second World War. Many of the founders of these companies did not have an academic background, nor did they mind the lack of one. A factor common to all of them was that they were good at creating positive formal and informal human relationships and were also skilled at setting ideals of production activity and in private life. They were familiar with the production capabilities and skills of their workers, and, more often than not, were the most skilled leading figures in their own lines of operation. Despite the inferior conditions of their facilities, they usually had a keen interest in productivity and were seriously conscious of evaluating the quality of their products as well as that of their competitors. These aspects came into being in the course of the development of SMEs and SMIs in Japan and eventually constituted the preconditions for full-scale economic growth after the Second World War. It might be incidentally noted, with the relevance to our own times, that most of those industries developed as labor-intensive sectors.

The Japanese are nowadays said to hold a leading position in the production of industrial robots.[6] In the major enterprises manufacturing these robots, traditional skills and manual dexterity are preserved and protected much more than might be imagined. For anyone who can appreciate that the quality of software fed into a robot's central processing unit (CPU) determines its market value, this is nothing to wonder at. There is naturally a huge difference between a set of software that represents the standardization of the work done by an average skilled worker and one deriving from that by the best skilled worker, incorporating even the delicate moves of his fingers and the judgment accompanying them. This holds equally true for an automatic machine turning out sophisticated knitted products as for a metal-processing robot. In the historical development of Japanese industries, manual skills have evolved into more sophisticated technologies. However, entrepreneurs at the same time found that they required far more skilled workers to manufacture the most advanced robots for present-day technological growth.

In most advanced countries, economic development has been promoted by substituting capital-intensive for labor-intensive ways of production and by the social division of labor between manual and mental labor. Japanese industrialists did not, however, always adopt the same course as other developed countries. Until the 1970s, they lacked adequate funds to adopt the latest models of modern and capital-intensive production in most manufacturing sectors. They needed to find as many substitutions as possible, especially in their own lines of production. The Japanese labor movement was not as militant as in other industrialized countries partly because workers were able to enjoy a higher valuation of their skills by their superiors and had a better chance at social mobility than their counterparts elsewhere and partly because radical left-wing movements were almost completely suppressed in the 1950s. Through this historical process, entrepreneurs managed to combine traditional with modern factors without engaging in a serious social struggle, and they also succeeded in establishing stable management in the context of dynamic technological development.

Human Capabilities and Modern Enterprise

To turn now to the fact that labor-intensive production was more efficient in a small-scale management context. In a number of instances in Japan, especially at the early stages of industrialization, large-scale production and mechanization alone were appreciated and pursued even when production processes could have been developed in a labor-intensive way. The results often proved a miserable failure. We can see that similar errors are still frequently being repeated today.

Judging from the Japanese experience, economic development does not always mean adopting large-scale organizations and industrial discipline, accompanied by the social compulsion necessary to enable them. As a matter of fact, the larger an organization becomes, the more intensively it needs to be supported by developing labor-intensive sub-sectors, not only externally but also internally. In addition, to make large economic organizations function in ways so as to expand the labor-intensive sub-sector seems to involve developing human capabilities that do not always coincide with modern capabilities. Labor-intensive sectors necessarily involve some mental and peripheral regions that depend on individual spontaneity and creativity, including latent regions that are still not perceived as such.

In Japan, many technical breakthroughs occurred as the result of the ideas of workers and craftsmen. They often did not mind functioning as engineers or managers without extra pay. On the contrary, owner-managers would frequently take on the role of domestic servants. One such entrepreneur was Konosuke Matushita, who later became a famous business leader. According to his biography, he used to clean the workers' toilet after they returned home. In most successful SMEs, owner-managers were not only administrative leaders but also leaders in life. They trained workers or apprentices how to live as well as how to work. A number of business leaders who recollect their apprentice days in their biographies have recalled how they had learned routine methods, mental arithmetic, calligraphy, bookkeeping, and so on from their masters or their wise apprentices. Whereas the development of such human capabilities has been an important asset to the present-day economy, it is also significant that their development was stimulated by a high potential of social mobility and by intense competition among SMEs and even among workers.

High social mobility deserves emphasis not only because of its effect on allowing individuals of different classes to exert more of their energies but also because it can present interesting facts for a comparative international study. Despite the radical transformation undergone by its economic system, Japan has experienced little social unrest or political turmoil. Intense competition among small manufacturers and processors, and for that matter within the same social stratum, can be an explanatory variable revealing the Japanese historical experience of political stability, even if it became a factor in making the Japanese transaction system tremendously complicated and informal in orientation.

Conclusion

The author does not always consider the Japanese experience of industrialization as typical. However, Japan's experience could provide ideas pertinent to the industrialization of other Asian countries, especially in the manufacturing sectors in which they need to accumulate various human resources and to arrange numerous social factors for the development of labor-intensive sectors. Small labor-intensive sectors could in the long run also have tremendous significance for the sophistication of industrial structures. At the same time, the public sector should take a decisive role in accomplishing effective technology transfer from abroad, especially in the field of heavy industry. Having taken the Japanese experience into account, this paper concludes with some tentative comments on the industrialization of Myanmar.

Large-Scale Enterprises

State-owned enterprises occupy by far the lion's share of large-scale enterprises in Myanmar, and this means that the public sector should take responsibility for obtaining new technology from abroad and diffusing it to small and very small businesses throughout the country. These firms should promote:

- higher capital and labor productivity to achieve adequate cost-management and efficiency that will eventually provide opportunities for their employees to found new businesses

- adequate staff training for the assessment of modern technology to be transferred from abroad and for the training of workers and young engineers
- sufficient breakthroughs to obtain adaptations for local manufacturers and small enterprises
- human resources in order for individuals eventually to spin out to be independent and prosperous manufacturers.

Small and Medium-Scale Enterprises

SMEs are the training school of modern entrepreneurship and rational attitudes are the decisive factor for achieving development into a modern economic society and for long-term development. However, in Myanmar where the accumulation of SMEs has been inadequate, the public sector must arrange certain initial conditions for their development. These conditions include:

- the promotion of privatization of publicly owned SMEs or the abolition of inefficient enterprises
- the arrangement of social policies for breeding small businesses in numerous agro-businesses and handicraft sectors that depend upon the country's abundant natural resources
- the nationwide establishment of a social system to supply adequate market information and to instruct on the new adaptation of technology and/or unfamiliar skills
- the establishment of a financing system for SMEs not directly financed by the public sector but arranged through the regional and autonomous movement of individuals in the community
- the provision of secondary vocational education and/or night school for adult education for basic vocational training and the diffusion of a highly sophisticated value system to appreciate these skills and products.

Regional Development Policy

Myanmar still needs to introduce new industrial sectors that are now very popular in neighboring countries like Thailand and to improve its basic social infrastructure. However, it will be far more important and difficult to obtain the human resources necessary to promote the above mentioned projects in the country, especially in the countryside. It is therefore necessary for the government to establish a regional system to raise regional and/or community leaders who will be responsible for promoting various projects as follows:

- regional elementary education for children of poor families not currently enrolled in school
- evening and/or night school for individuals in the community lacking an adequate educational background
- fostering regional industry to supply special products to the national and international market
- establishing regional public organizations to instruct people in the community how to improve the quality of their products and ensure market access.

The country will also need to foster the social attitudes of community leaders to be the organizers of the community movement. These individuals will be responsible for foster certain social factors, including: (1) social infrastructure fundamental for community life; (2) social education to obtain information about new products and the market; (3) modernizing the community's value system in order to improve its standard of living.

Role of Government Officials

From the point of view of national industrialization and community development, it will be necessary to train younger generations of high government officials so that their abilities are appreciated not by the scale of their projects but by the scope of regional development and their impact on the community. The central government needs to set up a regional development plan identifying detailed industrial sectors and production targets for each division and community. The plan's operational efficiency should be investigated at the level of each industrial sub-sector and community manufacturer. For these planning and investigation activities, young officials should be assigned to reside in and make intensive surveys of the countryside. Those who intend to fulfill their duty in remote or isolated areas should be more highly rewarded than those who select easily accessible regions, provided that their reports and planning are on a par. They should clarify items in their planning and investigations as follows:

- limited industrial sectors and/or sub-sectors to be selected for regional development
- initial conditions and difficulties to be taken into account for the development of new manufacturing and transactions
- impacts of introducing new products and/or businesses on the community
- strategies to improve community living standards and especially to utilize mass communications and social education efficiently.

Young officials in regional public offices are the human resources who are often going to reside with people in the community and to undertake the intensive investigations that will provide effective information for the planning of the regional and/or central governments. Their unique public task for regional development should include the following:

- diffusion and improvement of basic education for community children
- diffusion and improvement of social education
- utilization of mass communication and investigation of human activities and community movements to be selected for mass communication and social education

- acquisition and diffusion of market information for the development of regional and community industry
- investigation of the conditions required to enhance the effectiveness of regional transactions.

Notes

[1] *Bangkok Weekly*, 8-15 November 1996.

[2] *Ministry of National Planning and Economic Development, Union of Myanmar,* Review of Financial, Economic, and Social Conditions for 1995-96.

[3] Ministry of Planning and Finance, Report to the Pyithu Hluttaw by the Socialist Republic of the Union of Burma on Financial, Economic, and Social Conditions, Annual edition.

[4] See the paper in this volume by Aung Myint, "Investment Opportunities in the Processing and Manufacturing Sector in Myanmar."

[5] The level of social mobility has been falling in Japan along with economic growth in manufacturing sectors. This seems to be a highly relevant point for predicting the future of the Japanese economy, but this issue cannot be pursued here.

[6] Japanese technology has often been criticized for its relative lack of development of basic principles or creative ideas concerning whole systems. This criticism, however, leads to confusion between the treatment of problems with which Japan had to struggle while concentrating its efforts to catch up with advanced nations and that of a textbook classification of modern technological systems.

Contributors

TUN AYE, Vice-President and Founder of the Myanmar Industries Association, CEC Member of the Union of Myanmar Chamber of Commerce and Industries, graduated from the University of Rangoon. The Chairman of the Yadana Rice Milling Company, Yangon, he is engaged in numerous entrepreneurial activities and is currently involved in businesses related to corrugated iron sheets, videotapes, construction, and rice milling.

MINORU KIRYU, Professor of Economics at Osaka University of Industry, received an MA in Economics from the University of Dhaka in 1970. From 1979 to 1982 he served as Extra Chancellor at the Embassy of Japan in Rangoon. He was a consultant for the World Bank in 1983 and was Director of the Economic Development Unit of the Institute of Developing Economies from 1989 to 1991. He was an economic advisor to the Government of Burma on a United Nations Development Project during 1991-92.

TOSHIHIRO KUDO, Researcher, JETRO/Institute of Developing Economies, holds a BA from Tokyo University of Foreign Studies and an MA in Economics from Cambridge University with a speciality in Development Theory. He also attended the master's course at the Advanced School of the Institute of Developing Economies. Among his many published papers are "Investment-Capital Flow to Asia and the Role of Direct Capital" published by the Institute of Developing Economies in 1998 and "Myanmar: Current Status and Issues of Aid to It" in *World Trends*.

KITTI LIMSKUL, Deputy Director, Social Research Institute, Chulalongkorn University, Bangkok, and Director of the Socio-Economic Policy and Economic Forecasting Unit, has held various high-level posts including Director General of the Fiscal Policy Office, Ministry of Finance and as a member of the Committee on Current Account and Inflation. During 1987-88 he was a fellow at the Economic Research Center at Nagoya University. He is a research consultant to the United Nations Education, Science, and Cultural Organization (UNESCO).

TETUSO MINATO, Professor of Economics at Aoyama Gakuin University, Tokyo, specializes in comparative organizations, inter-firm transactions, and subcontracting systems and has done research on industrialized economies. He earned his MA and PhD (1973) at Osaka Prefectural University.

AUNG MYINT, President, Aung Aung & Associates Consultancy Services, Ltd, graduated from Rangoon University and earned two post-graduate degrees, in management and administration and in economic planning, from the Institute of Economics, Yangon. He was in the overseas training program in the factory management system of German enterprises during 1968-70 in the Federal Republic of Germany. He retired from the Directorate of Investment and Company Administration after forty-five years of service, including those as its Director General. He has served as the leader of various Myanmar delegations and study missions abroad.

CHIT SO, Project Coordinator, Itochu Corporation, Yangon, entered the Ministry of Foreign Affairs after graduating from the Rangoon University of Arts and Sciences. He received his PhD from the University of Tokyo. He has served at the Embassy of the Union of Myanmar in Tokyo, and before taking up his current position in 1996 held a variety of posts including a stint as a newspaper reporter in Los Angeles.

JOHZEN TAKEUCHI, Professor of Economics at Nagoya University, specializes in the Japanese economy, Japanese economic history, and economic development. Upon completing the doctoral course at the University of Tokyo, he became a Research Associate at Hiroshima University, where he was named Professor in 1987. He has also held visiting professorships at Delhi University and the University of Sheffield and was a Visiting Fellow at Cambridge University. He has held various positions on the Project Committee of the United Nations University, Tokyo.

YOSHIAKI UEDA, Professor of Economics in the Faculty of Information Sciences and Associate Professor in the Faculty of Commerce, University of Marketing and Distribution Sciences, Hanoi, graduated with an MBA from Kobe University where he also completed the doctoral course in 1983. From 1983 to 1988 he was an economist for the Japan Research Securities Institute.

TAKANORI WAJIMA, Consultant, CRC Research Institute, Tokyo, joined Deutsche Bank after graduating from Waseda University, Tokyo. He joined the Century Research Company, Ltd (now the CRC Research Institute) in 1988. In 1992, he had a research sabbatical focusing on European Community law at Tilburg University in the Netherlands. During 1993-95 he was seconded to the Research Division of Itochu Corporation. His work includes a published paper on "Policy Research on the Trade/Commerce of Various Countries (Myanmar)."

NU NU YIN, Dean and Associate Professor, MBA Program, Institute of Economics, Yangon, is a specialist in entrepreneurship and technology transfer. After graduating from the Institute of Economics, she went on to earn a PhD in commercial sciences from the Faculty of Commerce, Chuo University, Tokyo.